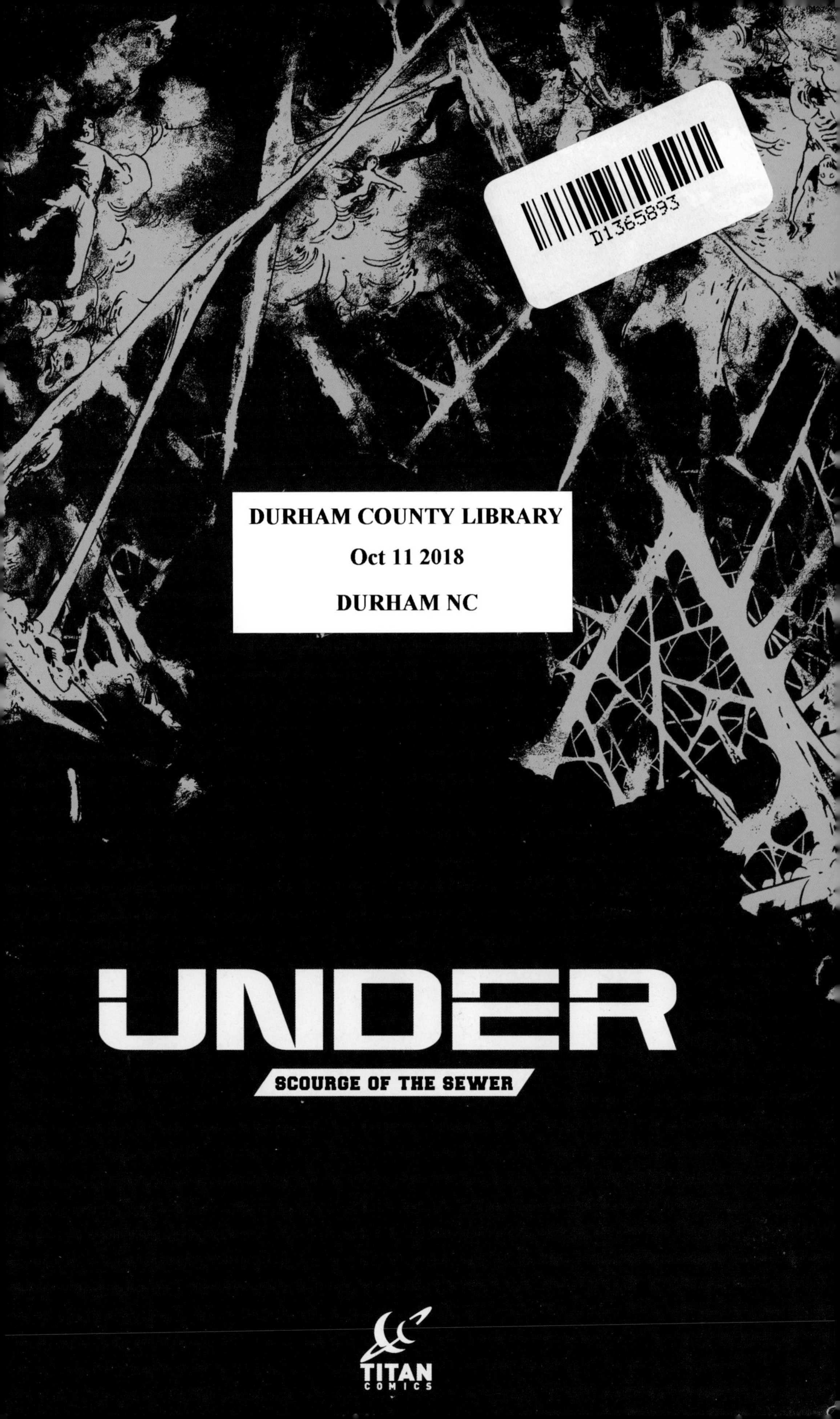

UNDER

SCOURGE OF THE SEWER

TITAN COMICS

UNDER

TITAN COMICS

EDITOR: LAUREN BOWES

Designer: Russell Seal
Managing & Launch Editor: Andrew James
Senior Production Controller: Jackie Flook
Production Supervisor: Maria Pearson
Production Controller: Peter James
Production Assistant: Natalie Bolger
Art Director: Oz Browne
Senior Sales Manager: Steve Tothill
Press Officer: Will O'Mullane
Direct Sales & Marketing Manager: Ricky Claydon
Commercial Manager: Michelle Fairlamb
Ads & Marketing Assistant: Tom Miller
Publishing Manager: Darryl Tothill
Publishing Director: Chris Teather
Operations Director: Leigh Baulch
Executive Director: Vivian Cheung
Publisher: Nick Landau

UNDER: SCOURGE OF THE SEWER
9781785864834
Published by Titan Comics
A division of Titan Publishing Group Ltd.
144 Southwark St., London, SE1 0UP

Under © BEC / RAFFAELE / ÉDITIONS DU LOMBARD (DARGAUD-LOMBARD S.A.)
Originally published as *Under: White Ladies* and *Under: Goliath*.

A CIP catalogue record for this title is available from the British Library.

10 9 8 7 6 5 4 3 2 1
First Published May 2018
Printed in China.
Titan Comics.

WWW.TITAN-COMICS.COM
Follow us on Twitter @ComicsTitan
Visit us at facebook.com/comicstitan

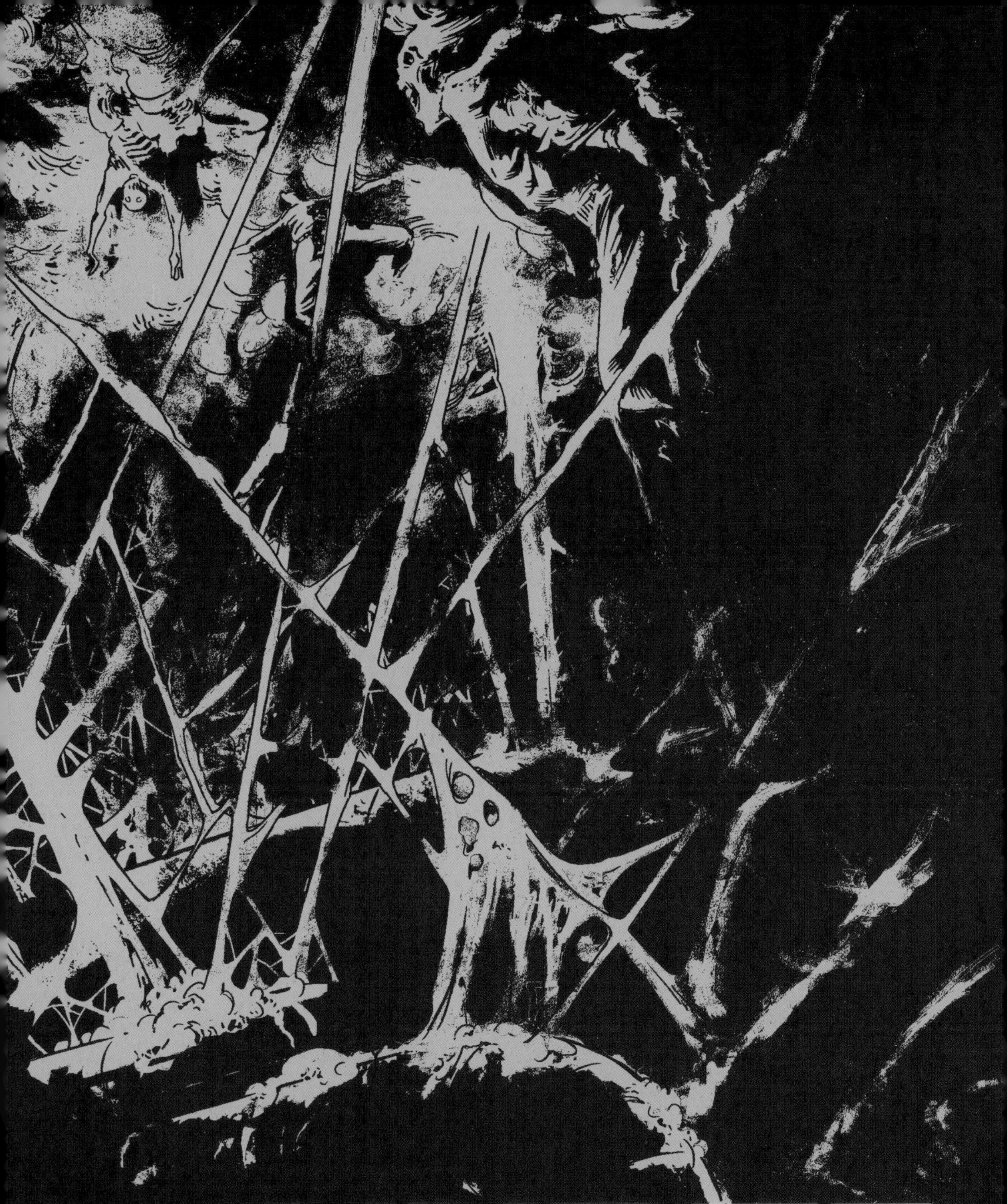

UNDER

SCOURGE OF THE SEWER

WRITTEN BY CHRISTOPHE BEC
ART BY STEFANO RAFFAELE
COLORS BY CHRISTIAN FAVRELLE

TRANSLATED BY Mark McKenzie-Ray

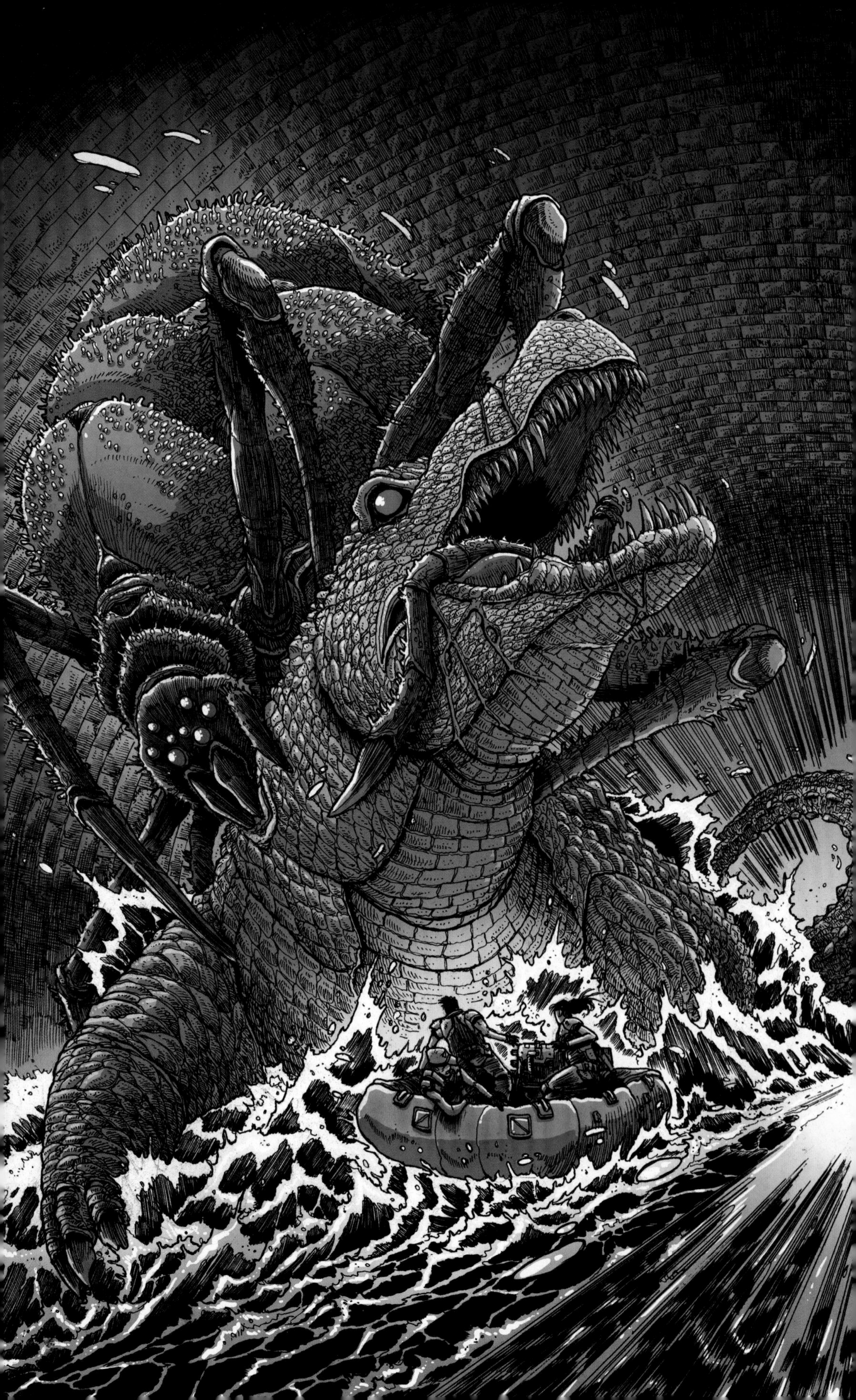

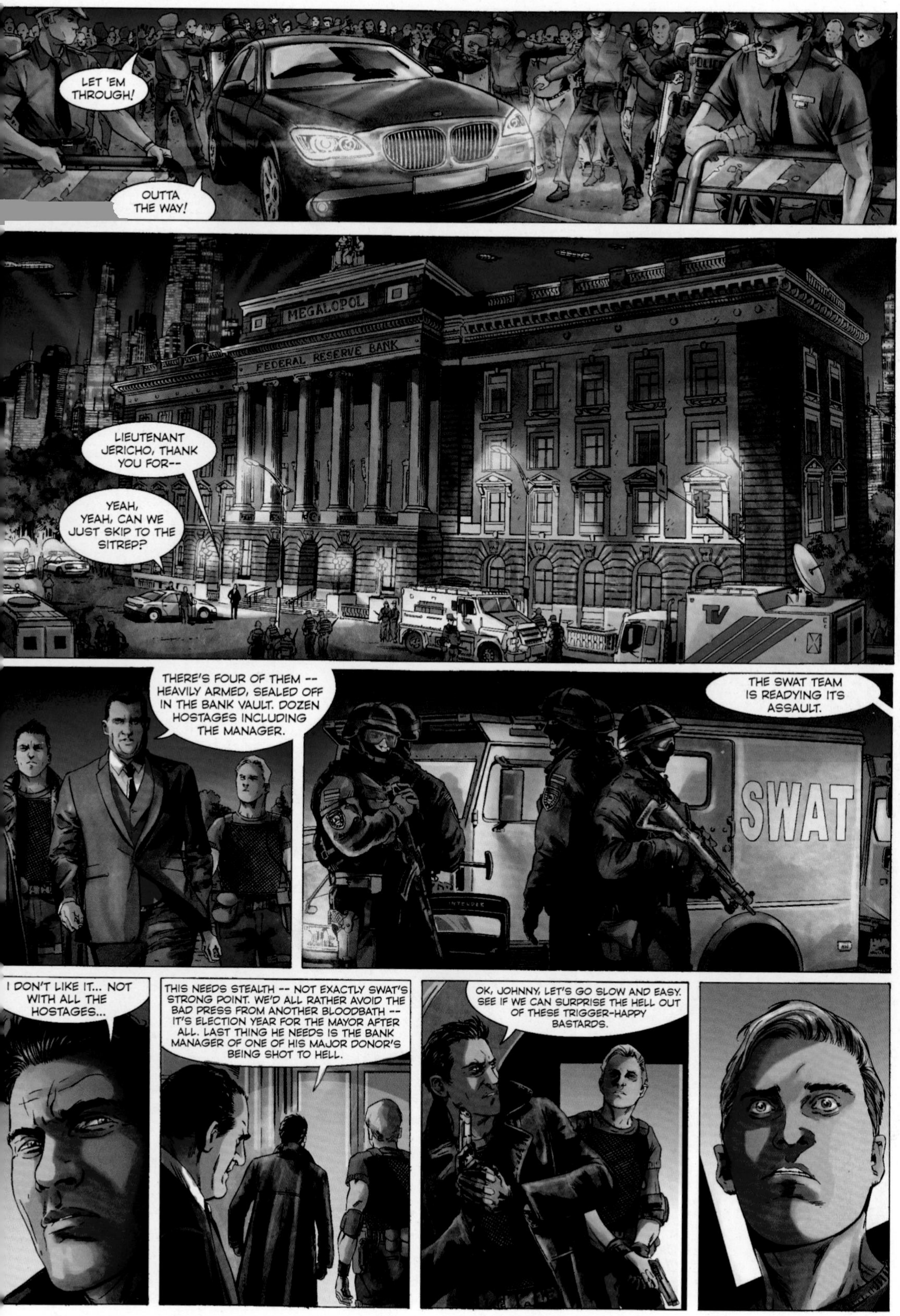
LET 'EM THROUGH!
OUTTA THE WAY!
MEGALOPOL
FEDERAL RESERVE BANK
LIEUTENANT JERICHO, THANK YOU FOR--
YEAH, YEAH, CAN WE JUST SKIP TO THE SITREP?
THERE'S FOUR OF THEM -- HEAVILY ARMED, SEALED OFF IN THE BANK VAULT. DOZEN HOSTAGES INCLUDING THE MANAGER.
THE SWAT TEAM IS READYING ITS ASSAULT.
SWAT
I DON'T LIKE IT... NOT WITH ALL THE HOSTAGES...
THIS NEEDS STEALTH -- NOT EXACTLY SWAT'S STRONG POINT. WE'D ALL RATHER AVOID THE BAD PRESS FROM ANOTHER BLOODBATH -- IT'S ELECTION YEAR FOR THE MAYOR AFTER ALL. LAST THING HE NEEDS IS THE BANK MANAGER OF ONE OF HIS MAJOR DONOR'S BEING SHOT TO HELL.
OK, JOHNNY, LET'S GO SLOW AND EASY. SEE IF WE CAN SURPRISE THE HELL OUT OF THESE TRIGGER-HAPPY BASTARDS.

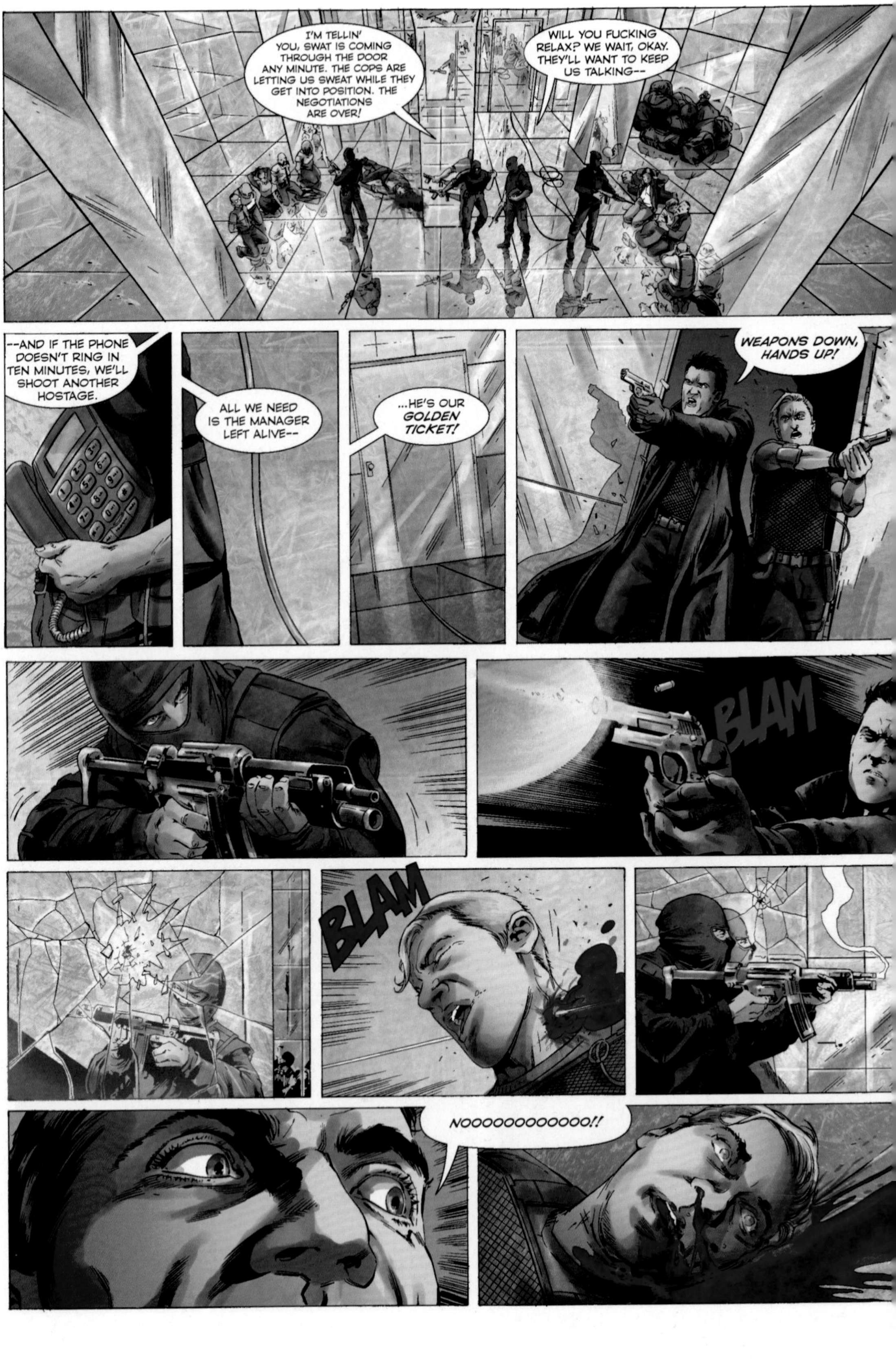
I'M TELLIN' YOU, SWAT IS COMING THROUGH THE DOOR ANY MINUTE. THE COPS ARE LETTING US SWEAT WHILE THEY GET INTO POSITION. THE NEGOTIATIONS ARE OVER!
WILL YOU FUCKING RELAX? WE WAIT, OKAY. THEY'LL WANT TO KEEP US TALKING--
--AND IF THE PHONE DOESN'T RING IN TEN MINUTES, WE'LL SHOOT ANOTHER HOSTAGE.
ALL WE NEED IS THE MANAGER LEFT ALIVE--
...HE'S OUR GOLDEN TICKET!
WEAPONS DOWN, HANDS UP!
BLAM
BLAM
NOOOOOOOOOOOO!!

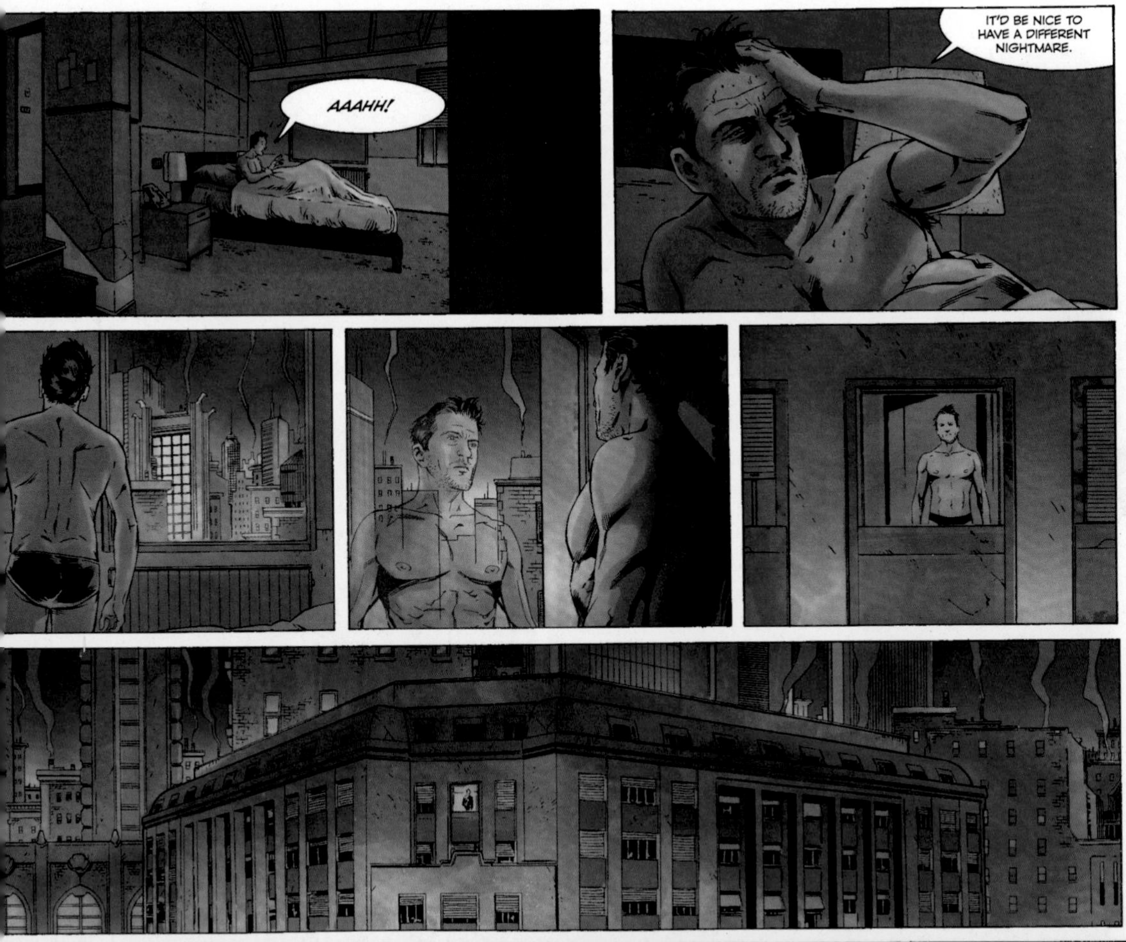
AAAHH!
IT'D BE NICE TO HAVE A DIFFERENT NIGHTMARE.

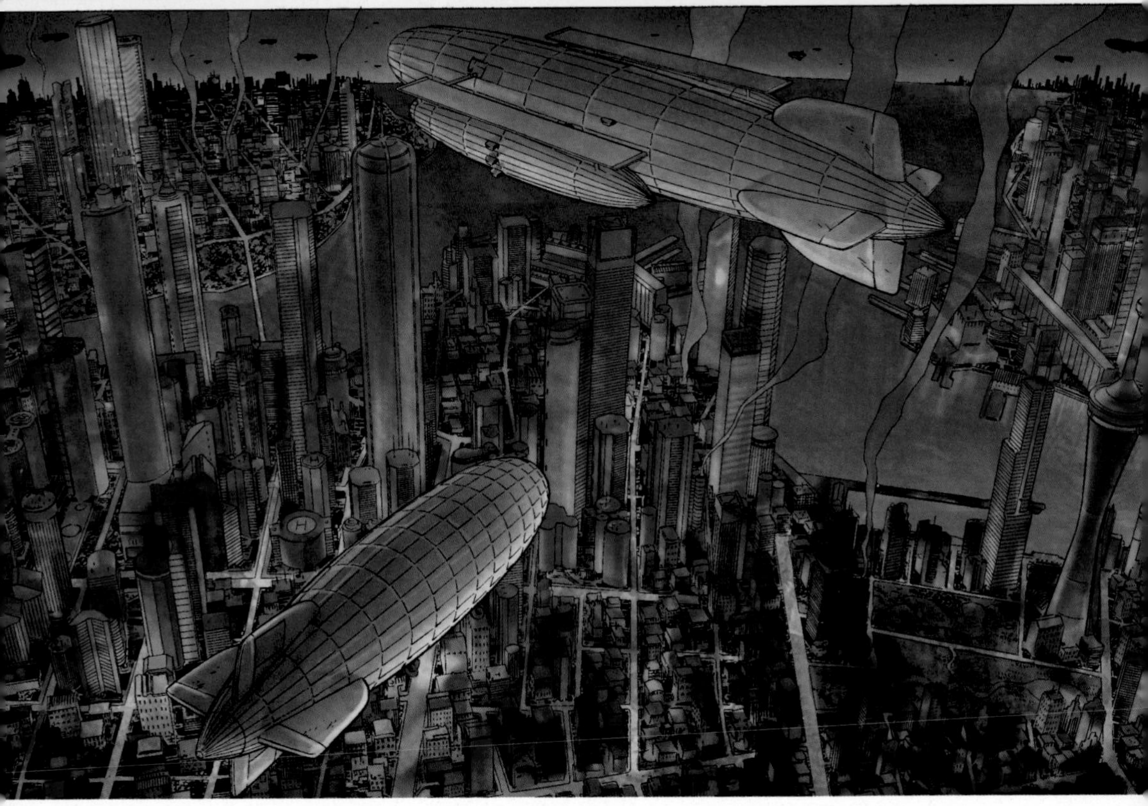

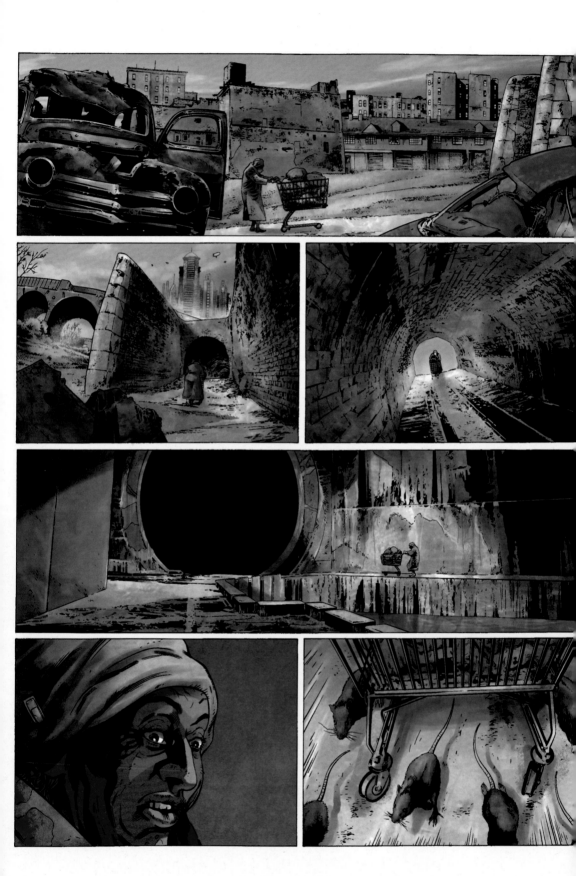

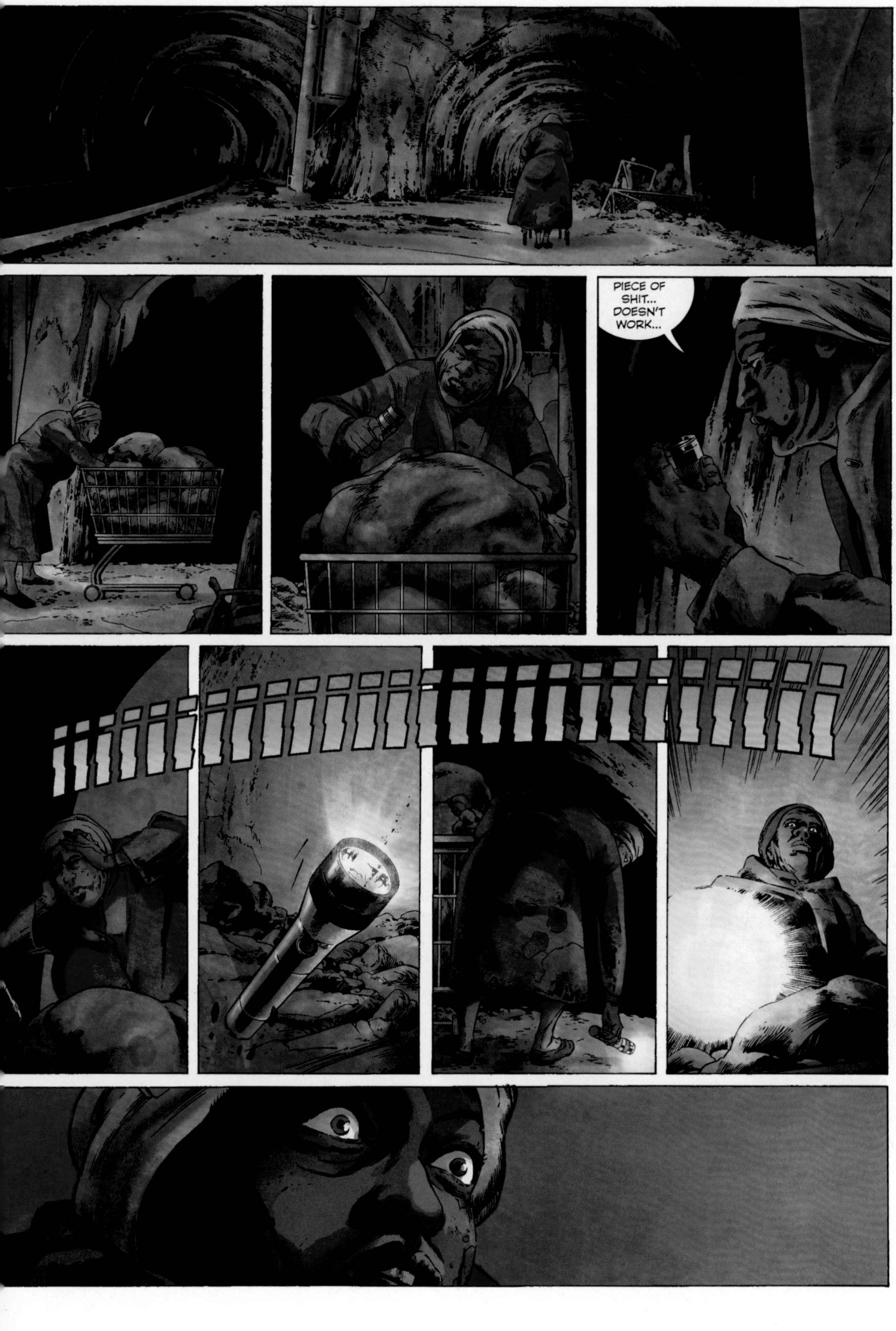
PIECE OF SHIT... DOESN'T WORK...

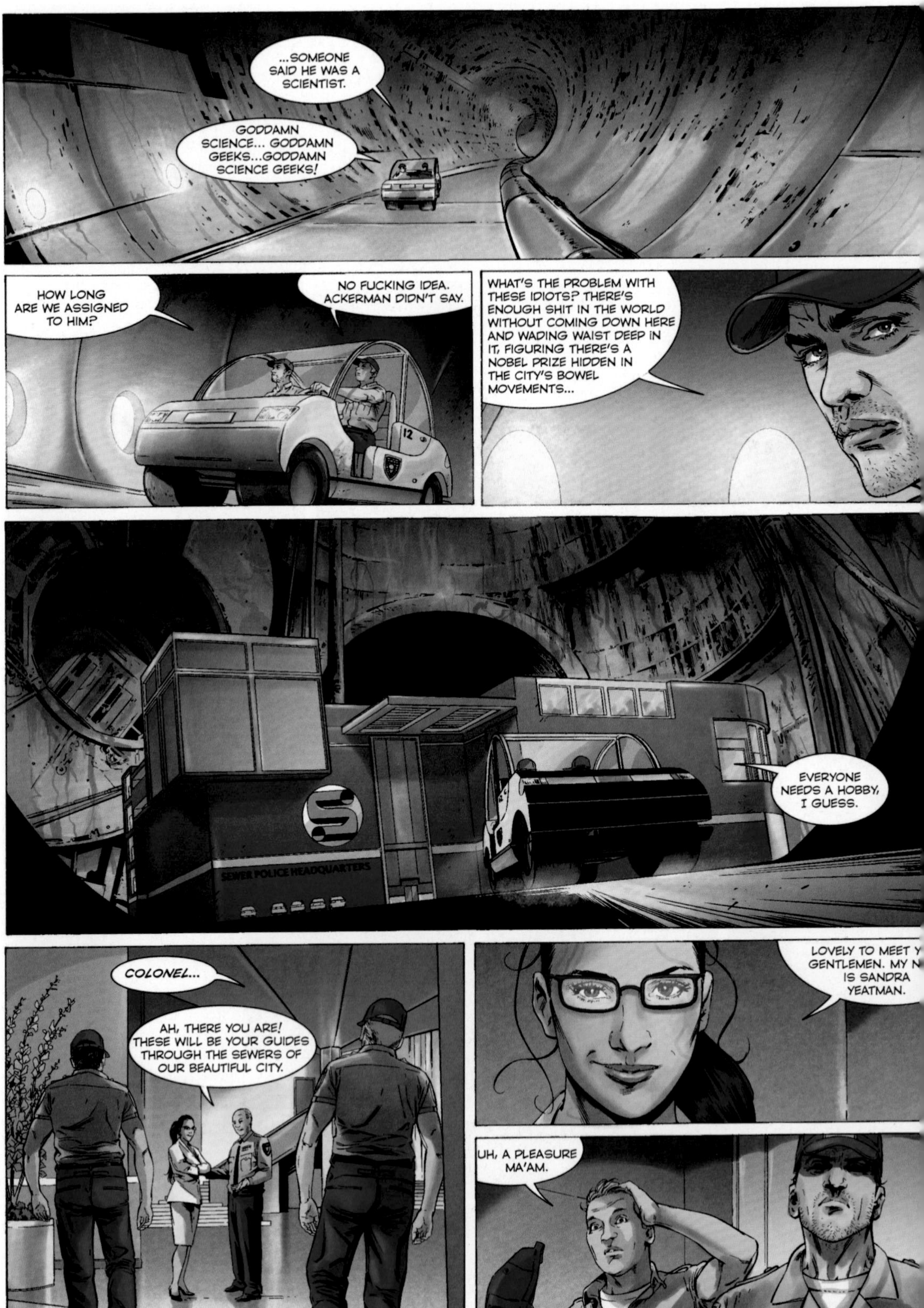
...SOMEONE SAID HE WAS A SCIENTIST.
GODDAMN SCIENCE... GODDAMN GEEKS...GODDAMN SCIENCE GEEKS!
HOW LONG ARE WE ASSIGNED TO HIM?
NO FUCKING IDEA. ACKERMAN DIDN'T SAY.
WHAT'S THE PROBLEM WITH THESE IDIOTS? THERE'S ENOUGH SHIT IN THE WORLD WITHOUT COMING DOWN HERE AND WADING WAIST DEEP IN IT, FIGURING THERE'S A NOBEL PRIZE HIDDEN IN THE CITY'S BOWEL MOVEMENTS...
SEWER POLICE HEADQUARTERS
EVERYONE NEEDS A HOBBY, I GUESS.
COLONEL...
AH, THERE YOU ARE! THESE WILL BE YOUR GUIDES THROUGH THE SEWERS OF OUR BEAUTIFUL CITY.
LOVELY TO MEET Y GENTLEMEN. MY N IS SANDRA YEATMAN.
UH, A PLEASURE MA'AM.

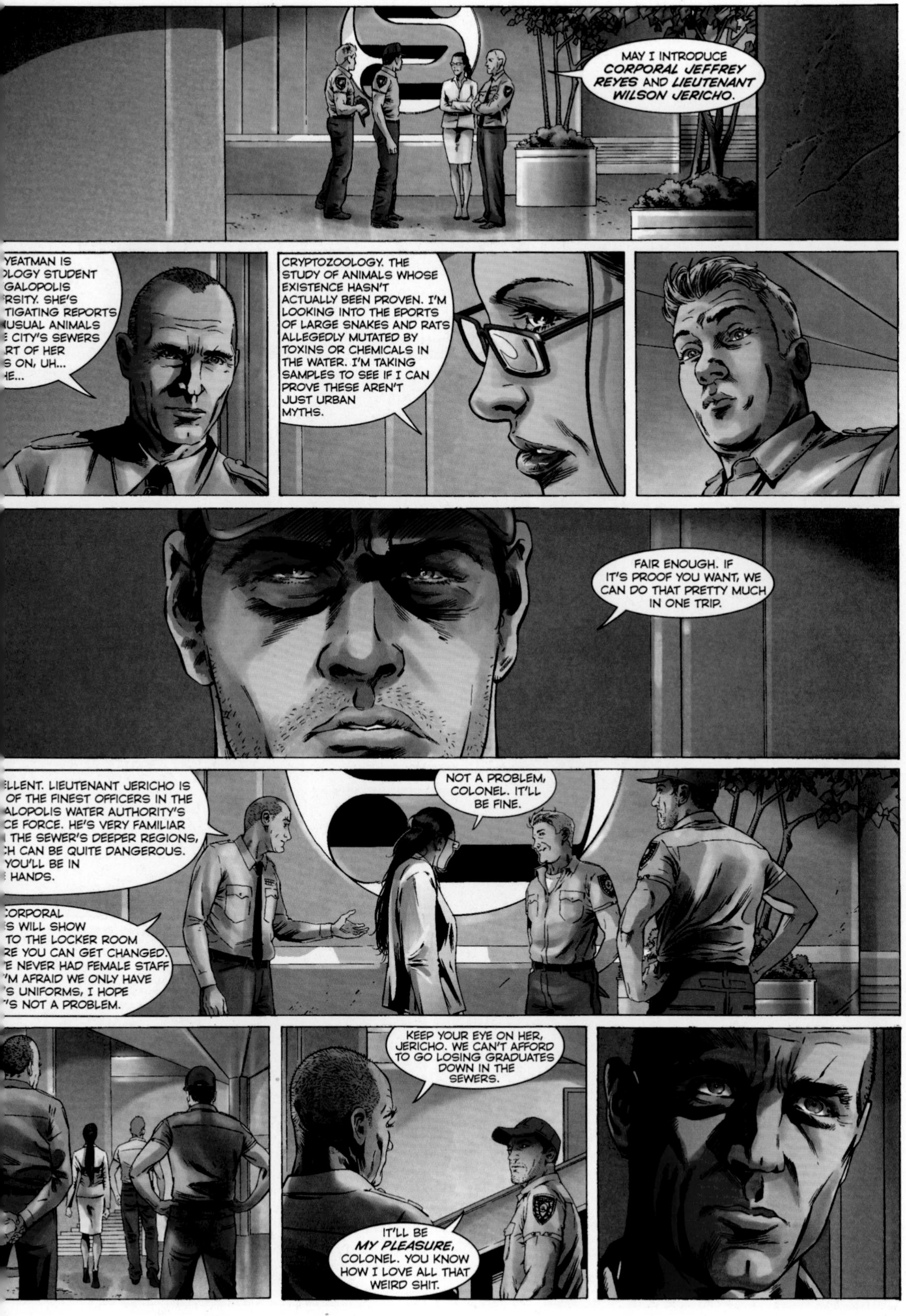
MAY I INTRODUCE CORPORAL JEFFREY REYES AND LIEUTENANT WILSON JERICHO.
YEATMAN IS OLOGY STUDENT GALOPOLIS RSITY. SHE'S TIGATING REPORTS USUAL ANIMALS E CITY'S SEWERS RT OF HER S ON, UH... HE...
CRYPTOZOOLOGY. THE STUDY OF ANIMALS WHOSE EXISTENCE HASN'T ACTUALLY BEEN PROVEN. I'M LOOKING INTO THE EPORTS OF LARGE SNAKES AND RATS ALLEGEDLY MUTATED BY TOXINS OR CHEMICALS IN THE WATER. I'M TAKING SAMPLES TO SEE IF I CAN PROVE THESE AREN'T JUST URBAN MYTHS.
FAIR ENOUGH. IF IT'S PROOF YOU WANT, WE CAN DO THAT PRETTY MUCH IN ONE TRIP.
LLENT. LIEUTENANT JERICHO IS OF THE FINEST OFFICERS IN THE ALOPOLIS WATER AUTHORITY'S CE FORCE. HE'S VERY FAMILIAR THE SEWER'S DEEPER REGIONS, CH CAN BE QUITE DANGEROUS. YOU'LL BE IN HANDS.
NOT A PROBLEM, COLONEL. IT'LL BE FINE.
CORPORAL S WILL SHOW TO THE LOCKER ROOM RE YOU CAN GET CHANGED. E NEVER HAD FEMALE STAFF 'M AFRAID WE ONLY HAVE 'S UNIFORMS, I HOPE 'S NOT A PROBLEM.
KEEP YOUR EYE ON HER, JERICHO. WE CAN'T AFFORD TO GO LOSING GRADUATES DOWN IN THE SEWERS.
IT'LL BE MY PLEASURE, COLONEL. YOU KNOW HOW I LOVE ALL THAT WEIRD SHIT.

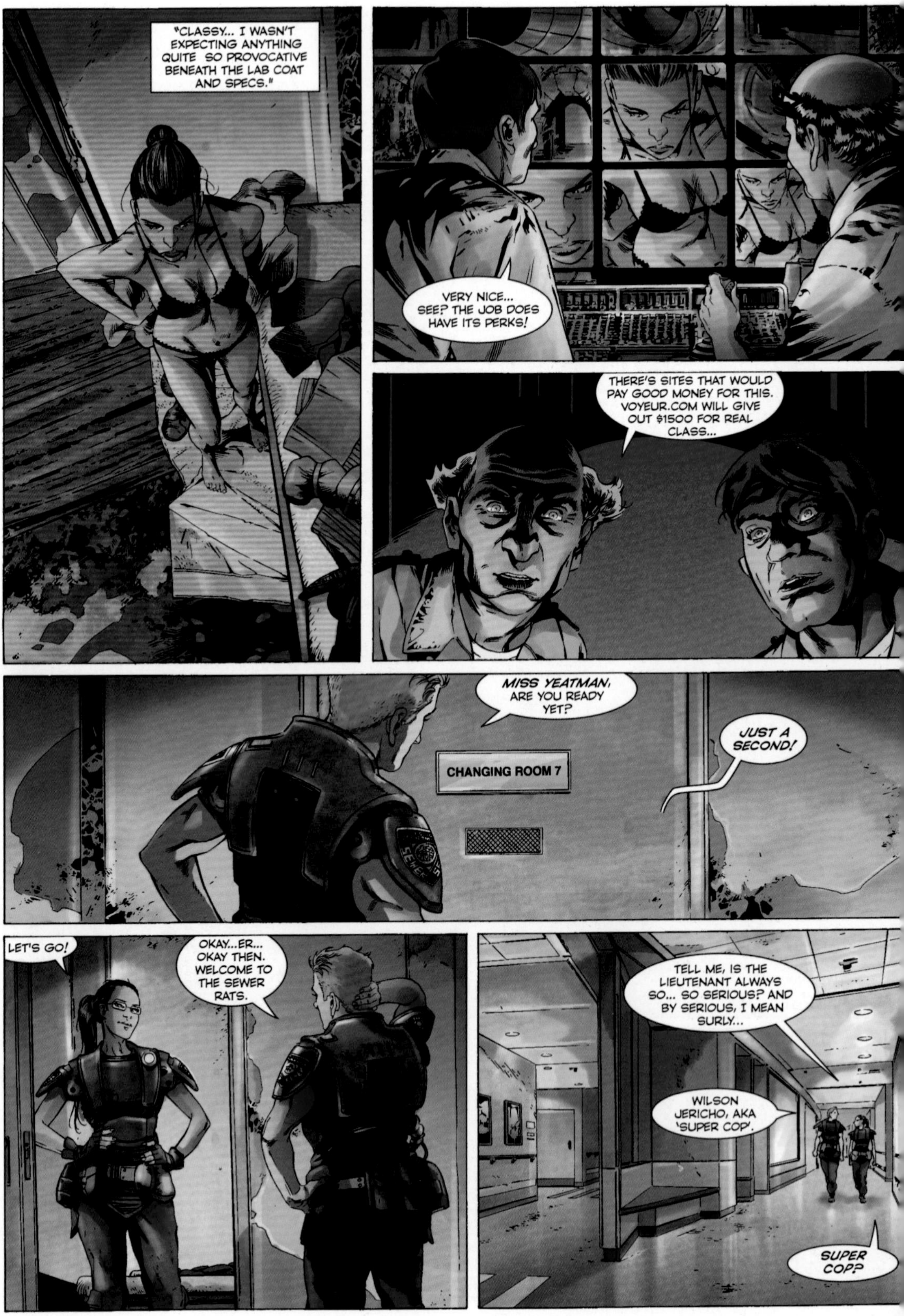
"CLASSY... I WASN'T EXPECTING ANYTHING QUITE SO PROVOCATIVE BENEATH THE LAB COAT AND SPECS."
VERY NICE... SEE? THE JOB DOES HAVE ITS PERKS!
THERE'S SITES THAT WOULD PAY GOOD MONEY FOR THIS. VOYEUR.COM WILL GIVE OUT $1500 FOR REAL CLASS...
MISS YEATMAN, ARE YOU READY YET?
CHANGING ROOM 7
JUST A SECOND!
LET'S GO!
OKAY...ER... OKAY THEN. WELCOME TO THE SEWER RATS.
TELL ME, IS THE LIEUTENANT ALWAYS SO... SO SERIOUS? AND BY SERIOUS, I MEAN SURLY...
WILSON JERICHO, AKA 'SUPER COP'.
SUPER COP?

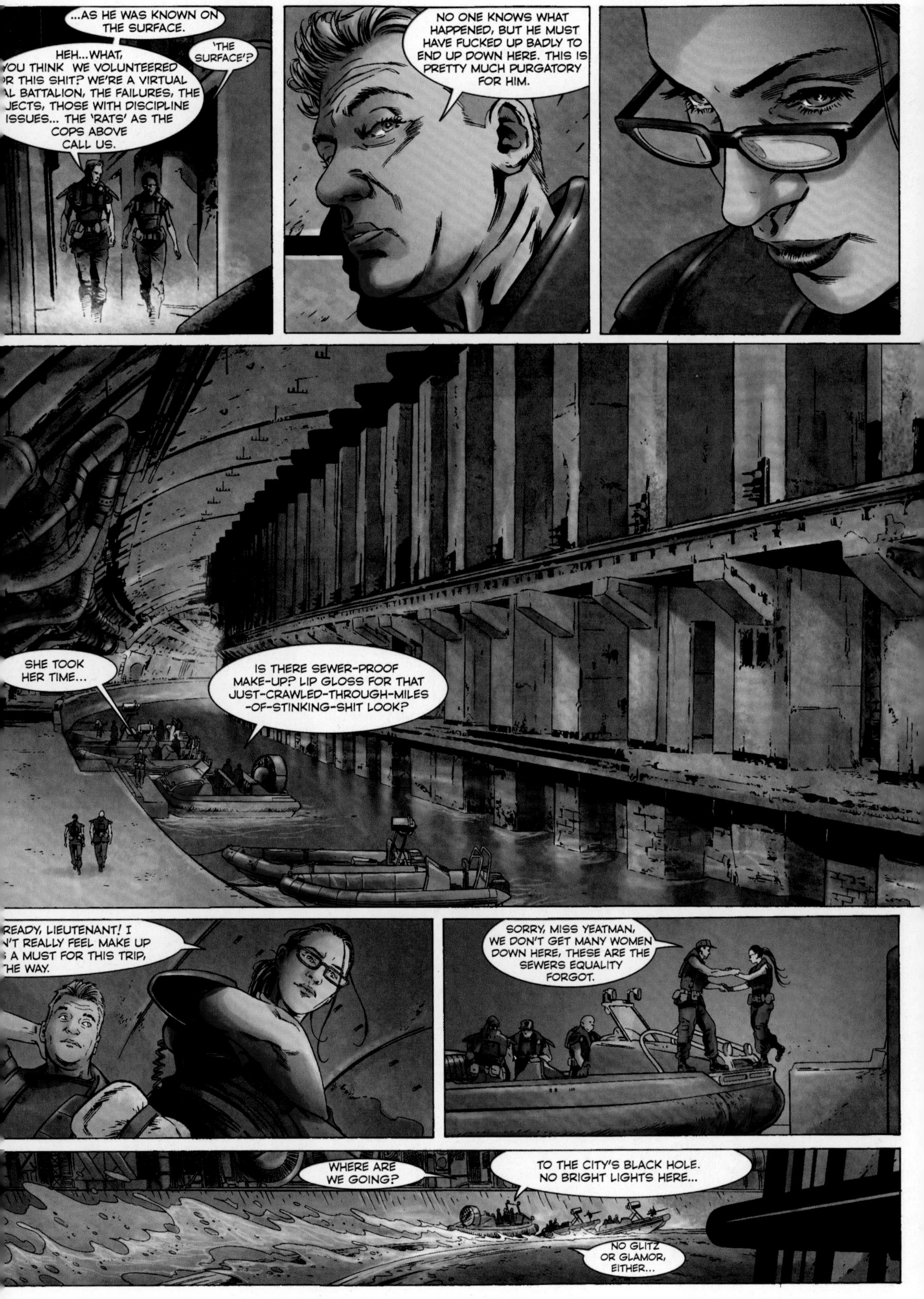

...AS HE WAS KNOWN ON THE SURFACE.
HEH...WHAT, YOU THINK WE VOLUNTEERED FOR THIS SHIT? WE'RE A VIRTUAL PENAL BATTALION, THE FAILURES, THE REJECTS, THOSE WITH DISCIPLINE ISSUES... THE 'RATS' AS THE COPS ABOVE CALL US.
'THE SURFACE'?
NO ONE KNOWS WHAT HAPPENED, BUT HE MUST HAVE FUCKED UP BADLY TO END UP DOWN HERE. THIS IS PRETTY MUCH PURGATORY FOR HIM.
SHE TOOK HER TIME...
IS THERE SEWER-PROOF MAKE-UP? LIP GLOSS FOR THAT JUST-CRAWLED-THROUGH-MILES-OF-STINKING-SHIT LOOK?
READY, LIEUTENANT! I DIDN'T REALLY FEEL MAKE UP WAS A MUST FOR THIS TRIP, BY THE WAY.
SORRY, MISS YEATMAN, WE DON'T GET MANY WOMEN DOWN HERE, THESE ARE THE SEWERS EQUALITY FORGOT.
WHERE ARE WE GOING?
TO THE CITY'S BLACK HOLE. NO BRIGHT LIGHTS HERE...
NO GLITZ OR GLAMOR, EITHER...

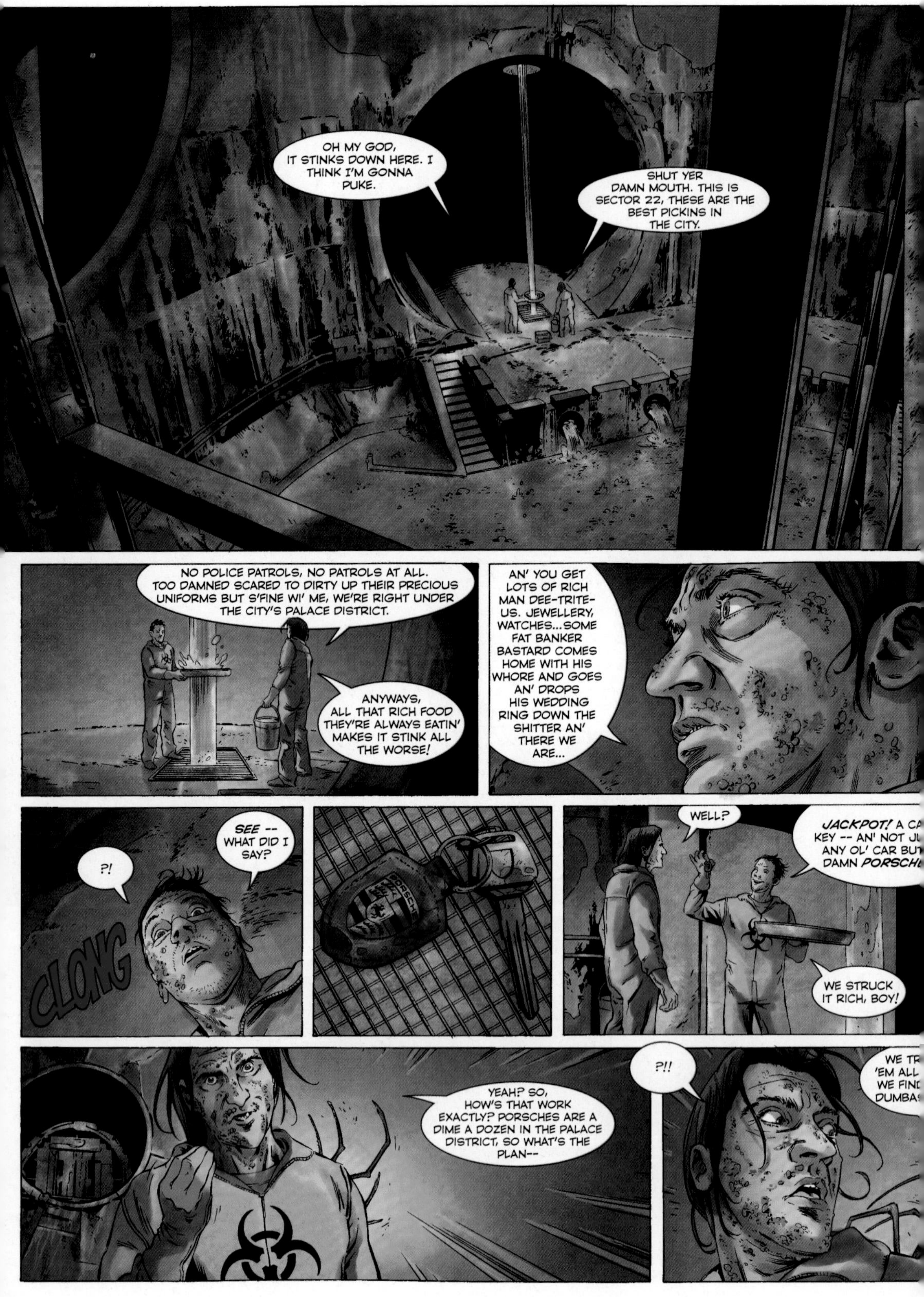
OH MY GOD, IT STINKS DOWN HERE. I THINK I'M GONNA PUKE.
SHUT YER DAMN MOUTH. THIS IS SECTOR 22, THESE ARE THE BEST PICKINS IN THE CITY.
NO POLICE PATROLS, NO PATROLS AT ALL. TOO DAMNED SCARED TO DIRTY UP THEIR PRECIOUS UNIFORMS BUT S'FINE WI' ME, WE'RE RIGHT UNDER THE CITY'S PALACE DISTRICT.
ANYWAYS, ALL THAT RICH FOOD THEY'RE ALWAYS EATIN' MAKES IT STINK ALL THE WORSE!
AN' YOU GET LOTS OF RICH MAN DEE-TRITE-US. JEWELLERY, WATCHES...SOME FAT BANKER BASTARD COMES HOME WITH HIS WHORE AND GOES AN' DROPS HIS WEDDING RING DOWN THE SHITTER AN' THERE WE ARE...
?!
SEE -- WHAT DID I SAY?
CLONG
PORSCHE
WELL?
JACKPOT! A CA KEY -- AN' NOT JU ANY OL' CAR BU DAMN PORSCH
WE STRUCK IT RICH, BOY!
YEAH? SO, HOW'S THAT WORK EXACTLY? PORSCHES ARE A DIME A DOZEN IN THE PALACE DISTRICT, SO WHAT'S THE PLAN--
?!!
WE TR 'EM ALL WE FIN DUMBA

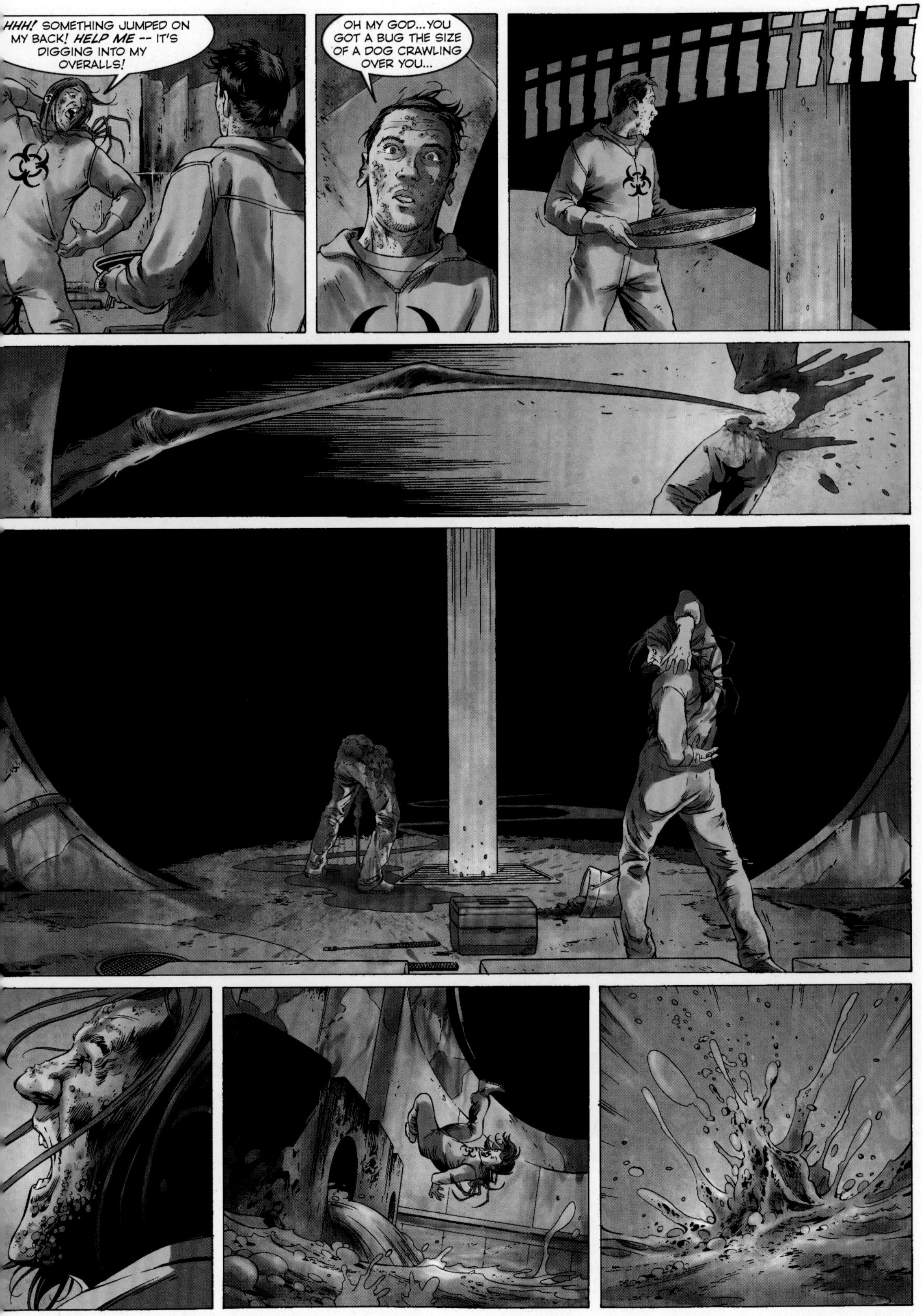
HHH! SOMETHING JUMPED ON MY BACK! HELP ME -- IT'S DIGGING INTO MY OVERALLS!
OH MY GOD...YOU GOT A BUG THE SIZE OF A DOG CRAWLING OVER YOU...

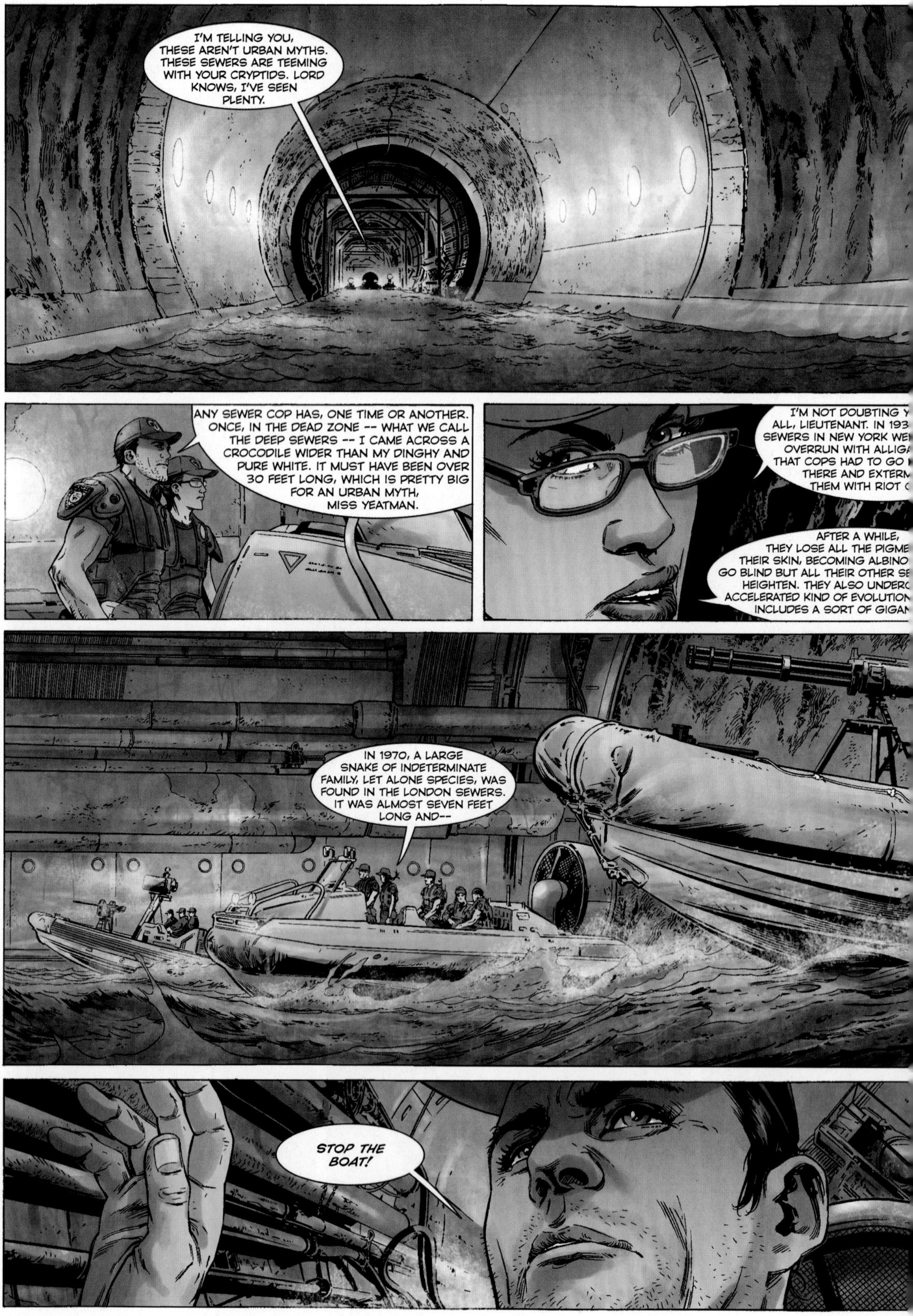
I'M TELLING YOU, THESE AREN'T URBAN MYTHS. THESE SEWERS ARE TEEMING WITH YOUR CRYPTIDS. LORD KNOWS, I'VE SEEN PLENTY.
ANY SEWER COP HAS, ONE TIME OR ANOTHER. ONCE, IN THE DEAD ZONE -- WHAT WE CALL THE DEEP SEWERS -- I CAME ACROSS A CROCODILE WIDER THAN MY DINGHY AND PURE WHITE. IT MUST HAVE BEEN OVER 30 FEET LONG, WHICH IS PRETTY BIG FOR AN URBAN MYTH, MISS YEATMAN.
I'M NOT DOUBTING Y ALL, LIEUTENANT. IN 193 SEWERS IN NEW YORK WE OVERRUN WITH ALLIGA THAT COPS HAD TO GO THERE AND EXTERM THEM WITH RIOT
AFTER A WHILE, THEY LOSE ALL THE PIGME THEIR SKIN, BECOMING ALBINO GO BLIND BUT ALL THEIR OTHER SE HEIGHTEN. THEY ALSO UNDERG ACCELERATED KIND OF EVOLUTION INCLUDES A SORT OF GIGAN
IN 1970, A LARGE SNAKE OF INDETERMINATE FAMILY, LET ALONE SPECIES, WAS FOUND IN THE LONDON SEWERS. IT WAS ALMOST SEVEN FEET LONG AND--
STOP THE BOAT!

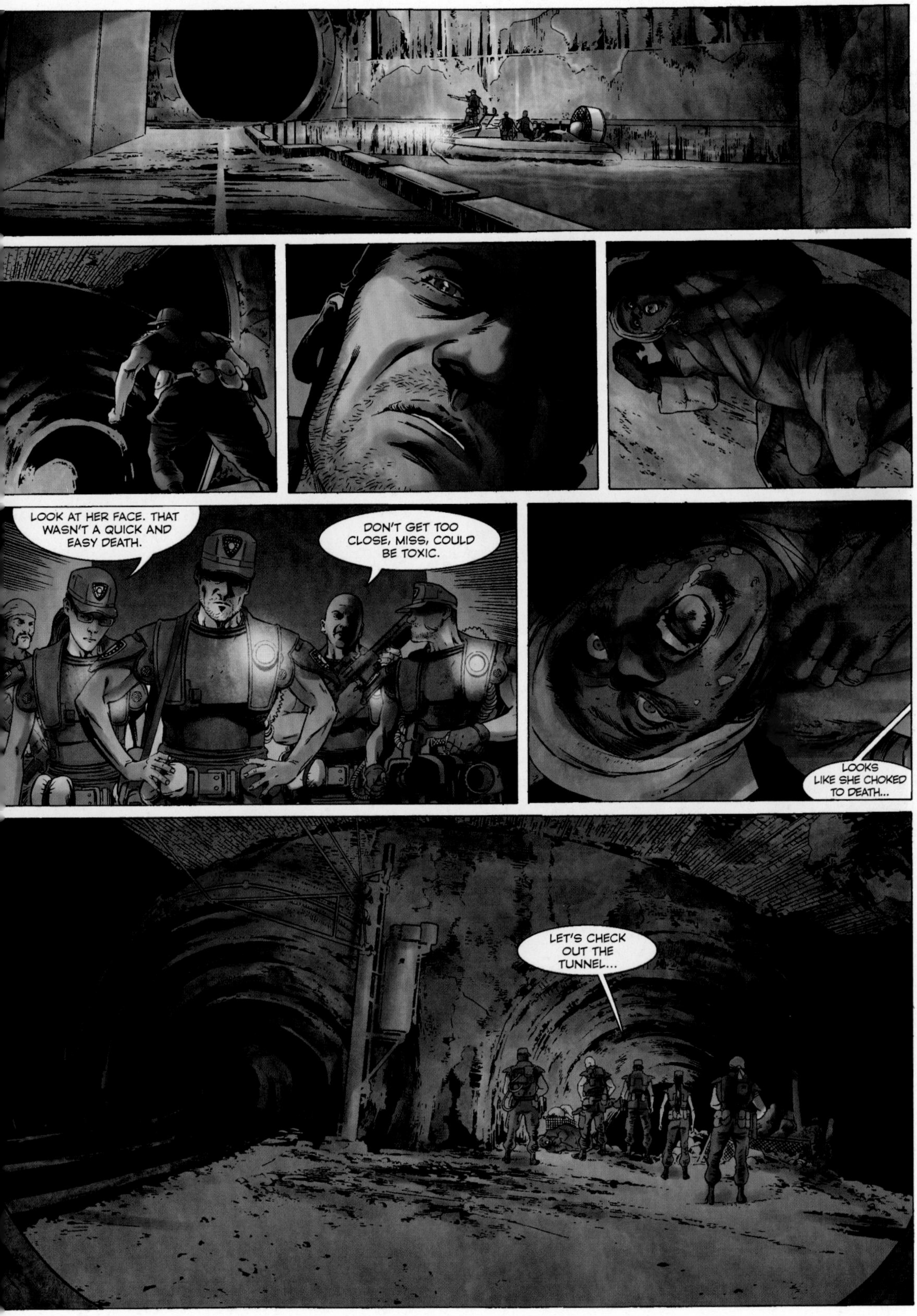
LOOK AT HER FACE. THAT WASN'T A QUICK AND EASY DEATH.
DON'T GET TOO CLOSE, MISS, COULD BE TOXIC.
LOOKS LIKE SHE CHOKED TO DEATH...
LET'S CHECK OUT THE TUNNEL...

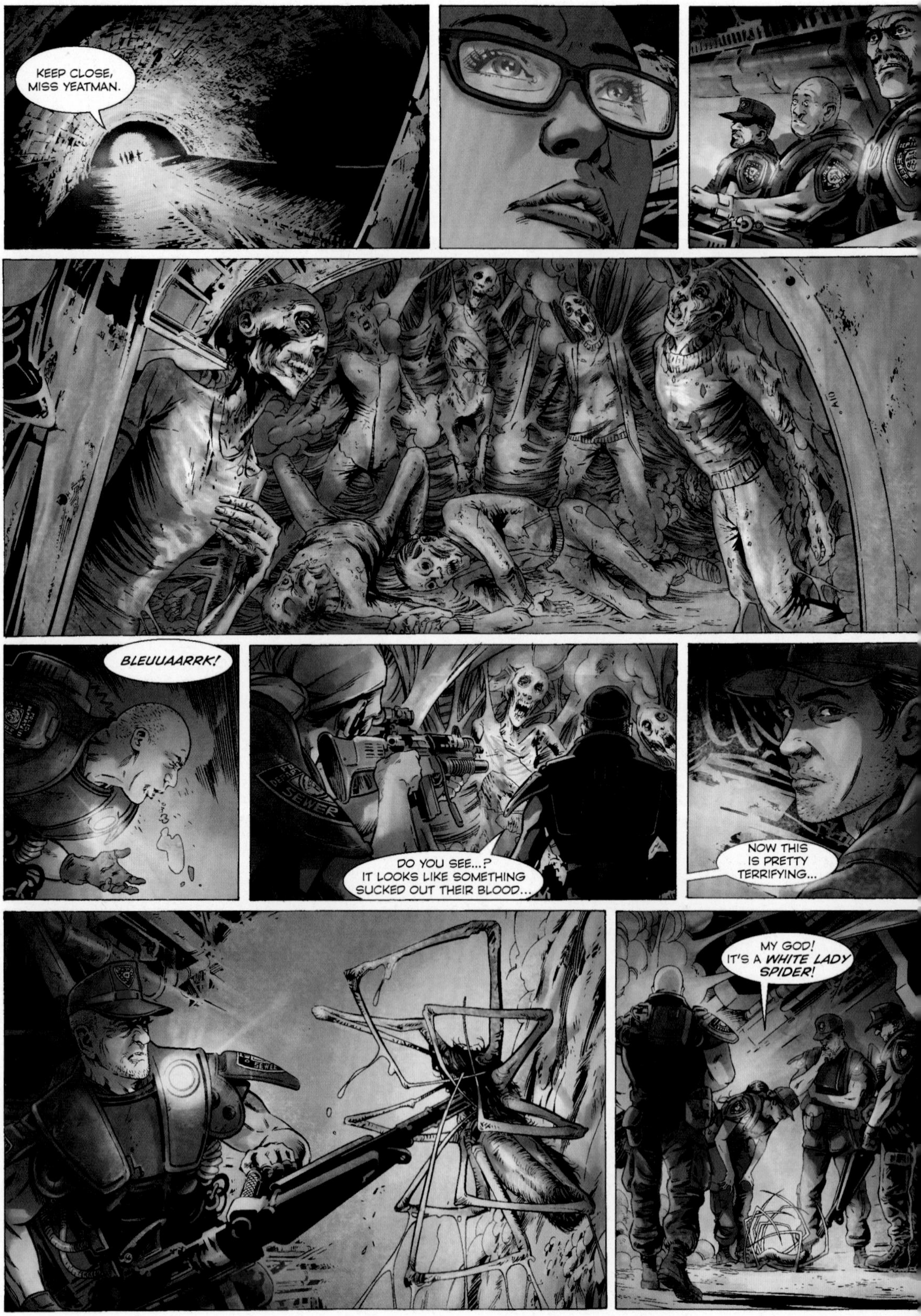
KEEP CLOSE, MISS YEATMAN.
BLEUUAARRK!
DO YOU SEE...? IT LOOKS LIKE SOMETHING SUCKED OUT THEIR BLOOD...
NOW THIS IS PRETTY TERRIFYING...
MY GOD! IT'S A *WHITE LADY SPIDER*!

TAKE
DOWN
HE
OGICAL
NUTE
AN AUTO-
SEE IF IT
Y IS A

MMM...

THERE'S MY BUS.
I SHOULD GO.

SEE YOU
TOMORROW!

YEAH, SURE --
SEE YOU THEN.

EVENING, JERICHO.
WANT THE WHOLE
BOTTLE?

THANKS.

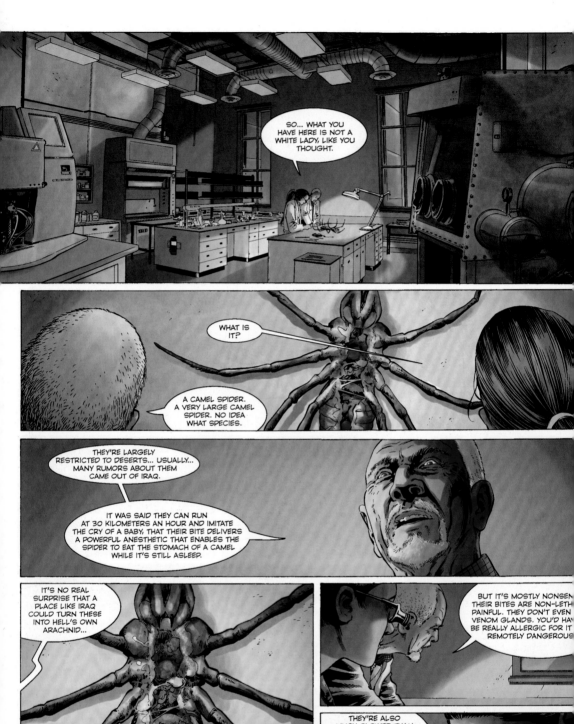

SO... WHAT YOU HAVE HERE IS NOT A WHITE LADY, LIKE YOU THOUGHT.

WHAT IS IT?

A CAMEL SPIDER. A VERY LARGE CAMEL SPIDER. NO IDEA WHAT SPECIES.

THEY'RE LARGELY RESTRICTED TO DESERTS... USUALLY... MANY RUMORS ABOUT THEM CAME OUT OF IRAQ.

IT WAS SAID THEY CAN RUN AT 30 KILOMETERS AN HOUR AND IMITATE THE CRY OF A BABY, THAT THEIR BITE DELIVERS A POWERFUL ANESTHETIC THAT ENABLES THE SPIDER TO EAT THE STOMACH OF A CAMEL WHILE IT'S STILL ASLEEP.

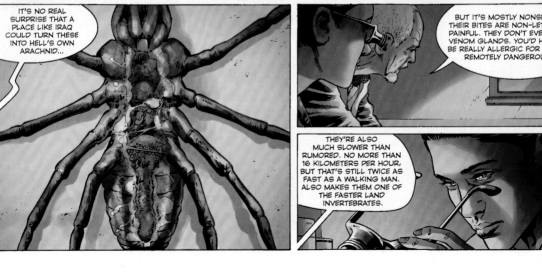

IT'S NO REAL SURPRISE THAT A PLACE LIKE IRAQ COULD TURN THESE INTO HELL'S OWN ARACHNID...

BUT IT'S MOSTLY NONSEN THEIR BITES ARE NON-LETH PAINFUL. THEY DON'T EVEN VENOM GLANDS. YOU'D HAV BE REALLY ALLERGIC FOR IT REMOTELY DANGEROUS

THEY'RE ALSO MUCH SLOWER THAN RUMORED. NO MORE THAN 16 KILOMETERS PER HOUR, BUT THAT'S STILL TWICE AS FAST AS A WALKING MAN. ALSO MAKES THEM ONE OF THE FASTER LAND INVERTEBRATES.

I HAVE NO IDEA WHERE THE BABY CRY LEGEND BEGAN. A SOLDIER DID ACCIDENTALLY BRING ONE BACK FROM AFGHANISTAN AND IT WAS RUMORED TO HAVE KILLED HIS DOG.

...LIKE THAT, THOUGH, MAYBE THEY COULD CUT INTO A CAMEL'S STOMACH...

?!

THE MOST INTRIGUING FEATURE OF THIS ONE IS ITS SIZE. GENERALLY, CAMEL SPIDERS ARE NO MORE THAN ABOUT 10 CMS IN DIAMETER. THIS ONE IS APPROXIMATELY 50...

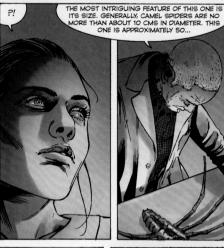

AND IN AN ENVIRONMENT IT IS COMPLETELY UNSUITED FOR. IT'S NOT AN UNKNOWN SPECIES BUT A MUTATED VERSION OF A COMMON GENUS.

AAAHHHHH!

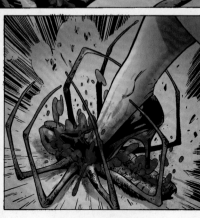

NICELY DONE, MISS YEATMAN. YOU'VE DESTROYED A UNIQUE SPECIMEN. I THOUGHT YOU WERE A SERIOUS SCIENTIST?

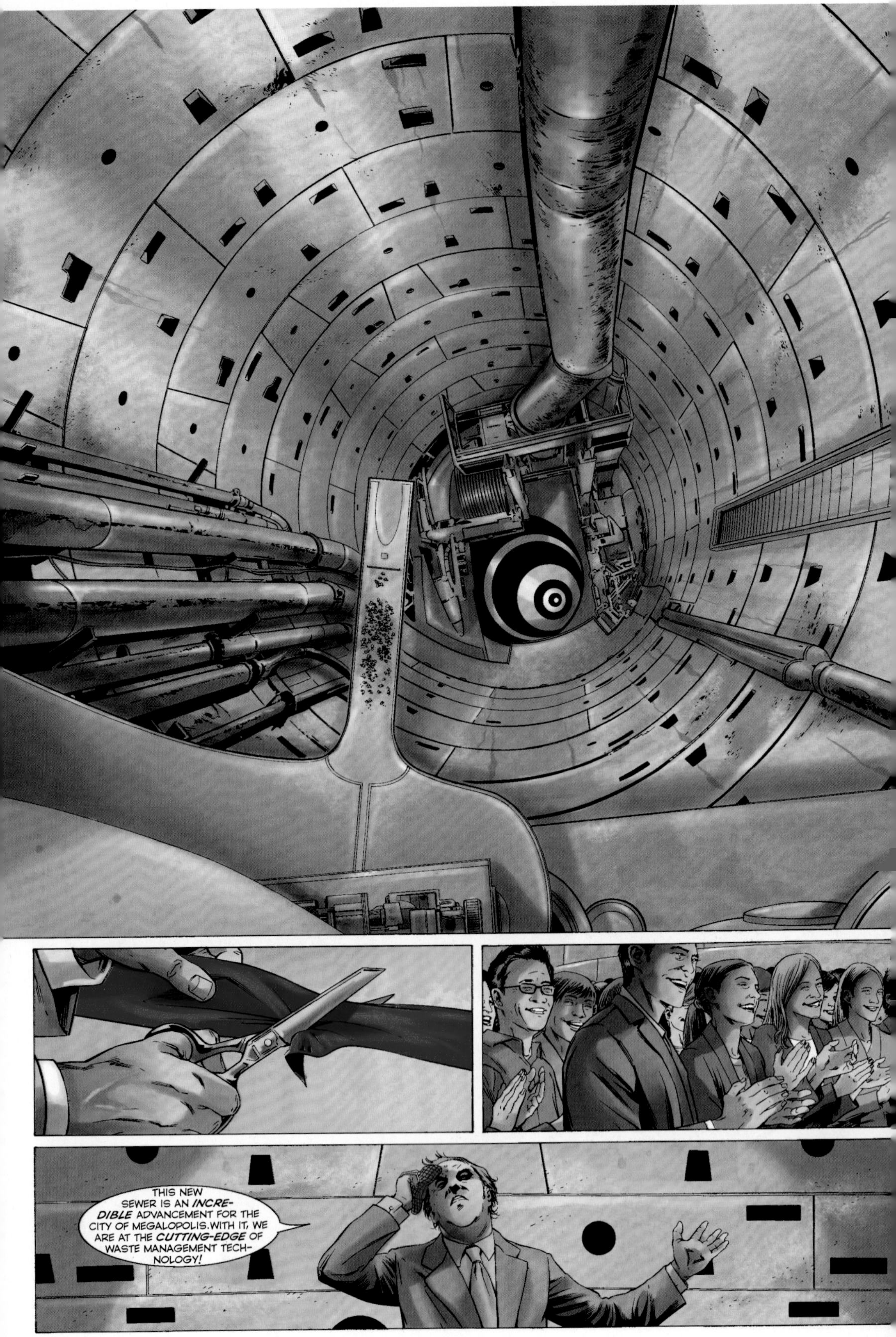
THIS NEW SEWER IS AN INCREDIBLE ADVANCEMENT FOR THE CITY OF MEGALOPOLIS. WITH IT, WE ARE AT THE CUTTING-EDGE OF WASTE MANAGEMENT TECHNOLOGY!

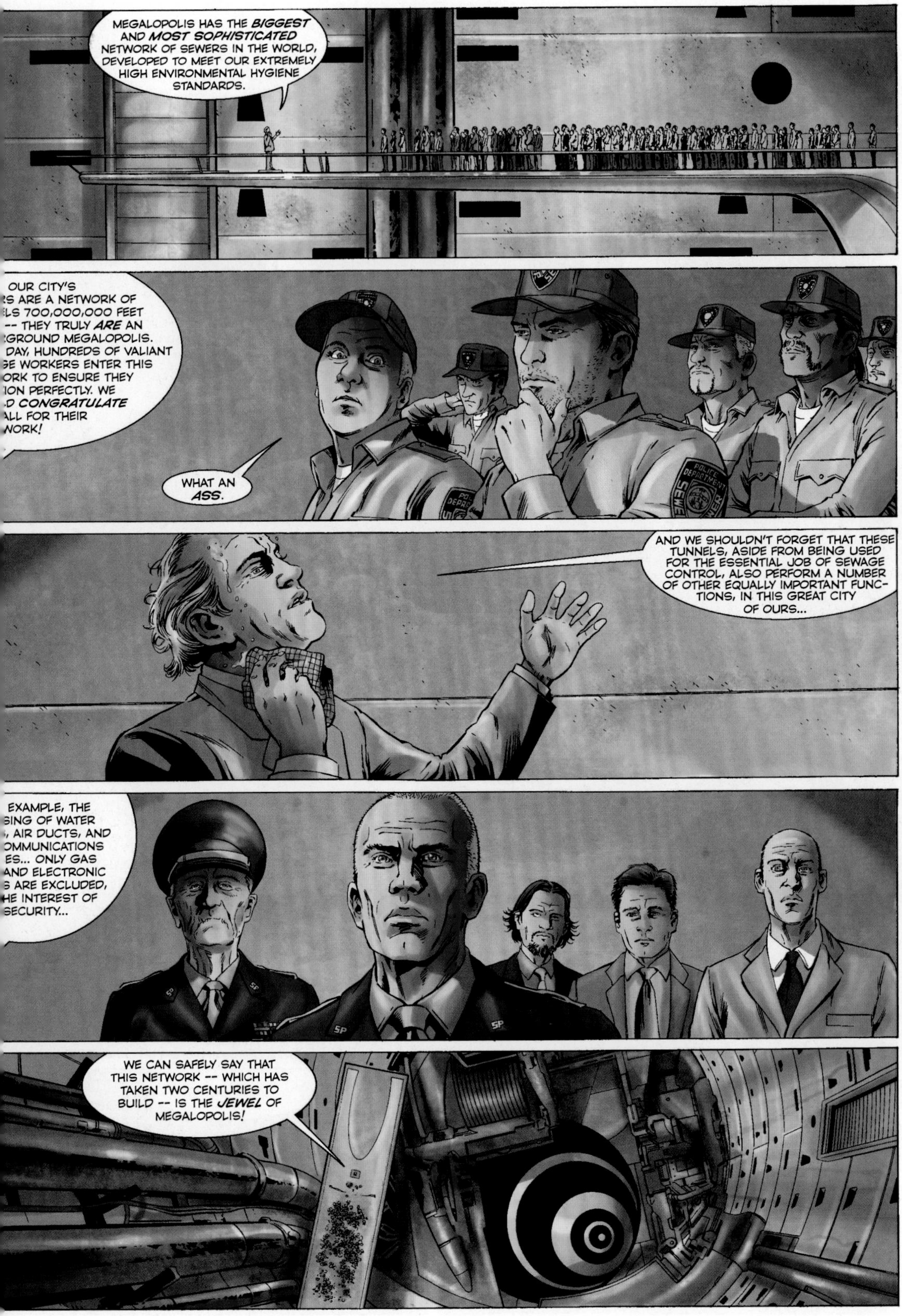
MEGALOPOLIS HAS THE *BIGGEST* AND *MOST SOPHISTICATED* NETWORK OF SEWERS IN THE WORLD, DEVELOPED TO MEET OUR EXTREMELY HIGH ENVIRONMENTAL HYGIENE STANDARDS.
OUR CITY'S ARE A NETWORK OF 700,000,000 FEET -- THEY TRULY *ARE* AN MEGALOPOLIS. DAY, HUNDREDS OF VALIANT WORKERS ENTER THIS TO ENSURE THEY PERFECTLY. WE *CONGRATULATE* ALL FOR THEIR
WHAT AN *ASS*.
AND WE SHOULDN'T FORGET THAT THESE TUNNELS, ASIDE FROM BEING USED FOR THE ESSENTIAL JOB OF SEWAGE CONTROL, ALSO PERFORM A NUMBER OF OTHER EQUALLY IMPORTANT FUNCTIONS, IN THIS GREAT CITY OF OURS...
EXAMPLE, THE OF WATER AIR DUCTS, AND ONLY GAS AND ELECTRONIC ARE EXCLUDED, INTEREST OF
WE CAN SAFELY SAY THAT THIS NETWORK -- WHICH HAS TAKEN TWO CENTURIES TO BUILD -- IS THE *JEWEL* OF MEGALOPOLIS!

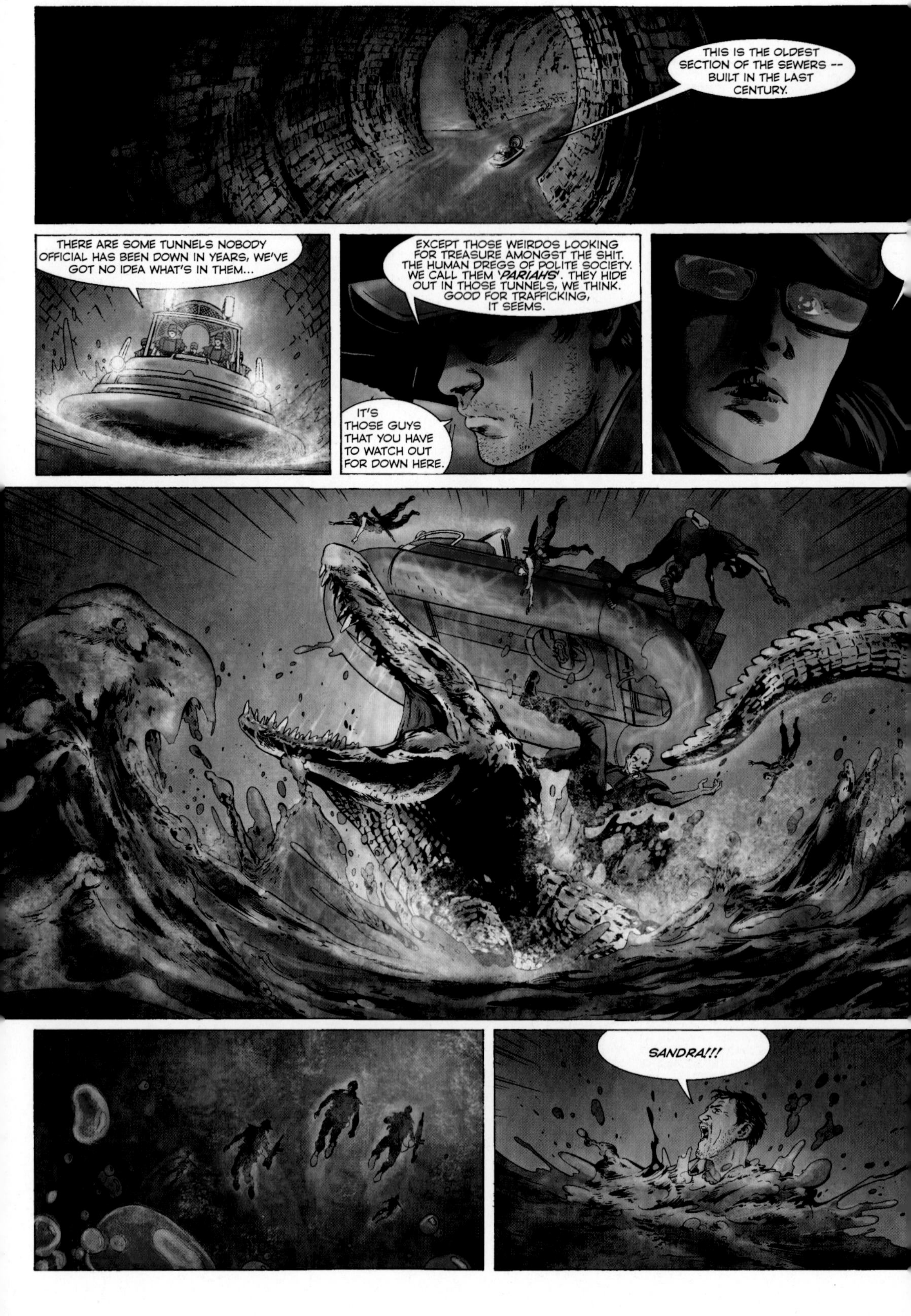
THIS IS THE OLDEST SECTION OF THE SEWERS -- BUILT IN THE LAST CENTURY.
THERE ARE SOME TUNNELS NOBODY OFFICIAL HAS BEEN DOWN IN YEARS, WE'VE GOT NO IDEA WHAT'S IN THEM...
EXCEPT THOSE WEIRDOS LOOKING FOR TREASURE AMONGST THE SHIT. THE HUMAN DREGS OF POLITE SOCIETY. WE CALL THEM 'PARIAHS'. THEY HIDE OUT IN THOSE TUNNELS, WE THINK. GOOD FOR TRAFFICKING, IT SEEMS.
IT'S THOSE GUYS THAT YOU HAVE TO WATCH OUT FOR DOWN HERE.
SANDRA!!!

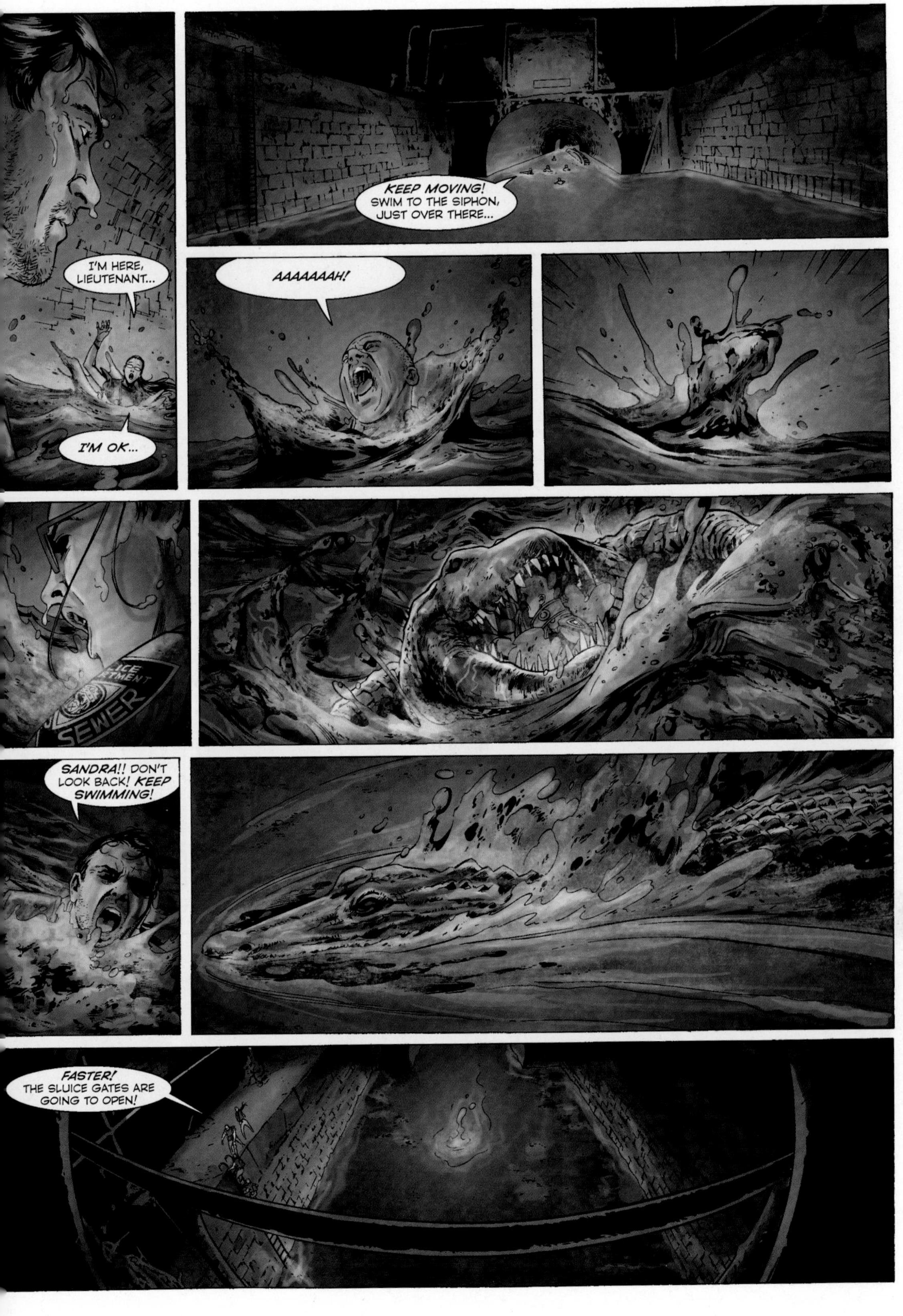
KEEP MOVING! SWIM TO THE SIPHON, JUST OVER THERE...
I'M HERE, LIEUTENANT...
I'M OK...
AAAAAAAH!
SEWER
SANDRA!! DON'T LOOK BACK! KEEP SWIMMING!
FASTER! THE SLUICE GATES ARE GOING TO OPEN!

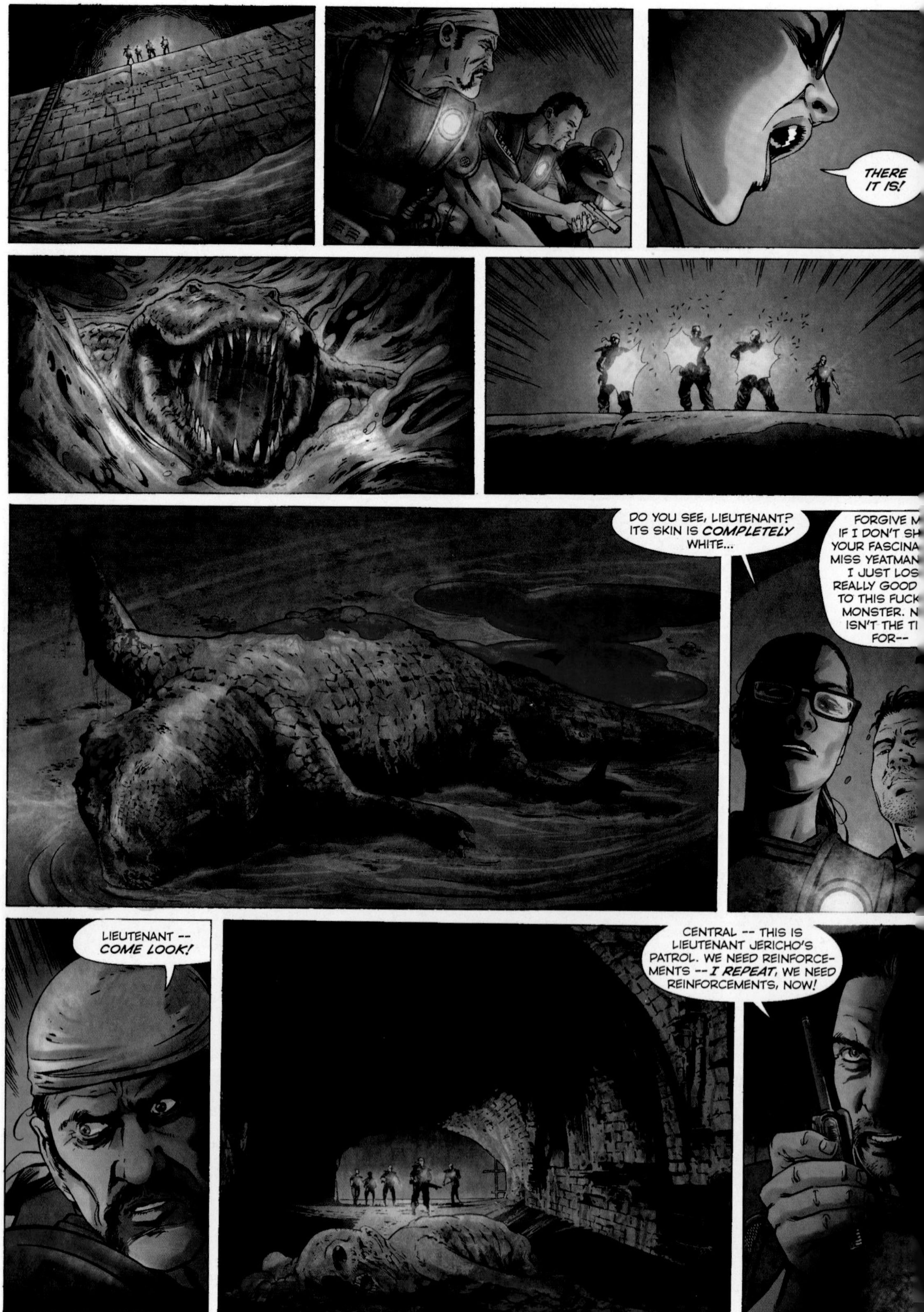
THERE IT IS!
DO YOU SEE, LIEUTENANT? ITS SKIN IS COMPLETELY WHITE...
FORGIVE M IF I DON'T SH YOUR FASCINA MISS YEATMAN I JUST LOS REALLY GOOD TO THIS FUCK MONSTER. N ISN'T THE TI FOR--
LIEUTENANT -- COME LOOK!
CENTRAL -- THIS IS LIEUTENANT JERICHO'S PATROL. WE NEED REINFORCEMENTS -- I REPEAT, WE NEED REINFORCEMENTS, NOW!

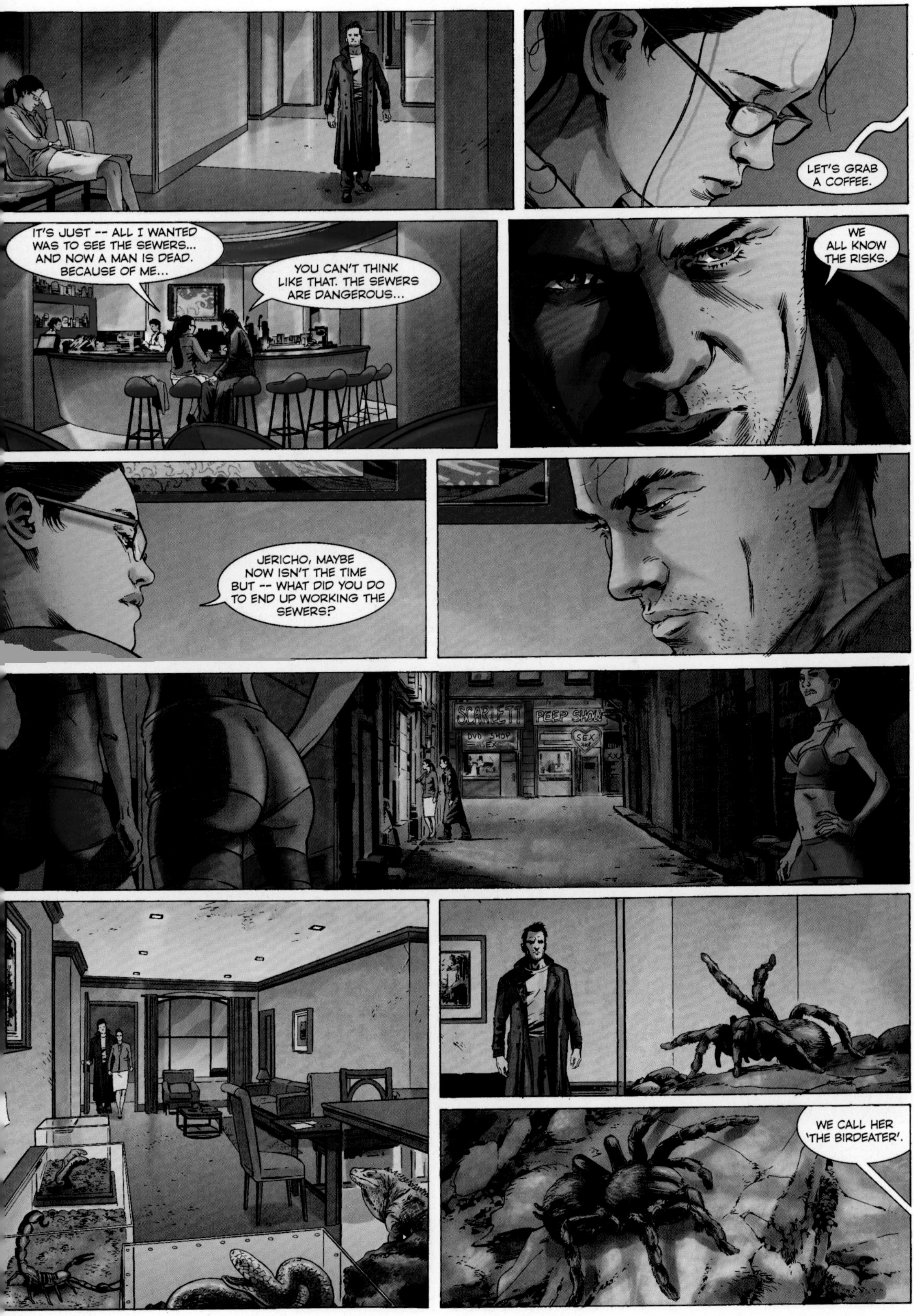
LET'S GRAB A COFFEE.
IT'S JUST -- ALL I WANTED WAS TO SEE THE SEWERS... AND NOW A MAN IS DEAD. BECAUSE OF ME...
YOU CAN'T THINK LIKE THAT. THE SEWERS ARE DANGEROUS...
WE ALL KNOW THE RISKS.
JERICHO, MAYBE NOW ISN'T THE TIME BUT -- WHAT DID YOU DO TO END UP WORKING THE SEWERS?
SCARLETT
PEEP SHOW
DVD SHOP
SEX
SEX
WE CALL HER 'THE BIRDEATER'.

SHE'S A MYGALE GOLIATH. SHE'S 11 INCHES WIDE, BUT OTHER SPIDERS FROM THAT SPECIES USUALLY AVERAGE OUT AT ABOUT FIVE INCHES.

IN THEIR NATURAL HABITATS, TH MYGALE SPIDERS ARE MOST ACTI DURING THE NIGHT. THEIR HAIRS C DETECT EVEN THE TINIEST DANGE BECAUSE THEIR EYESIGHT IS SO BAD MALES DON'T NORMALLY LIVE MORE FIVE YEARS, BUT THE FEMALES CA MAKE IT PAST 20.

SHE'S PRETTY OLD NOW, SHE'LL DIE SOON. THIS IS WHEN THEY'RE MOST VULNE-RABLE TO ATTACK, THEY ROLL ONTO THEIR BACKS...

I THOUGHT SPIDERS HAD EIGHT LEGS... THERE ARE ONLY SEVEN?

YES, NORMALLY, ALL *ARACHNIDS* ARE BORN WITH EIGHT LEGS. THESE GUYS MAIM THEMSELVES, AND WITH SURGICAL PRECISION. WE'VE GOT NO IDEA WHY, YET.

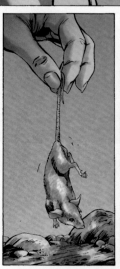

THOSE TWO TEETH C EITHER SIDE OF HER MO ARE *CHELICERAES* -- T ARTICULATED. THE O BETWEEN THEM CONTA THE VENOM.

ALL SPIDERS NEED TO *LIQUEFY* THEIR PREY IN ORDER TO INGEST THEM. THE OESOPHAGUS IS VERY TIGHT.

AFTER PARALYSING ITS PREY, THE MYGALE SPIDER MOISTENS ITS VICTIM WITH A SUBSTANCE THAT DISSOLVES THE TISSUE. THIS PULP IS THEN FILTERED BY THE HAIRS ON ITS MOUTH, WHICH REMOVES THE BIGGER PIECES...

THE REST IS CHEWED UP BY THE CHELICERAES.

MAKES YOU THINK, DOESN'T IT?

IT REALLY DOES.

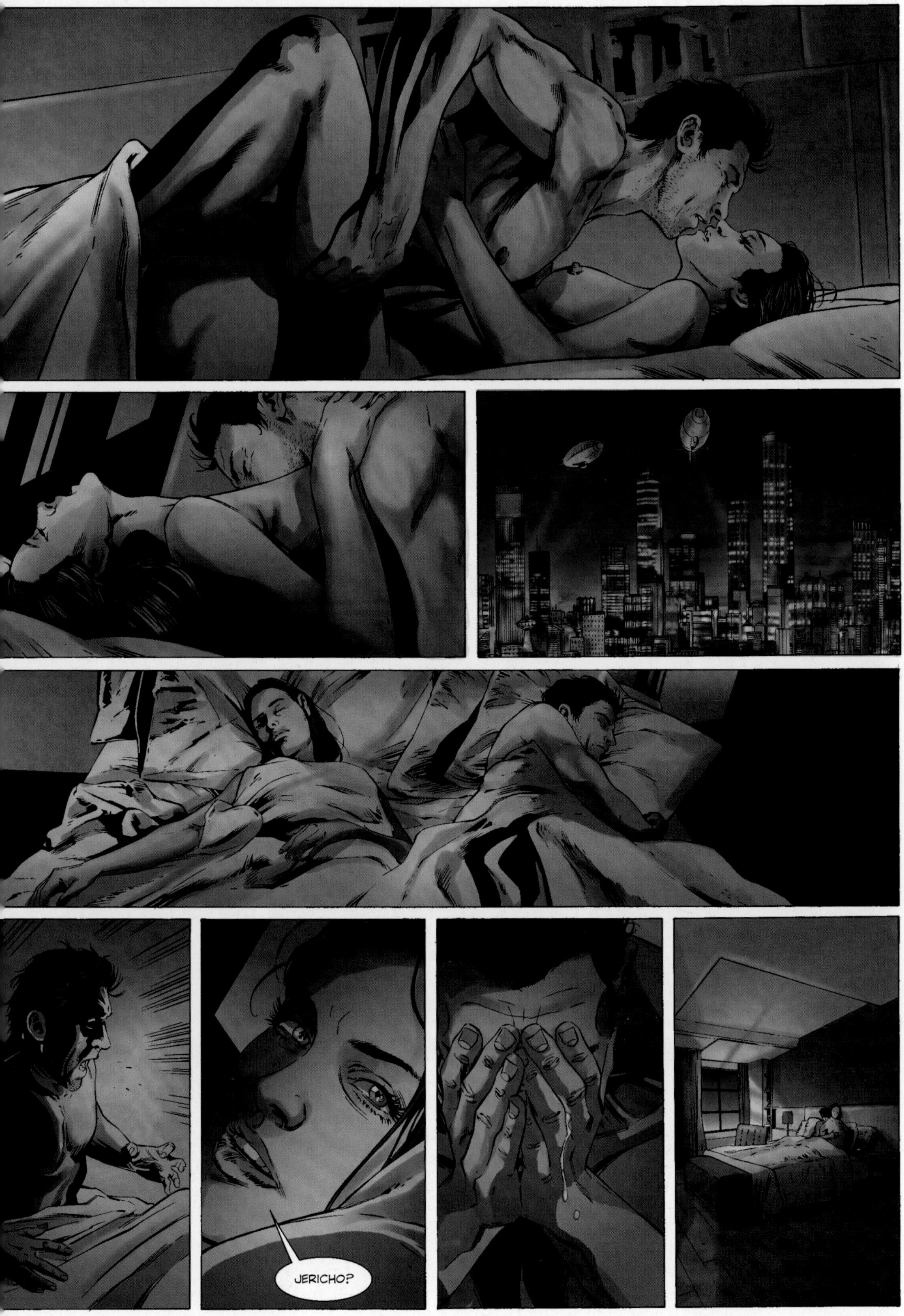

JERICHO?

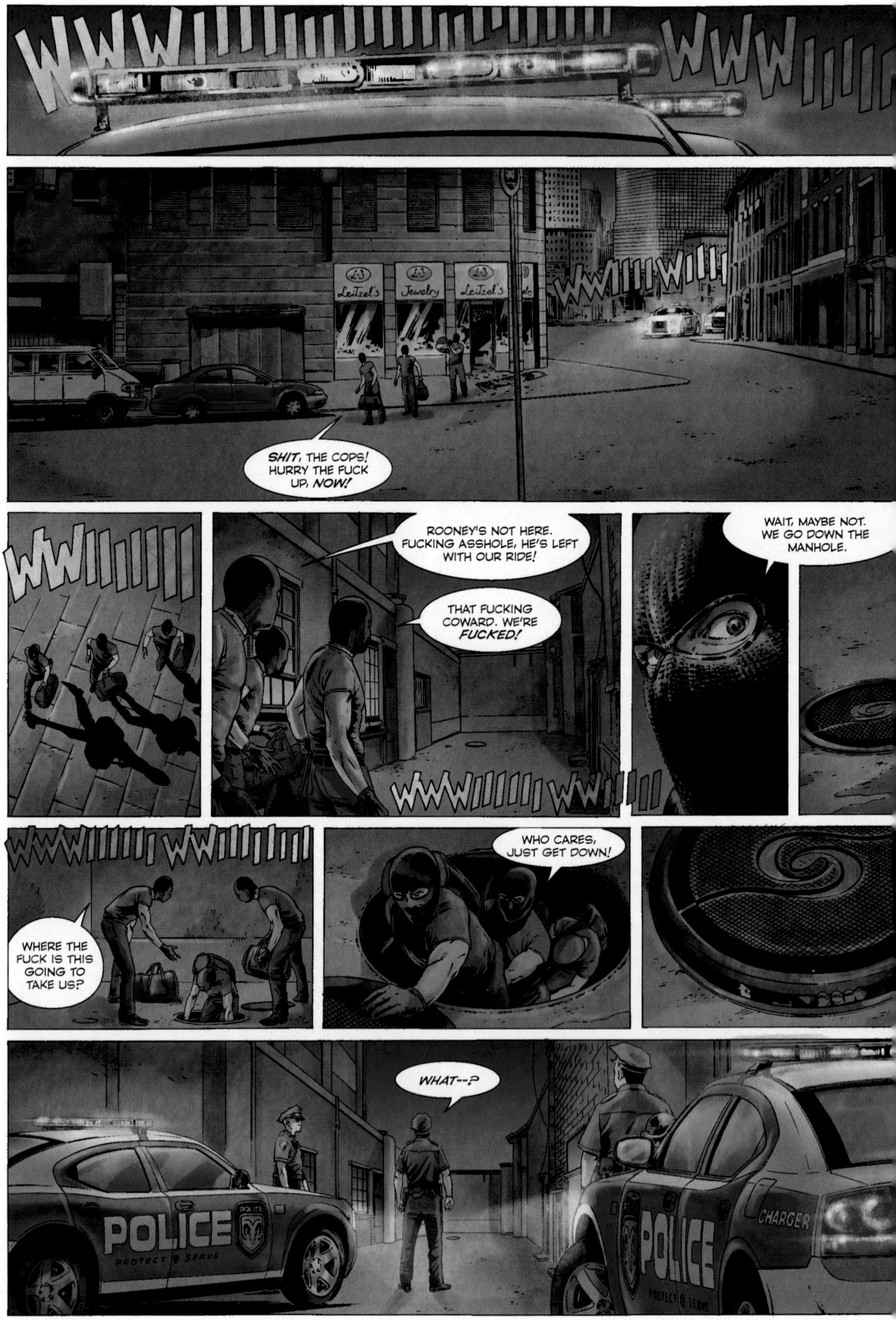
WWWIIIIIIIIIIIIIIIIIII
WWWIIIII
SHIT, THE COPS! HURRY THE FUCK UP, NOW!
WWWIIIIIWIIII
WWIIIIIIII
ROONEY'S NOT HERE. FUCKING ASSHOLE, HE'S LEFT WITH OUR RIDE!
THAT FUCKING COWARD. WE'RE FUCKED!
WWWIIIIII WWIIIII
WAIT, MAYBE NOT. WE GO DOWN THE MANHOLE.
WWWIIIIII WWIIIIIII
WHERE THE FUCK IS THIS GOING TO TAKE US?
WHO CARES, JUST GET DOWN!
WHAT--?
POLICE
PROTECT SERVE
CHARGER
POLICE
PROTECT SERVE

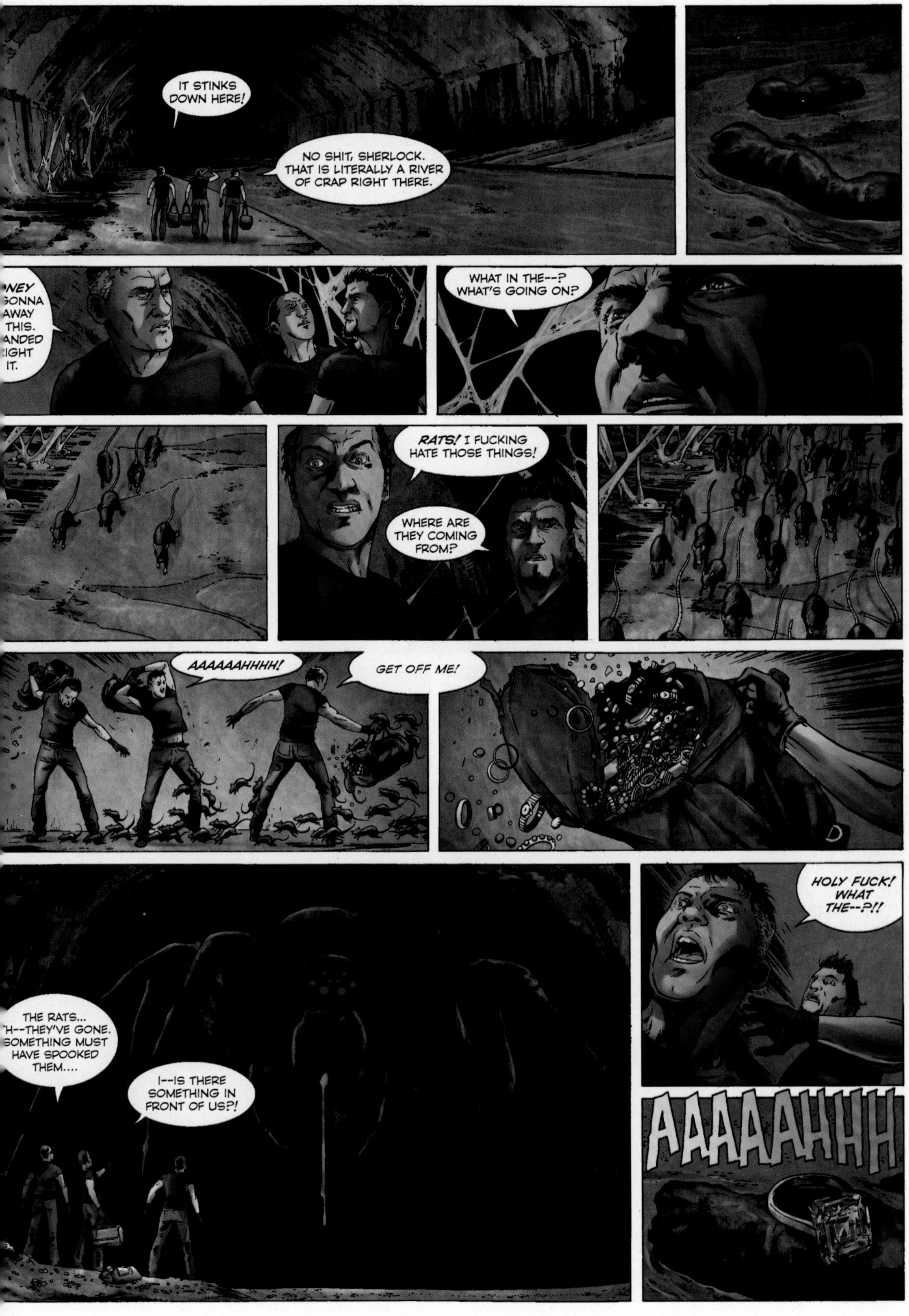

IT STINKS DOWN HERE!
NO SHIT, SHERLOCK. THAT IS LITERALLY A RIVER OF CRAP RIGHT THERE.
ONEY GONNA AWAY THIS. ANDED IGHT IT.
WHAT IN THE--? WHAT'S GOING ON?
RATS! I FUCKING HATE THOSE THINGS!
WHERE ARE THEY COMING FROM?
AAAAAAHHHH!
GET OFF ME!
THE RATS... H--THEY'VE GONE. SOMETHING MUST HAVE SPOOKED THEM....
I--IS THERE SOMETHING IN FRONT OF US?!
HOLY FUCK! WHAT THE--?!!
AAAAAHHH

NOW, THIS MAN WAS FOUND DEAD, FLOATING ON THE SURFACE OF THE CANAL. DROWNED, YOU'D ASSUME, YES, COLONEL?

BUT, THERE WAS SOMETHING OFF, WHICH FORCED ME TO REVISE MY INITIAL ASSESSMENT. DO YOU SEE THESE *MARKS* ALL OVER THE BODY, COLONEL ACKERMAN...?

HERE, LIKE LARGE INSECT BITES?

YES, I SEE THEM.

THE *SAME* MARKS WERE ON THE BODY THAT YOUR TEAM DISCOVERED.

ANOTHER EXAMPLE. HERE A HOMELESS MALE WHO L[...] AROUND THE SEWERS. HIS [...] IS SIMILAR TO THAT OF T[...] FIRST MAN.

AN INJECTION OF *VENOM*, LIKE THAT OF A SCORPION OR SPIDER. THE BLOOD HAS THEN BEEN ENTIRELY DRAINED VIA THE PUNCTURES THAT YOU CAN SEE, LOCATED AT VERY PRECISE POINTS ON THE BODY.

YOU SEE THE PUNCTURES, COLONEL? THEY ARE *EXACTLY THE SAME!*

I SEE.

AS FOR THIS OTHER MAN... WELL, THIS CASE IS NOT QUITE SO SIMPLE.

SIMPLE?

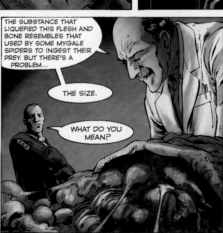

THE SUBSTANCE THAT LIQUEFIED THIS FLESH AND BONE RESEMBLES THAT USED BY SOME MYGALE SPIDERS TO INGEST THEIR PREY. BUT THERE'S A PROBLEM...

THE SIZE.

WHAT DO YOU MEAN?

SCIENCE HAS NO KNOWLEDGE OF A SPIDER THAT IS BIG ENOUGH TO DO THIS TO A FULLY GROWN MAN.

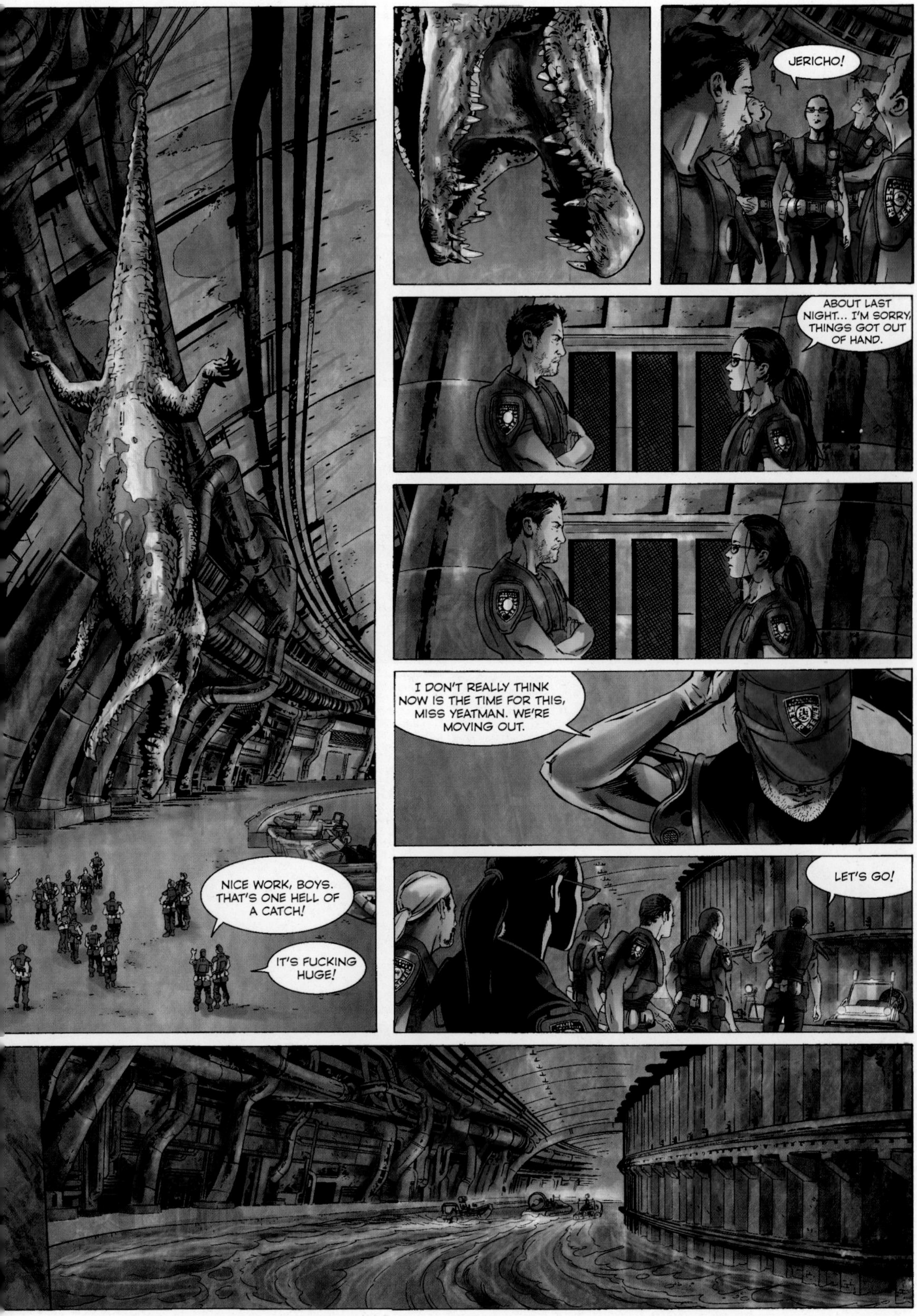NICE WORK, BOYS. THAT'S ONE HELL OF A CATCH!
IT'S FUCKING HUGE!
JERICHO!
ABOUT LAST NIGHT... I'M SORRY, THINGS GOT OUT OF HAND.
I DON'T REALLY THINK NOW IS THE TIME FOR THIS, MISS YEATMAN. WE'RE MOVING OUT.
LET'S GO!

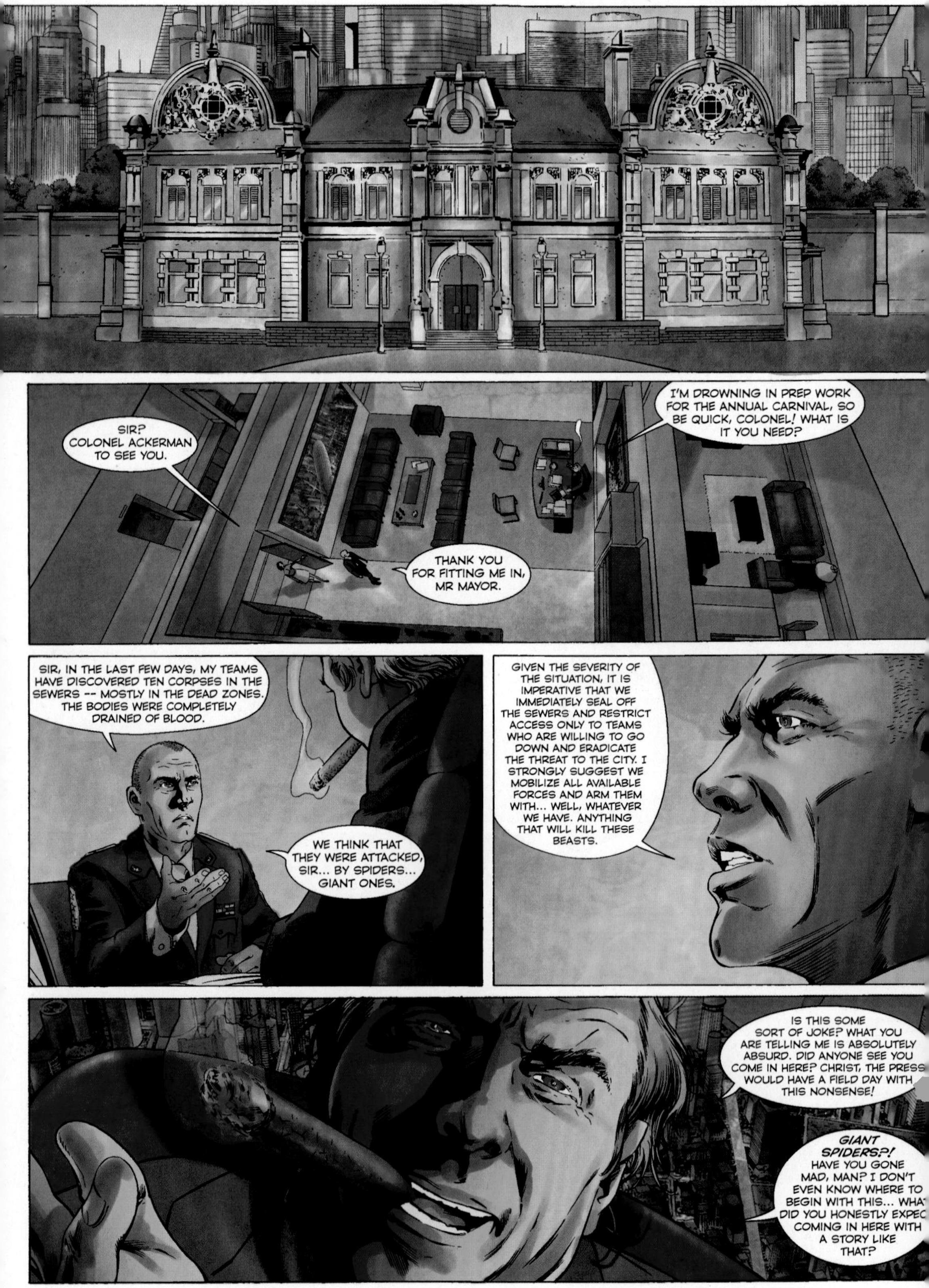
SIR? COLONEL ACKERMAN TO SEE YOU.
I'M DROWNING IN PREP WORK FOR THE ANNUAL CARNIVAL, SO BE QUICK, COLONEL! WHAT IS IT YOU NEED?
THANK YOU FOR FITTING ME IN, MR MAYOR.
SIR, IN THE LAST FEW DAYS, MY TEAMS HAVE DISCOVERED TEN CORPSES IN THE SEWERS -- MOSTLY IN THE DEAD ZONES. THE BODIES WERE COMPLETELY DRAINED OF BLOOD.
WE THINK THAT THEY WERE ATTACKED, SIR... BY SPIDERS... GIANT ONES.
GIVEN THE SEVERITY OF THE SITUATION, IT IS IMPERATIVE THAT WE IMMEDIATELY SEAL OFF THE SEWERS AND RESTRICT ACCESS ONLY TO TEAMS WHO ARE WILLING TO GO DOWN AND ERADICATE THE THREAT TO THE CITY. I STRONGLY SUGGEST WE MOBILIZE ALL AVAILABLE FORCES AND ARM THEM WITH... WELL, WHATEVER WE HAVE. ANYTHING THAT WILL KILL THESE BEASTS.
IS THIS SOME SORT OF JOKE? WHAT YOU ARE TELLING ME IS ABSOLUTELY ABSURD. DID ANYONE SEE YOU COME IN HERE? CHRIST, THE PRESS WOULD HAVE A FIELD DAY WITH THIS NONSENSE!
GIANT SPIDERS?! HAVE YOU GONE MAD, MAN? I DON'T EVEN KNOW WHERE TO BEGIN WITH THIS... WHA DID YOU HONESTLY EXPEC COMING IN HERE WITH A STORY LIKE THAT?

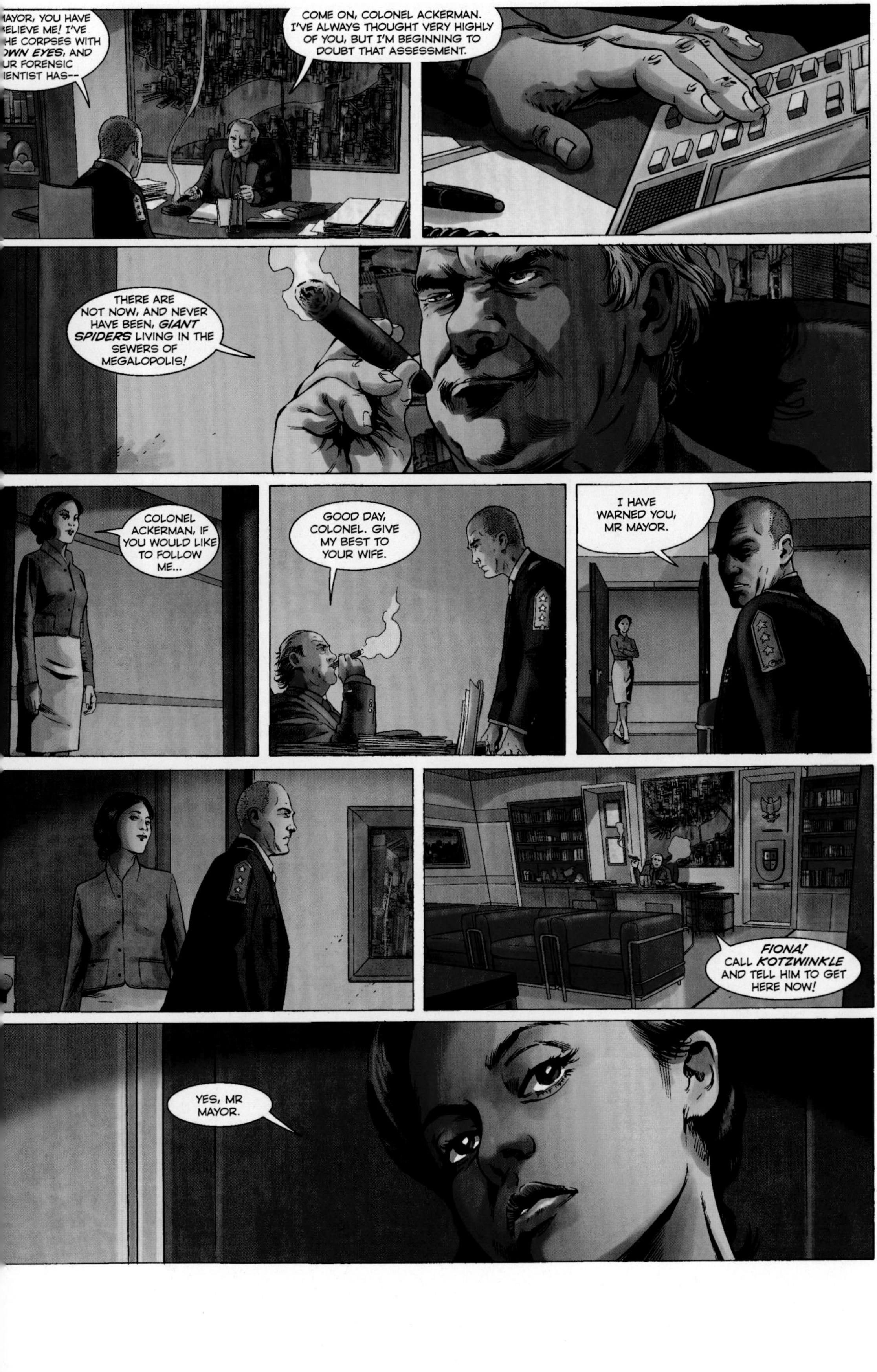
MAYOR, YOU HAVE ELIEVE ME! I'VE HE CORPSES WITH OWN EYES, AND UR FORENSIC IENTIST HAS--
COME ON, COLONEL ACKERMAN. I'VE ALWAYS THOUGHT VERY HIGHLY OF YOU, BUT I'M BEGINNING TO DOUBT THAT ASSESSMENT.
THERE ARE NOT NOW, AND NEVER HAVE BEEN, GIANT SPIDERS LIVING IN THE SEWERS OF MEGALOPOLIS!
COLONEL ACKERMAN, IF YOU WOULD LIKE TO FOLLOW ME...
GOOD DAY, COLONEL. GIVE MY BEST TO YOUR WIFE.
I HAVE WARNED YOU, MR MAYOR.
FIONA! CALL KOTZWINKLE AND TELL HIM TO GET HERE NOW!
YES, MR MAYOR.

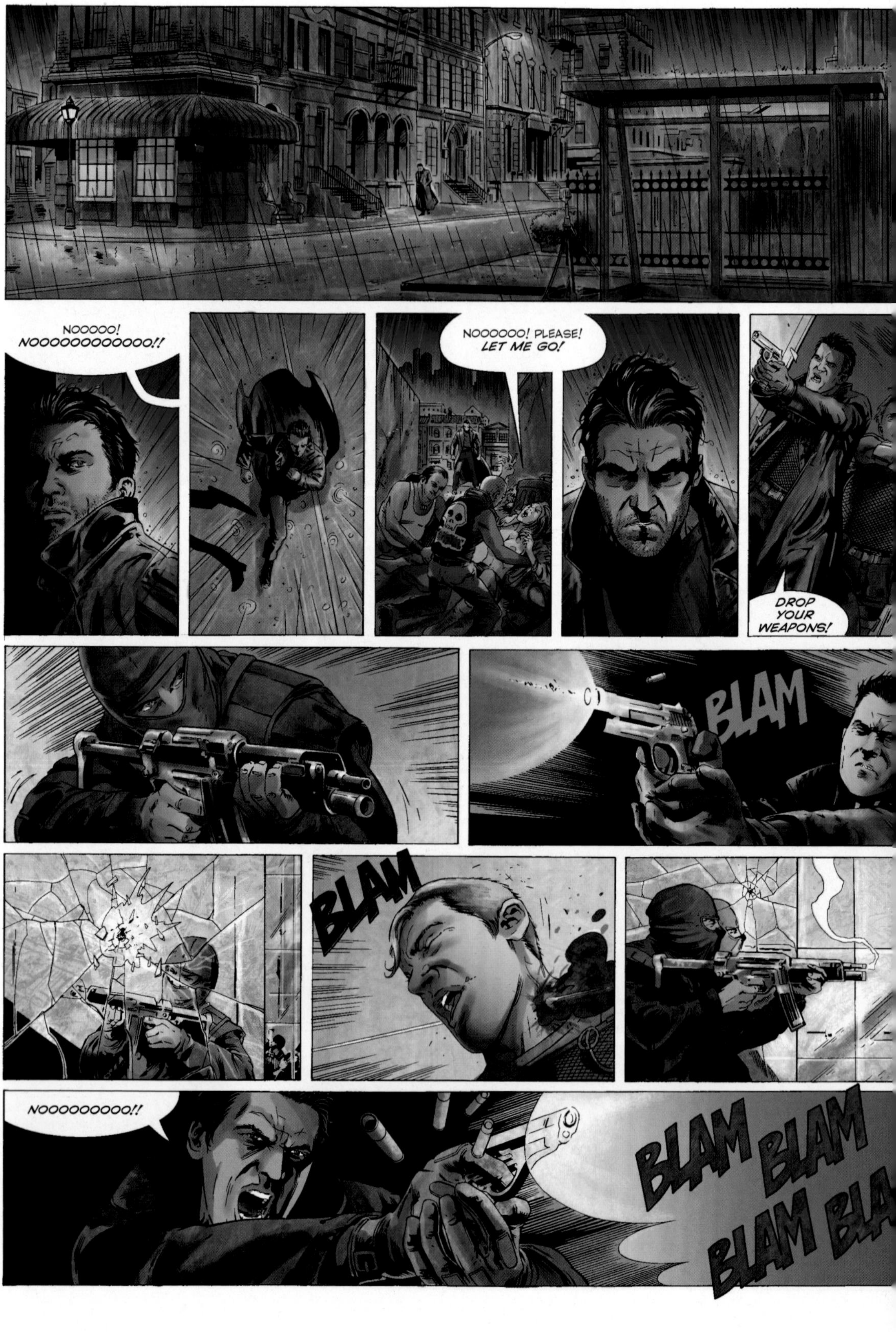
NOOOOO!
NOOOOOOOOOOOO!!
NOOOOOO! PLEASE! LET ME GO!
DROP YOUR WEAPONS!
BLAM
BLAM
NOOOOOOOOO!!
BLAM BLAM
BLAM

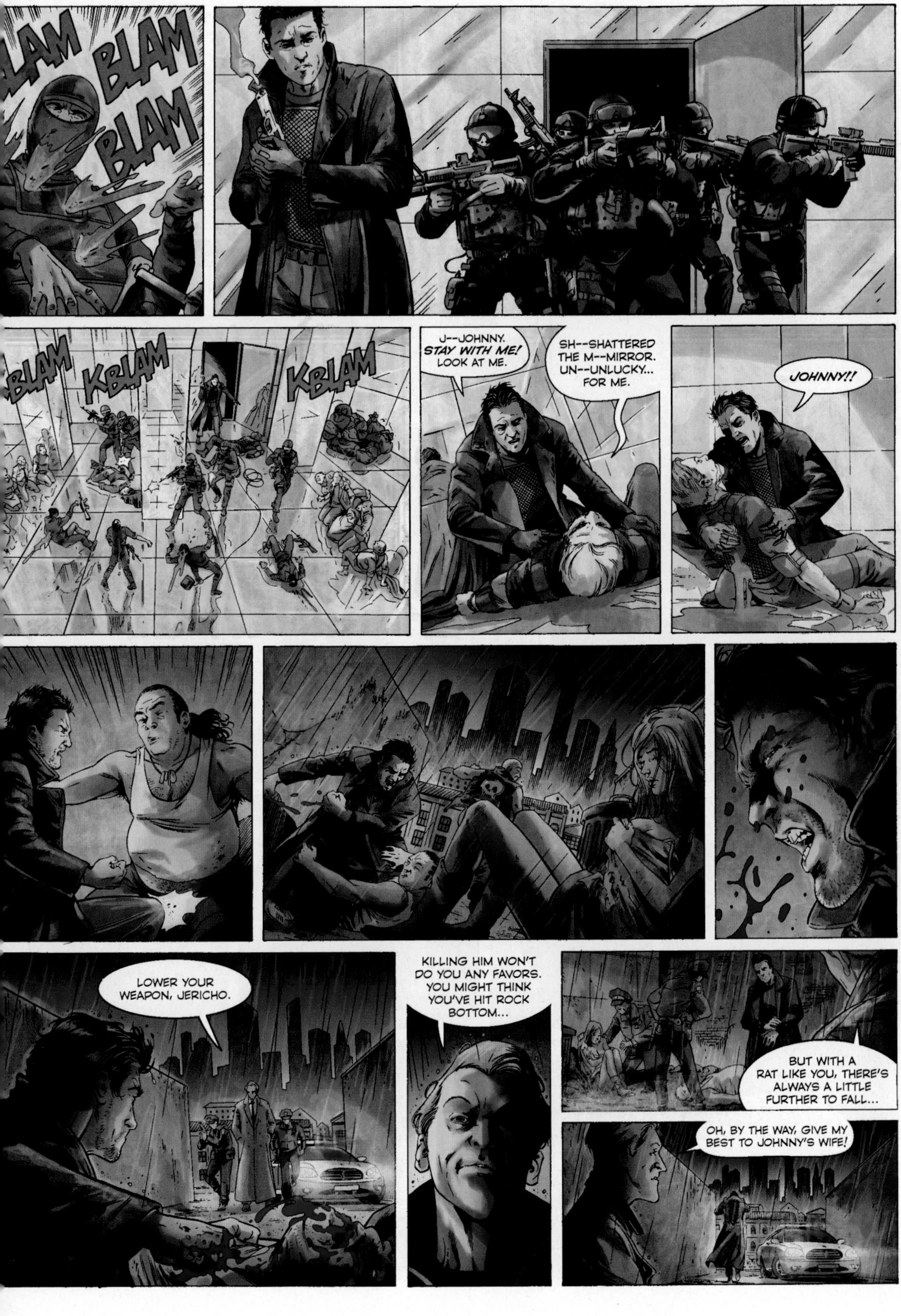
BLAM
BLAM
BLAM
BLAM
BLAM
KBLAM
KBLAM
J--JOHNNY. STAY WITH ME! LOOK AT ME.
SH--SHATTERED THE M--MIRROR. UN--UNLUCKY... FOR ME.
JOHNNY!!
LOWER YOUR WEAPON, JERICHO.
KILLING HIM WON'T DO YOU ANY FAVORS. YOU MIGHT THINK YOU'VE HIT ROCK BOTTOM...
BUT WITH A RAT LIKE YOU, THERE'S ALWAYS A LITTLE FURTHER TO FALL...
OH, BY THE WAY, GIVE MY BEST TO JOHNNY'S WIFE!

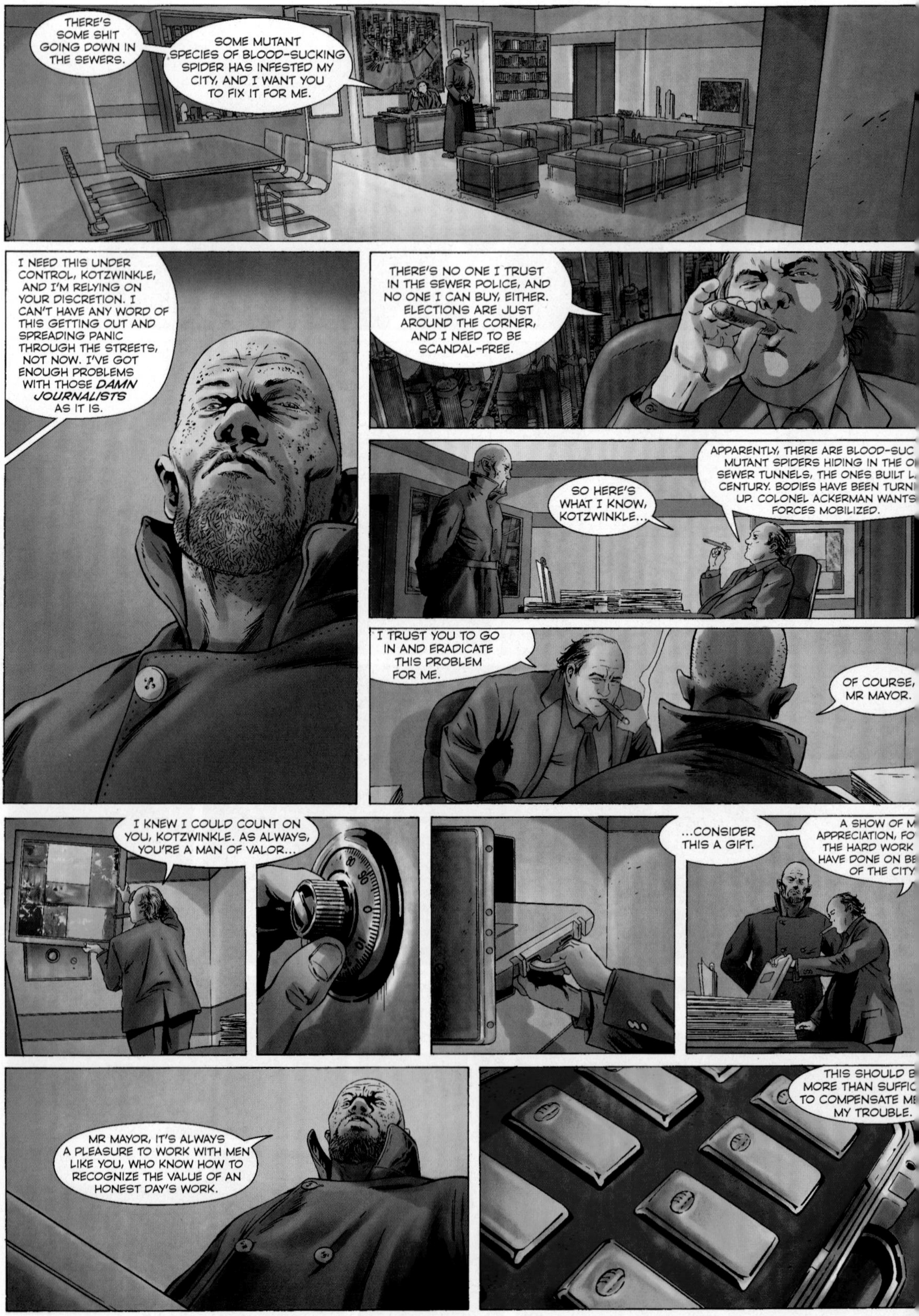
THERE'S SOME SHIT GOING DOWN IN THE SEWERS.
SOME MUTANT SPECIES OF BLOOD-SUCKING SPIDER HAS INFESTED MY CITY, AND I WANT YOU TO FIX IT FOR ME.
I NEED THIS UNDER CONTROL, KOTZWINKLE, AND I'M RELYING ON YOUR DISCRETION. I CAN'T HAVE ANY WORD OF THIS GETTING OUT AND SPREADING PANIC THROUGH THE STREETS, NOT NOW. I'VE GOT ENOUGH PROBLEMS WITH THOSE DAMN JOURNALISTS AS IT IS.
THERE'S NO ONE I TRUST IN THE SEWER POLICE, AND NO ONE I CAN BUY, EITHER. ELECTIONS ARE JUST AROUND THE CORNER, AND I NEED TO BE SCANDAL-FREE.
SO HERE'S WHAT I KNOW, KOTZWINKLE...
APPARENTLY, THERE ARE BLOOD-SUC MUTANT SPIDERS HIDING IN THE O SEWER TUNNELS, THE ONES BUILT L CENTURY. BODIES HAVE BEEN TURN UP. COLONEL ACKERMAN WANTS FORCES MOBILIZED.
I TRUST YOU TO GO IN AND ERADICATE THIS PROBLEM FOR ME.
OF COURSE, MR MAYOR.
I KNEW I COULD COUNT ON YOU, KOTZWINKLE. AS ALWAYS, YOU'RE A MAN OF VALOR...
...CONSIDER THIS A GIFT.
A SHOW OF M APPRECIATION, FO THE HARD WORK HAVE DONE ON BE OF THE CITY
MR MAYOR, IT'S ALWAYS A PLEASURE TO WORK WITH MEN LIKE YOU, WHO KNOW HOW TO RECOGNIZE THE VALUE OF AN HONEST DAY'S WORK.
THIS SHOULD B MORE THAN SUFFIC TO COMPENSATE M MY TROUBLE.

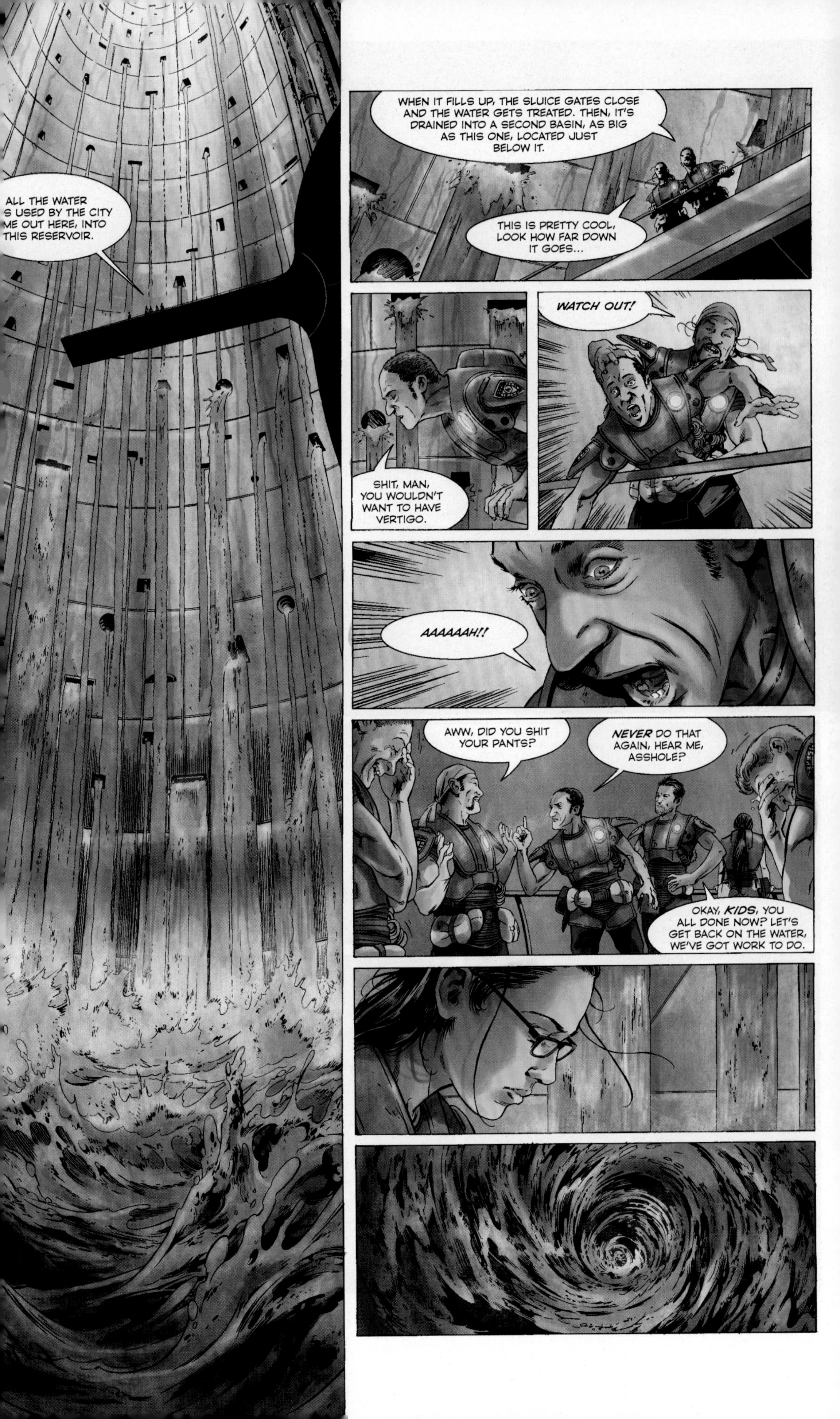
ALL THE WATER
S USED BY THE CITY
ME OUT HERE, INTO
THIS RESERVOIR.
WHEN IT FILLS UP, THE SLUICE GATES CLOSE AND THE WATER GETS TREATED. THEN, IT'S DRAINED INTO A SECOND BASIN, AS BIG AS THIS ONE, LOCATED JUST BELOW IT.
THIS IS PRETTY COOL, LOOK HOW FAR DOWN IT GOES...
SHIT, MAN, YOU WOULDN'T WANT TO HAVE VERTIGO.
WATCH OUT!
AAAAAAH!!
AWW, DID YOU SHIT YOUR PANTS?
NEVER DO THAT AGAIN, HEAR ME, ASSHOLE?
OKAY, KIDS, YOU ALL DONE NOW? LET'S GET BACK ON THE WATER, WE'VE GOT WORK TO DO.

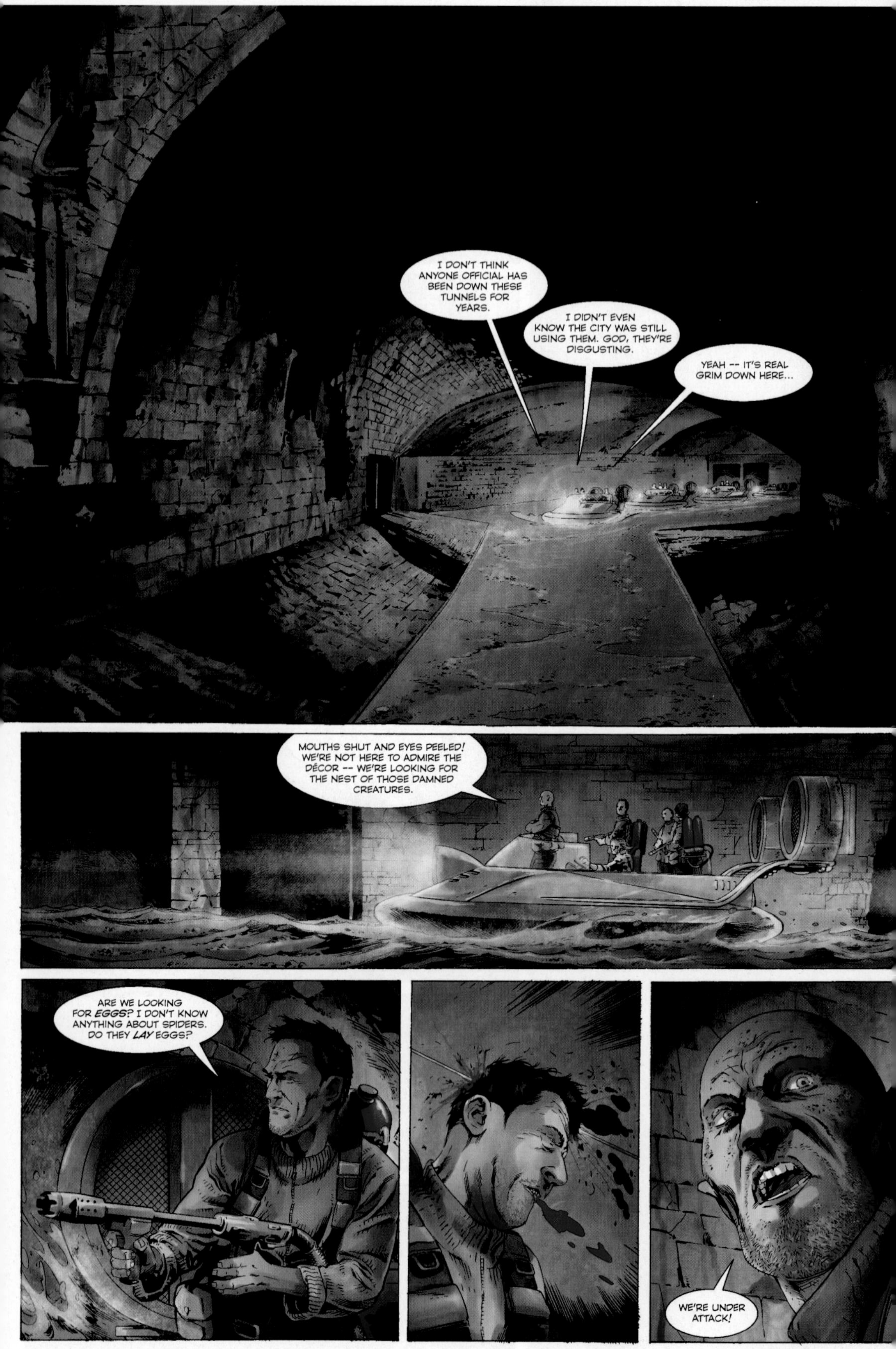
I DON'T THINK ANYONE OFFICIAL HAS BEEN DOWN THESE TUNNELS FOR YEARS.
I DIDN'T EVEN KNOW THE CITY WAS STILL USING THEM. GOD, THEY'RE DISGUSTING.
YEAH -- IT'S REAL GRIM DOWN HERE...
MOUTHS SHUT AND EYES PEELED! WE'RE NOT HERE TO ADMIRE THE DÉCOR -- WE'RE LOOKING FOR THE NEST OF THOSE DAMNED CREATURES.
ARE WE LOOKING FOR *EGGS*? I DON'T KNOW ANYTHING ABOUT SPIDERS. DO THEY *LAY* EGGS?
WE'RE UNDER ATTACK!

FUCK! SOMEONE'S FIRING AT US!

PARIAHS!

THEY'RE ALL AROUND US!

DAMMIT! WHY THE FUCK ARE THERE SO MANY OF THEM? WHAT DO THE FUCKING SEWER POLICE ACTUALLY FUCKING DO?

WE HAVE TO GET OUT OF HERE!

LET'S MOVE IT!

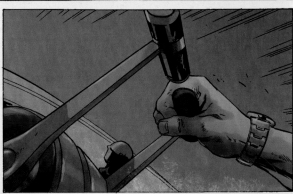

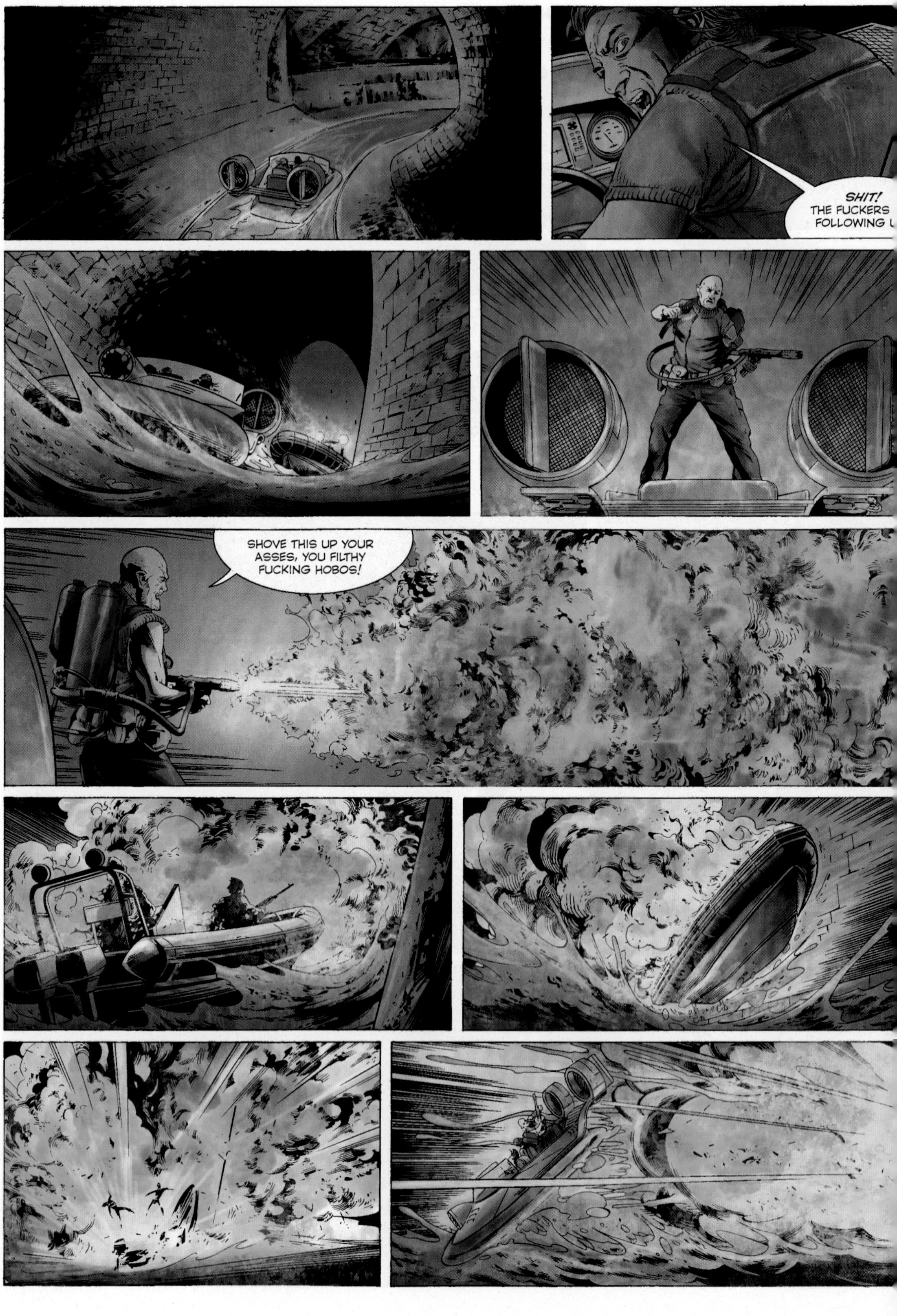
SHIT!
THE FUCKERS
FOLLOWING
SHOVE THIS UP YOUR ASSES, YOU FILTHY FUCKING HOBOS!

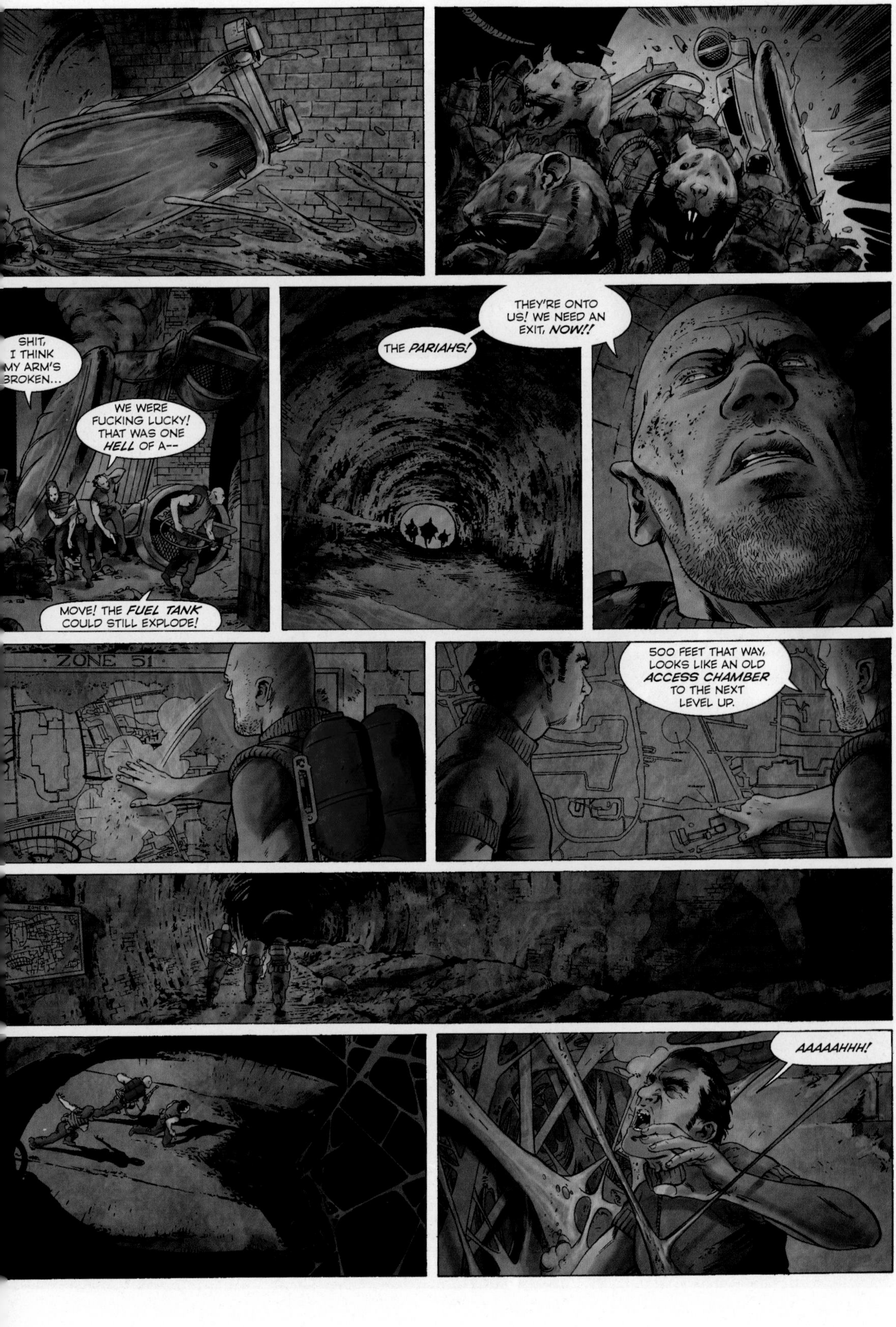
SHIT, I THINK MY ARM'S BROKEN...
WE WERE FUCKING LUCKY! THAT WAS ONE HELL OF A--
MOVE! THE FUEL TANK COULD STILL EXPLODE!
THE PARIAHS!
THEY'RE ONTO US! WE NEED AN EXIT, NOW!!
ZONE 51
500 FEET THAT WAY, LOOKS LIKE AN OLD ACCESS CHAMBER TO THE NEXT LEVEL UP.
AAAAAHHH!

FUCK! WHAT THE HELL IS THIS SHIT?

?!!

IS THAT THING WHAT WE'VE BEEN LOOKING FOR?

IT'S DISGUSTING!

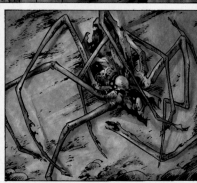

THOSE PARIAHS AREN'T FAR BEHIND US! WE'LL HAVE TO GO THROUGH THE WEB.

DESPERATE TIMES...

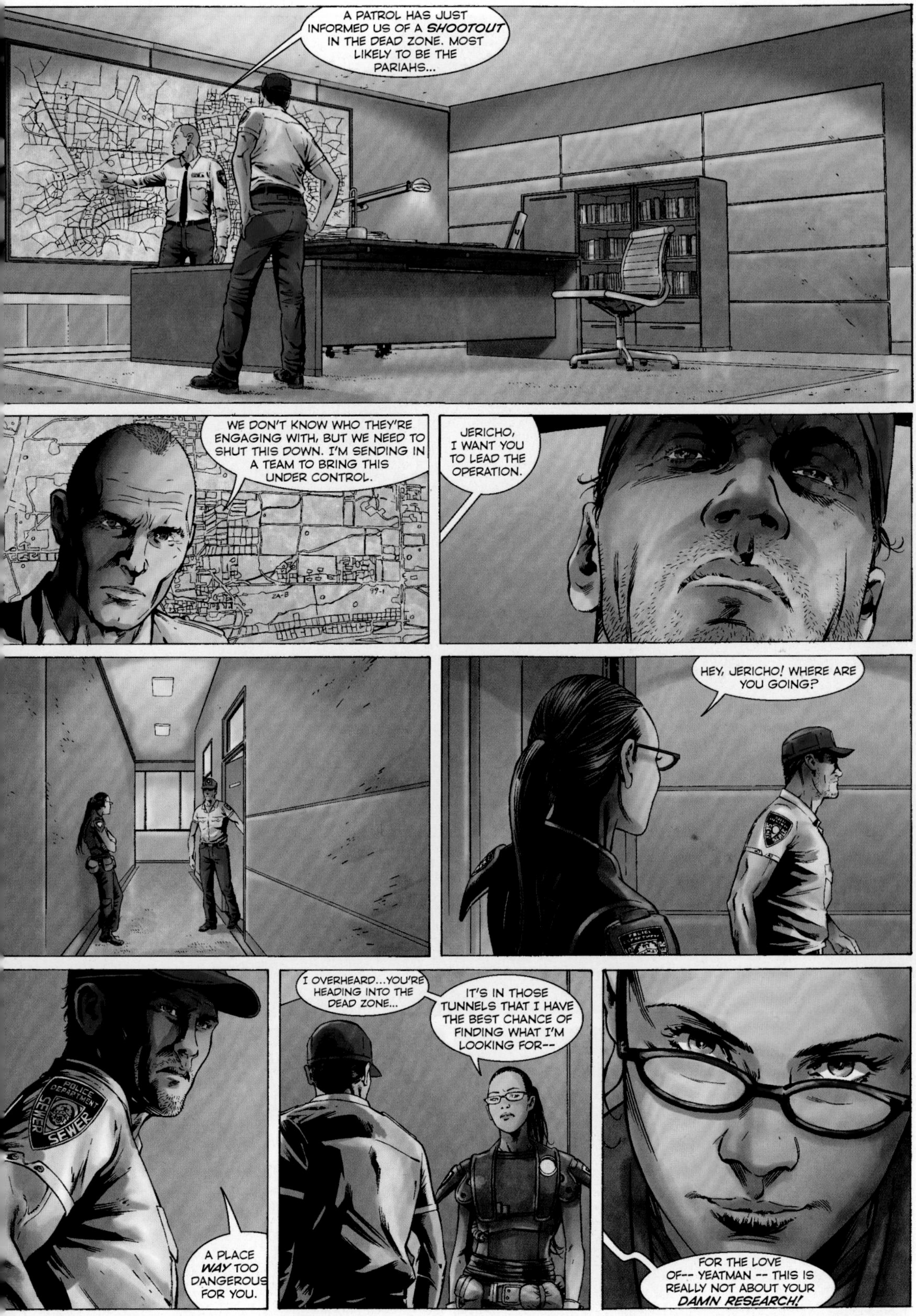
A PATROL HAS JUST INFORMED US OF A SHOOTOUT IN THE DEAD ZONE. MOST LIKELY TO BE THE PARIAHS...
WE DON'T KNOW WHO THEY'RE ENGAGING WITH, BUT WE NEED TO SHUT THIS DOWN. I'M SENDING IN A TEAM TO BRING THIS UNDER CONTROL.
JERICHO, I WANT YOU TO LEAD THE OPERATION.
HEY, JERICHO! WHERE ARE YOU GOING?
A PLACE WAY TOO DANGEROUS FOR YOU.
I OVERHEARD...YOU'RE HEADING INTO THE DEAD ZONE...
IT'S IN THOSE TUNNELS THAT I HAVE THE BEST CHANCE OF FINDING WHAT I'M LOOKING FOR--
FOR THE LOVE OF-- YEATMAN -- THIS IS REALLY NOT ABOUT YOUR DAMN RESEARCH!

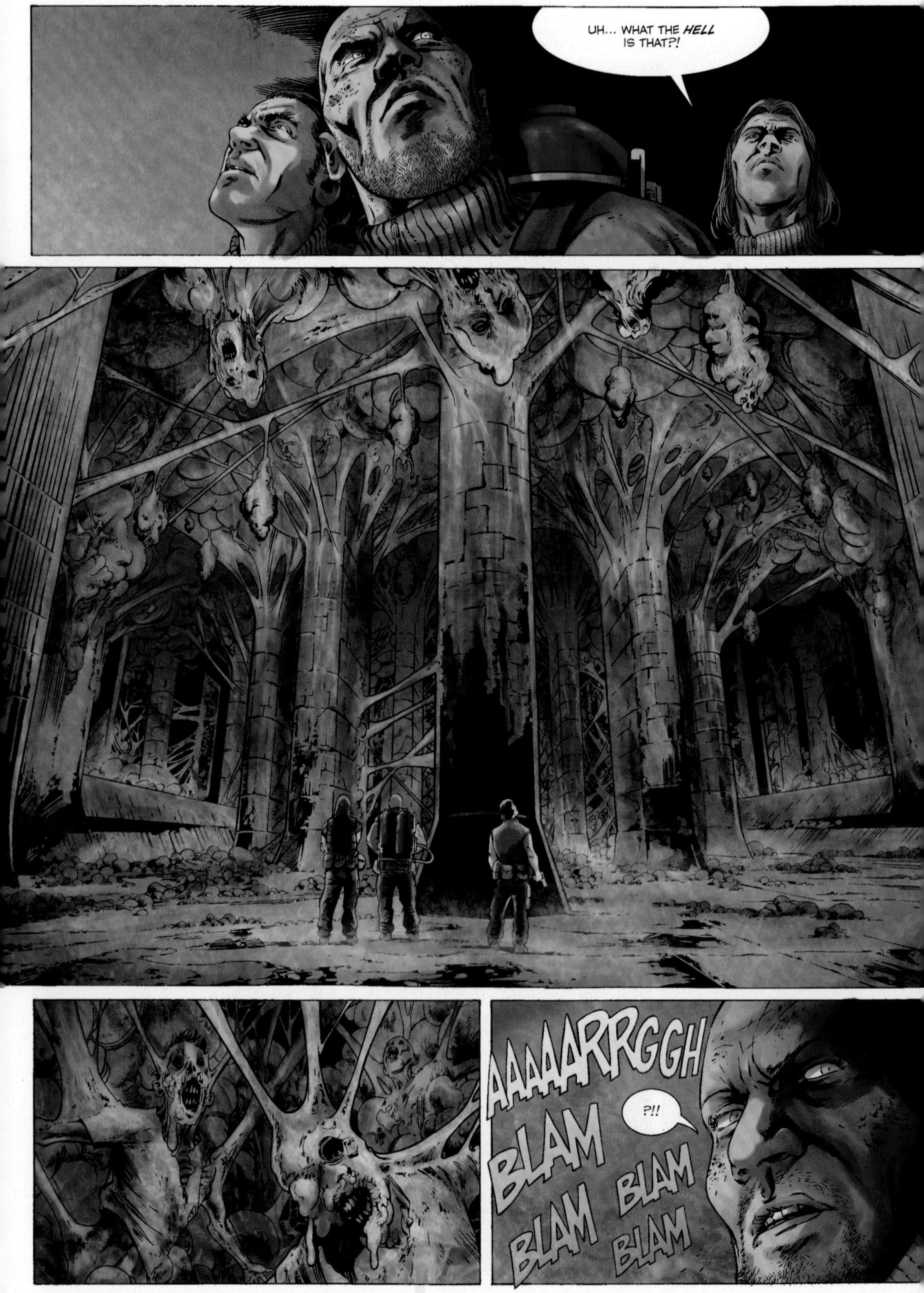
UH... WHAT THE *HELL* IS THAT?!
AAAAARRGGH
?!!
BLAM
BLAM BLAM
BLAM
BLAM

FUCK! WHAT IS GOING ON!?

IT'S THE PARIAHS! WE'LL HAVE TO ENGAGE FROM HERE!

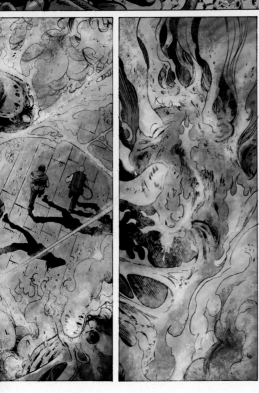

THERE! THE ACCESS HATCH!

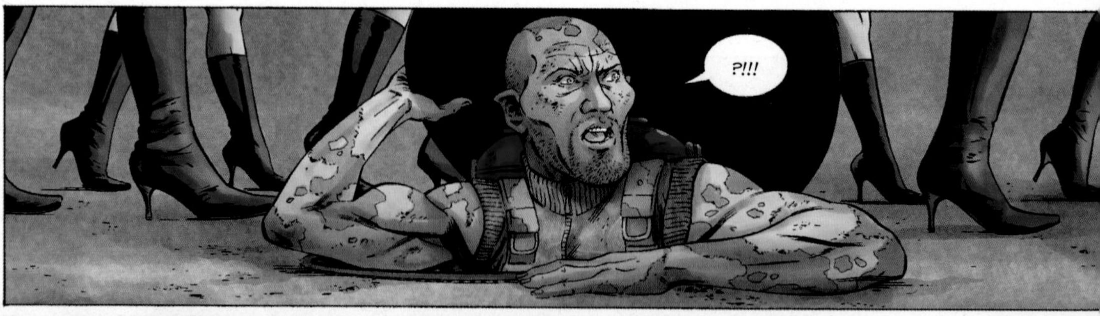
?!!!

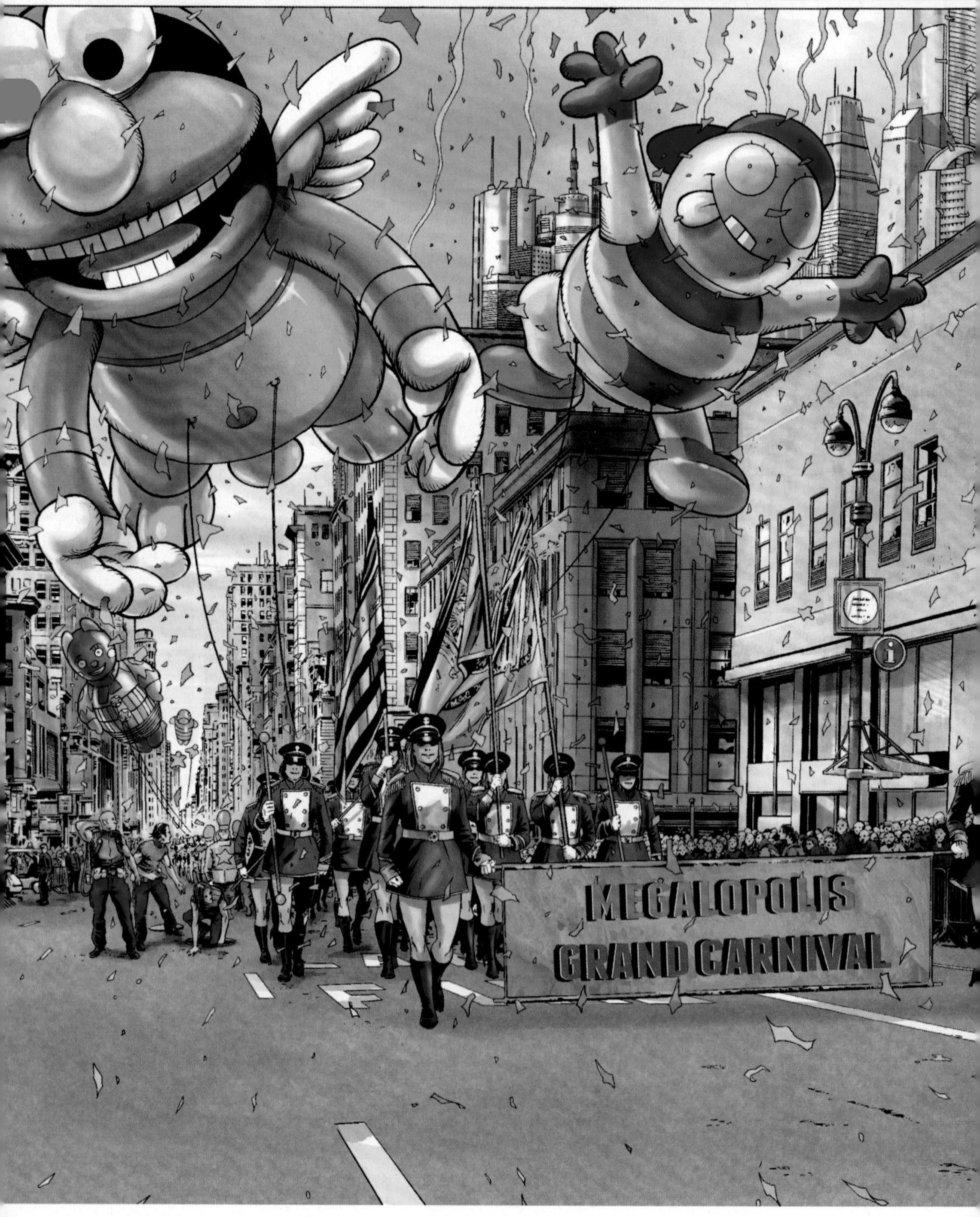
MEGALOPOLIS
GRAND CARNIVAL

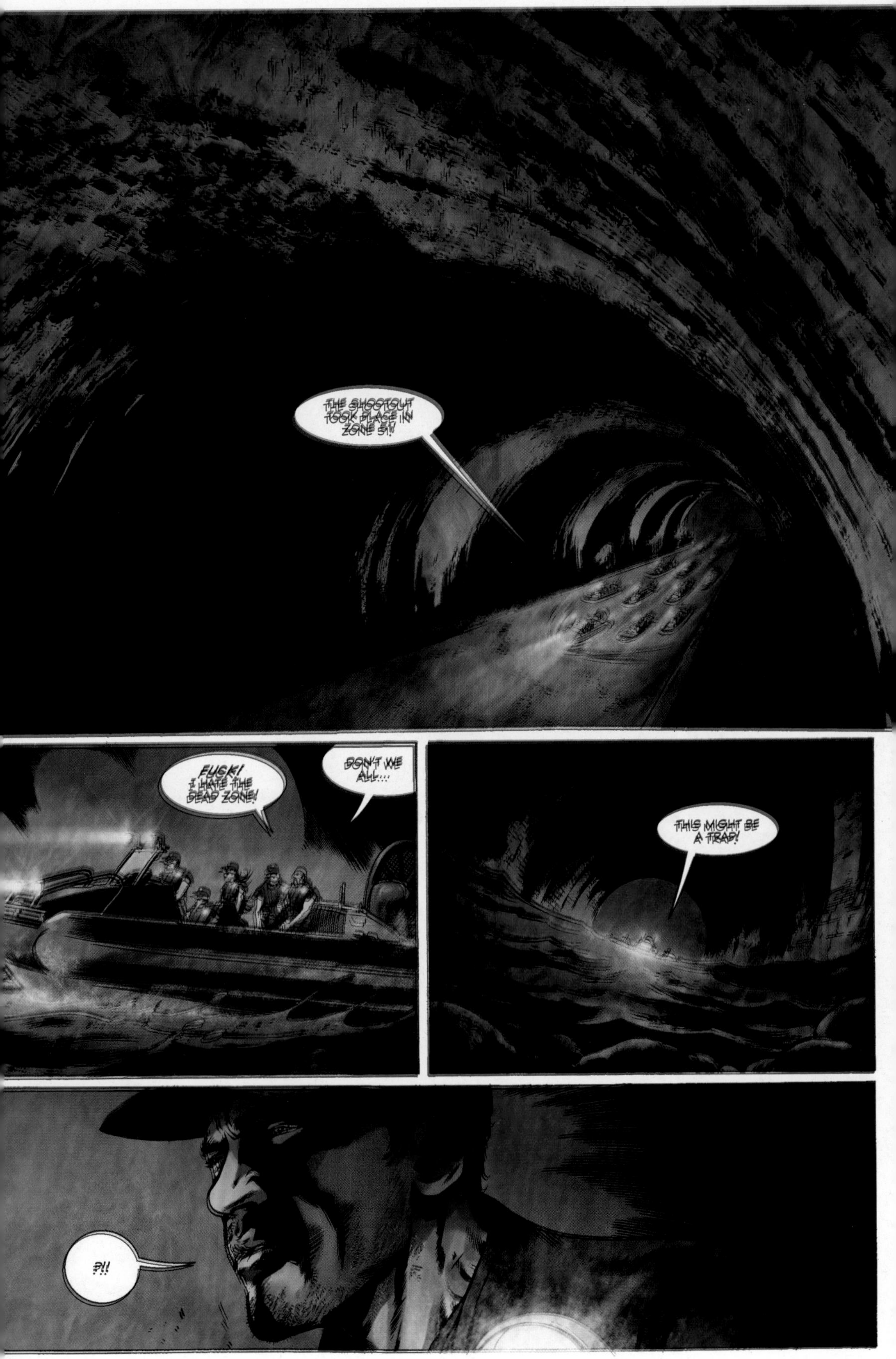
THE SHOOTOUT TOOK PLACE IN ZONE 51!
FUCK! I HATE THE DEAD ZONE!
DON'T WE ALL...
THIS MIGHT BE A TRAP!
?!!

STOP!
WHAT IS THAT?
MY GOD!
IT--IT'S MOVING!
IT'S ALIVE!

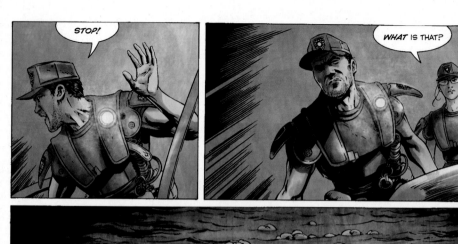

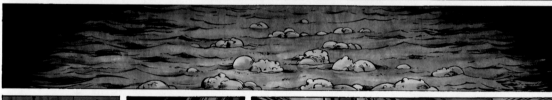

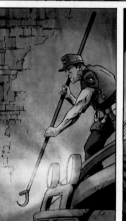

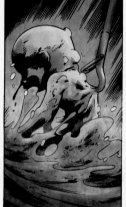

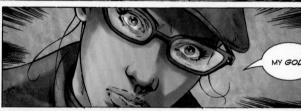

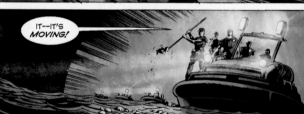

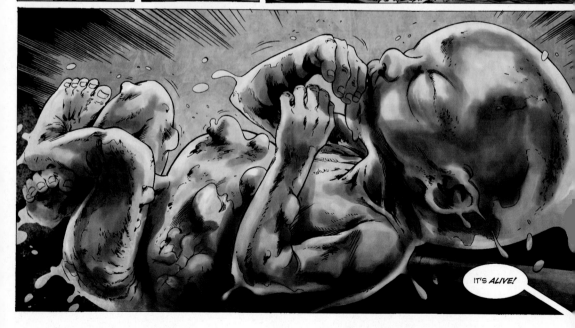

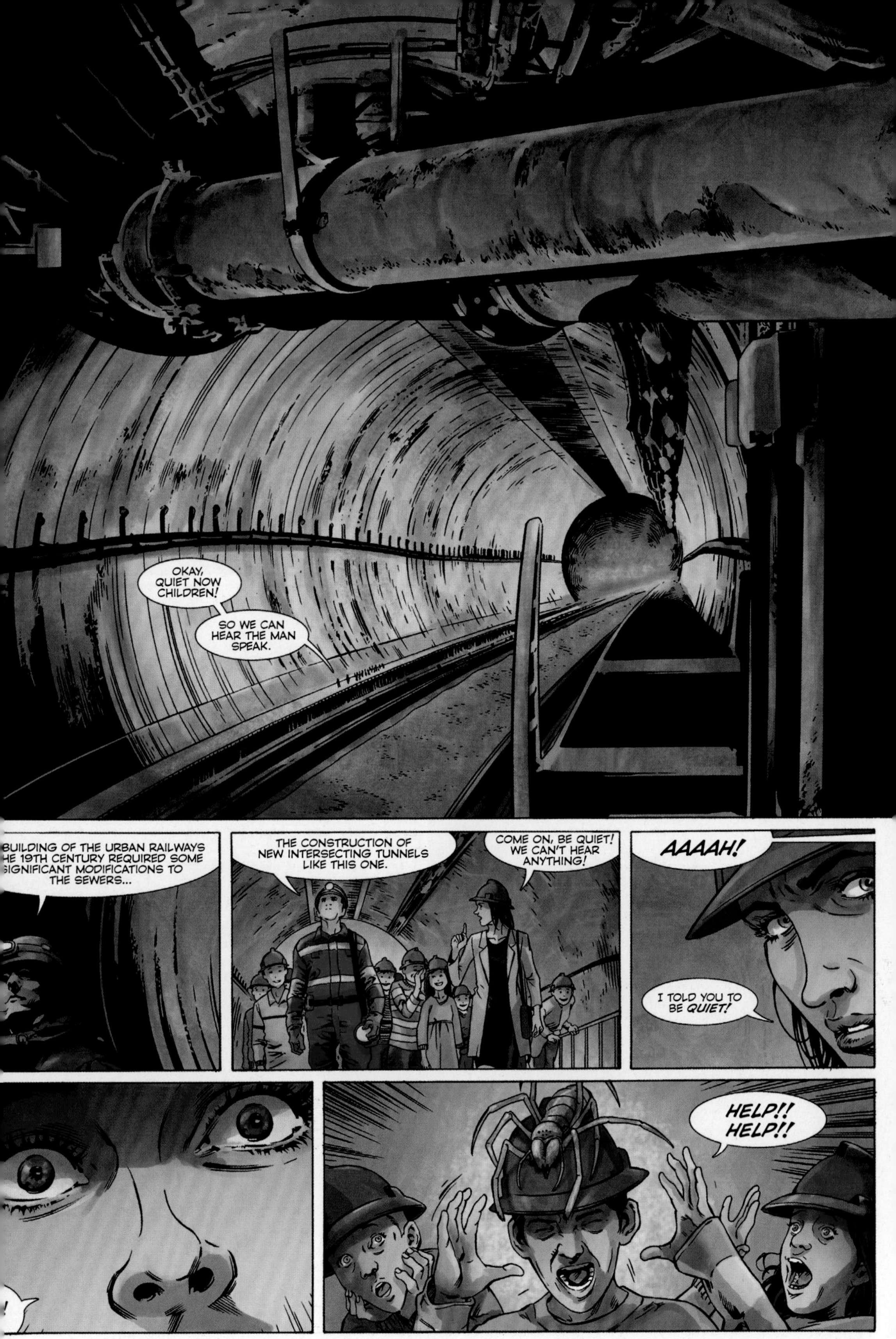
OKAY, QUIET NOW CHILDREN!
SO WE CAN HEAR THE MAN SPEAK.
BUILDING OF THE URBAN RAILWAYS HE 19TH CENTURY REQUIRED SOME SIGNIFICANT MODIFICATIONS TO THE SEWERS...
THE CONSTRUCTION OF NEW INTERSECTING TUNNELS LIKE THIS ONE.
COME ON, BE QUIET! WE CAN'T HEAR ANYTHING!
AAAAH!
I TOLD YOU TO BE QUIET!
HELP!! HELP!!

SPRROOTCH

GOOD GOD?!

THOUSANDS OF ANTS!

EEEEEK!

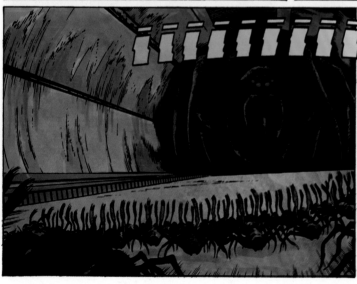

THEY LEAVIN

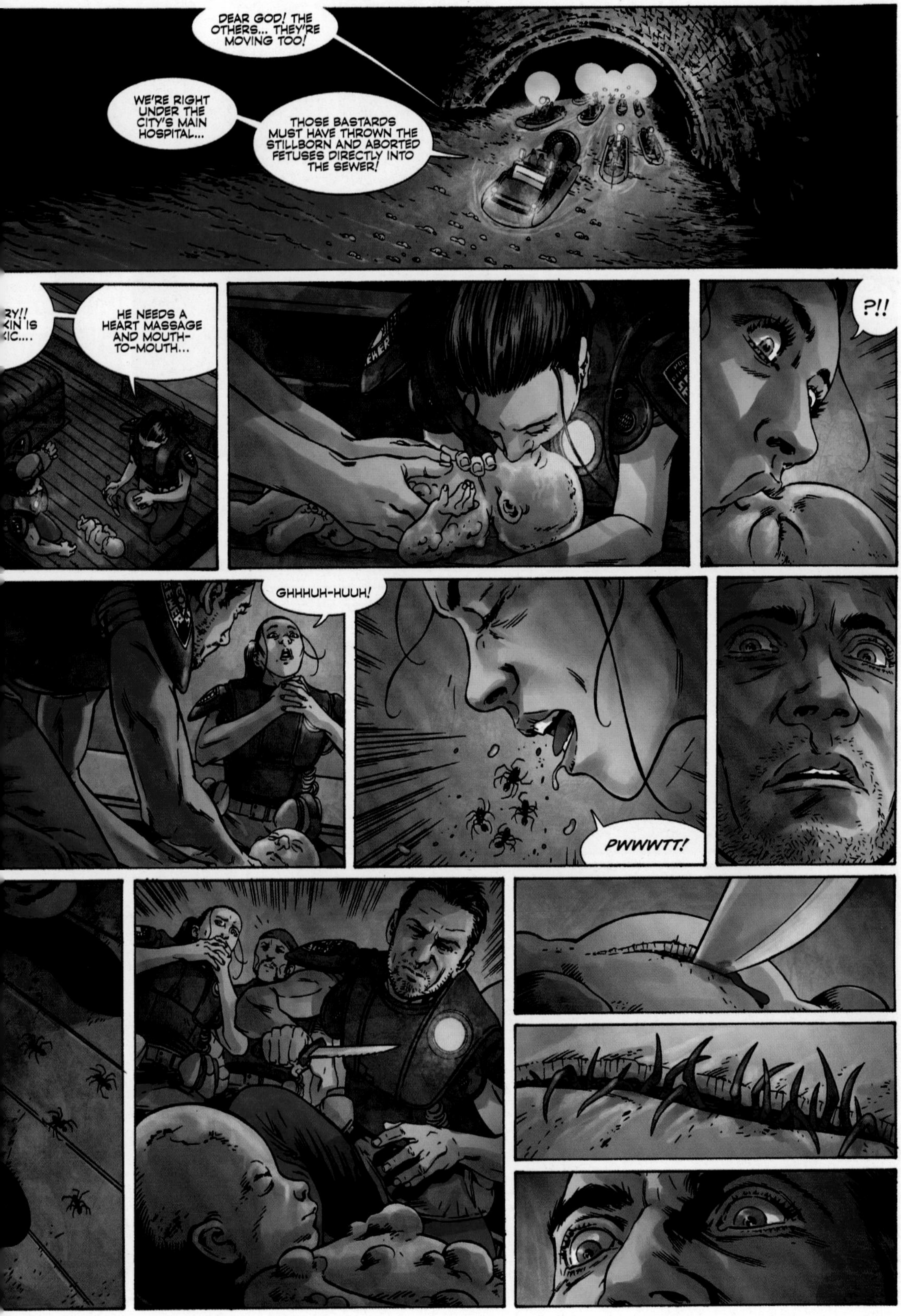

DEAR GOD! THE OTHERS... THEY'RE MOVING TOO!
WE'RE RIGHT UNDER THE CITY'S MAIN HOSPITAL...
THOSE BASTARDS MUST HAVE THROWN THE STILLBORN AND ABORTED FETUSES DIRECTLY INTO THE SEWER!
HE NEEDS A HEART MASSAGE AND MOUTH-TO-MOUTH...
?!!
GHHHUH-HUUH!
PWWWTT!

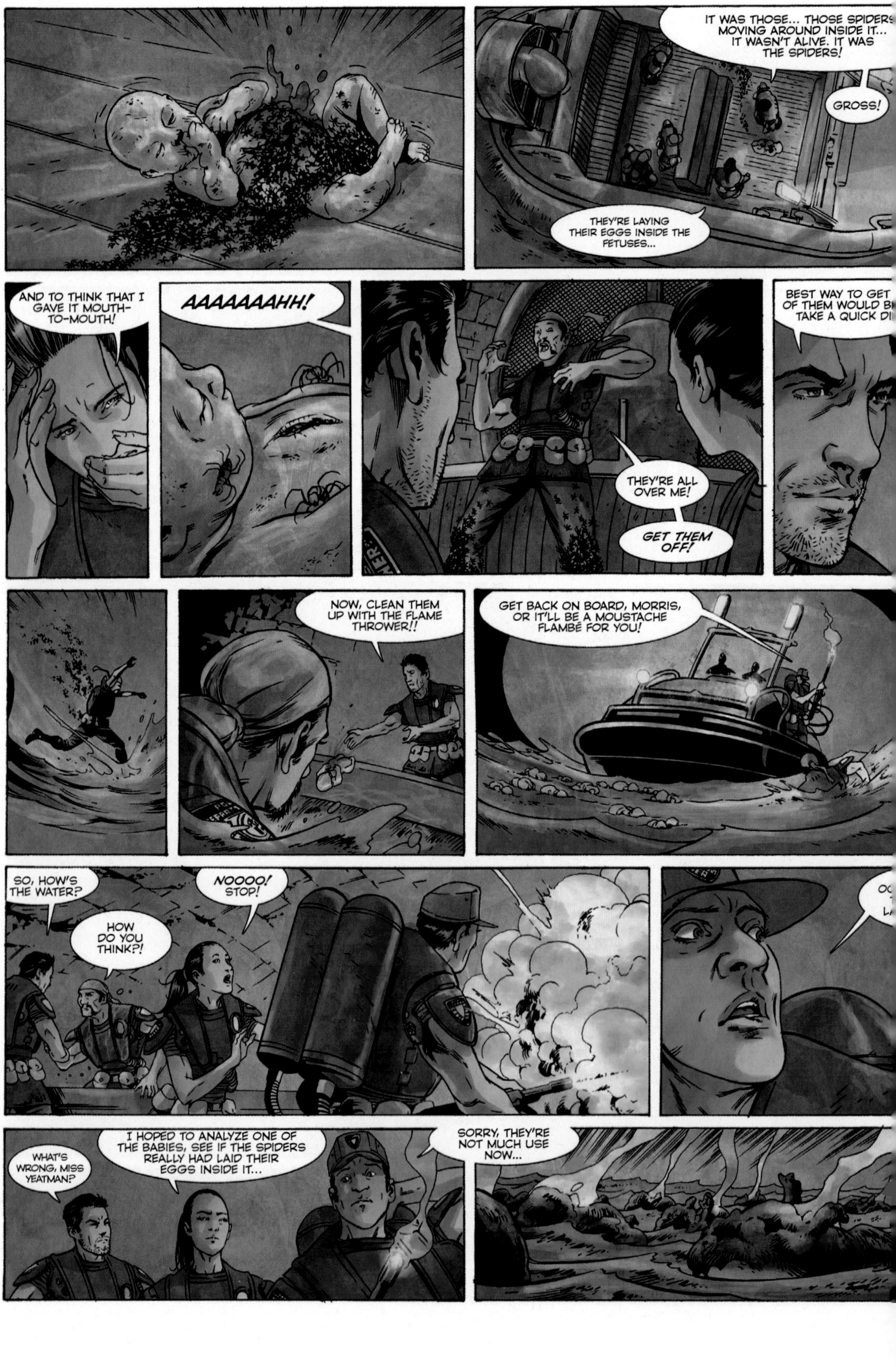
IT WAS THOSE... THOSE SPIDER MOVING AROUND INSIDE IT... IT WASN'T ALIVE. IT WAS THE SPIDERS!
GROSS!
THEY'RE LAYING THEIR EGGS INSIDE THE FETUSES...
AND TO THINK THAT I GAVE IT MOUTH-TO-MOUTH!
AAAAAAAHH!
THEY'RE ALL OVER ME!
GET THEM OFF!
BEST WAY TO GET OF THEM WOULD B TAKE A QUICK DI
NOW, CLEAN THEM UP WITH THE FLAME THROWER!!
GET BACK ON BOARD, MORRIS, OR IT'LL BE A MOUSTACHE FLAMBÉ FOR YOU!
SO, HOW'S THE WATER?
HOW DO YOU THINK?!
NOOOO! STOP!
WHAT'S WRONG, MISS YEATMAN?
I HOPED TO ANALYZE ONE OF THE BABIES, SEE IF THE SPIDERS REALLY HAD LAID THEIR EGGS INSIDE IT...
SORRY, THEY'RE NOT MUCH USE NOW...

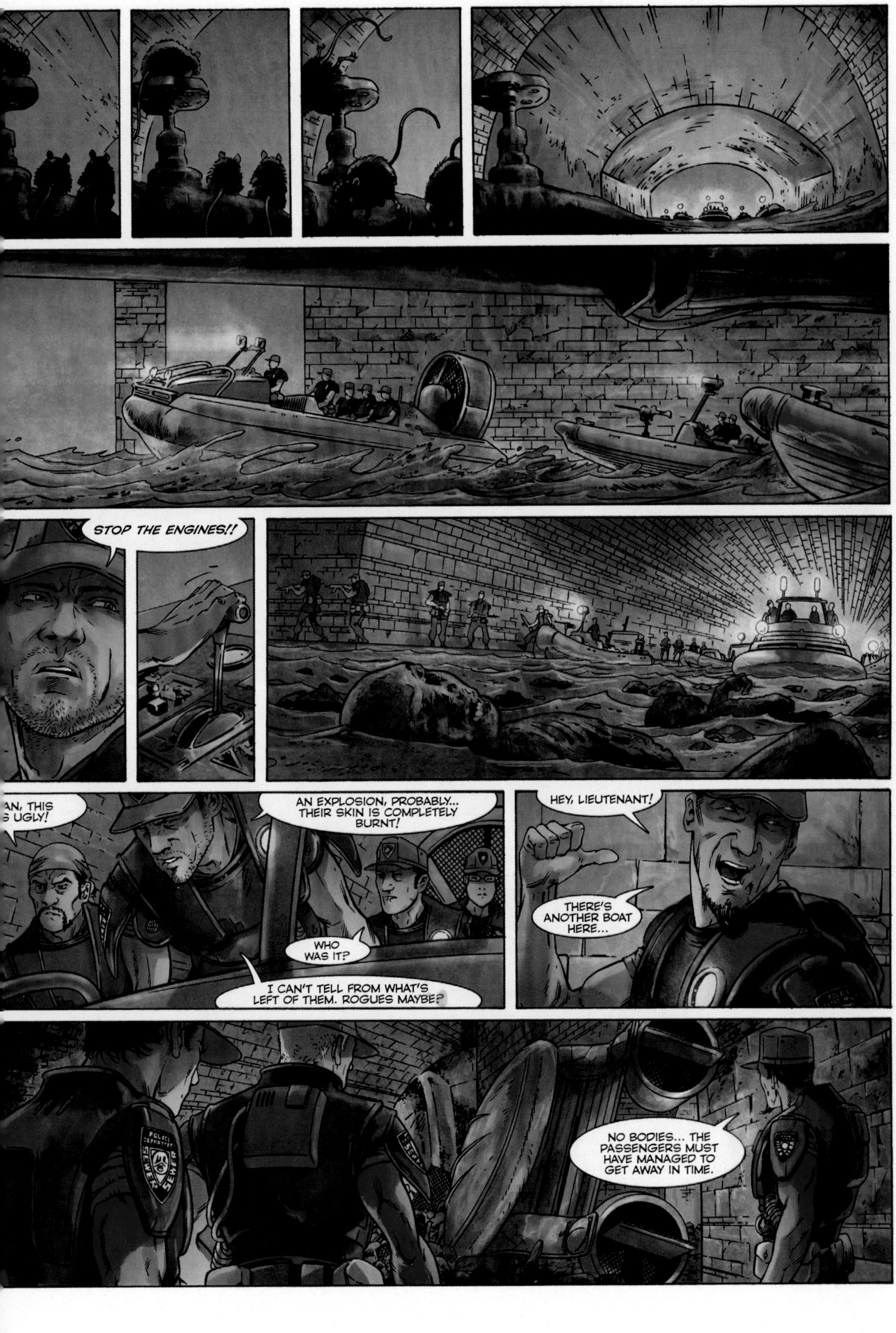
STOP THE ENGINES!!
AN, THIS
S UGLY!
AN EXPLOSION, PROBABLY... THEIR SKIN IS COMPLETELY BURNT!
WHO WAS IT?
I CAN'T TELL FROM WHAT'S LEFT OF THEM. ROGUES MAYBE?
HEY, LIEUTENANT!
THERE'S ANOTHER BOAT HERE...
NO BODIES... THE PASSENGERS MUST HAVE MANAGED TO GET AWAY IN TIME.

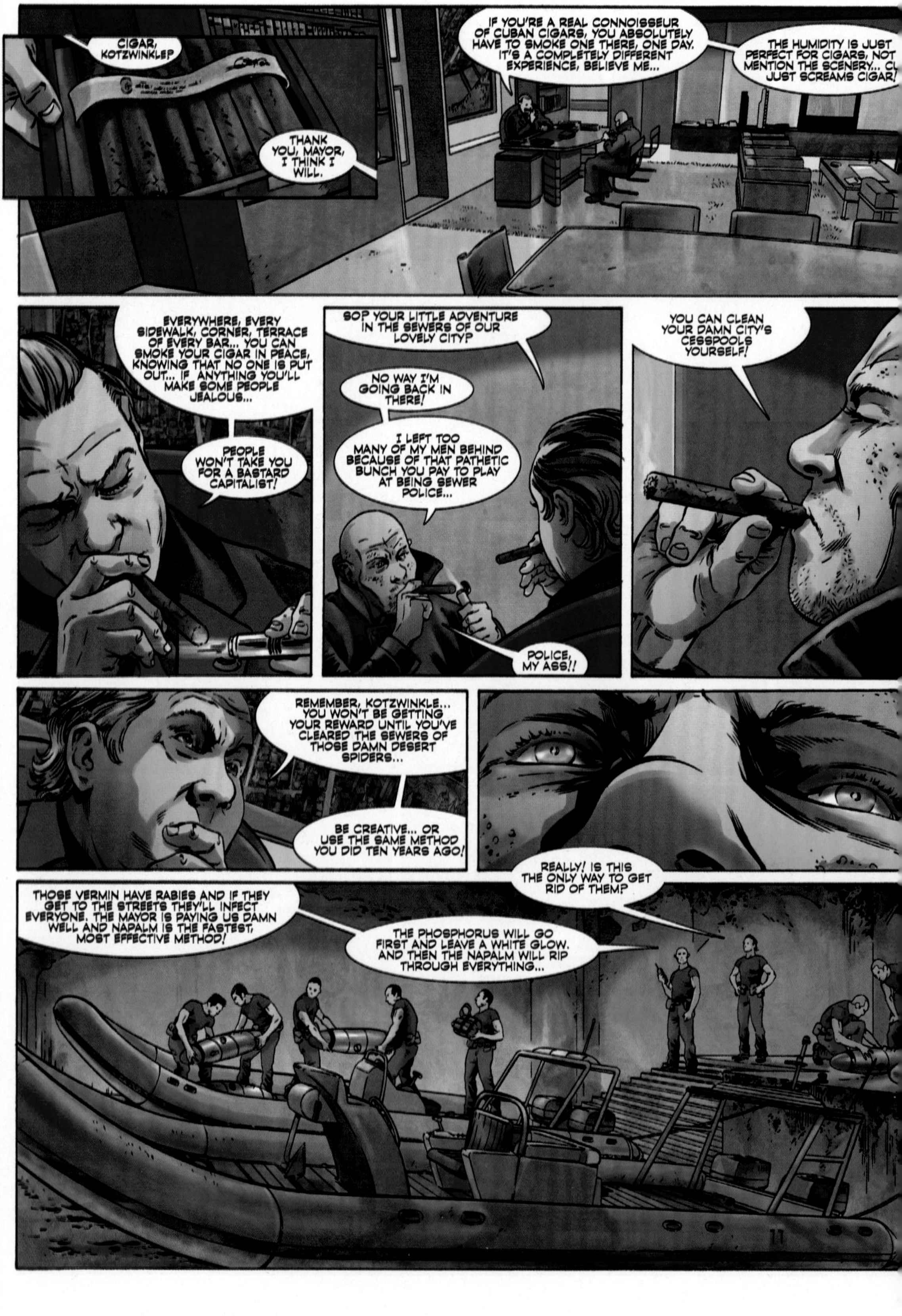
CIGAR, KOTZWINKLE?
THANK YOU, MAYOR, I THINK I WILL.
IF YOU'RE A REAL CONNOISSEUR OF CUBAN CIGARS, YOU ABSOLUTELY HAVE TO SMOKE ONE THERE, ONE DAY. IT'S A COMPLETELY DIFFERENT EXPERIENCE, BELIEVE ME...
THE HUMIDITY IS JUST PERFECT FOR CIGARS, NOT MENTION THE SCENERY... CU JUST SCREAMS CIGAR!
EVERYWHERE, EVERY SIDEWALK, CORNER, TERRACE OF EVERY BAR... YOU CAN SMOKE YOUR CIGAR IN PEACE, KNOWING THAT NO ONE IS PUT OUT... IF ANYTHING YOU'LL MAKE SOME PEOPLE JEALOUS...
PEOPLE WON'T TAKE YOU FOR A BASTARD CAPITALIST!
SO? YOUR LITTLE ADVENTURE IN THE SEWERS OF OUR LOVELY CITY?
NO WAY I'M GOING BACK IN THERE!
I LEFT TOO MANY OF MY MEN BEHIND BECAUSE OF THAT PATHETIC BUNCH YOU PAY TO PLAY AT BEING SEWER POLICE...
POLICE, MY ASS!!
YOU CAN CLEAN YOUR DAMN CITY'S CESSPOOLS YOURSELF!
REMEMBER, KOTZWINKLE... YOU WON'T BE GETTING YOUR REWARD UNTIL YOU'VE CLEARED THE SEWERS OF THOSE DAMN DESERT SPIDERS...
BE CREATIVE... OR USE THE SAME METHOD YOU DID TEN YEARS AGO!
REALLY! IS THIS THE ONLY WAY TO GET RID OF THEM?
THOSE VERMIN HAVE RABIES AND IF THEY GET TO THE STREETS THEY'LL INFECT EVERYONE. THE MAYOR IS PAYING US DAMN WELL AND NAPALM IS THE FASTEST, MOST EFFECTIVE METHOD!
THE PHOSPHORUS WILL GO FIRST AND LEAVE A WHITE GLOW. AND THEN THE NAPALM WILL RIP THROUGH EVERYTHING...

THERE'LL BE A HUGE FIREBALL THAT WILL SPEED DOWN THE TUNNELS... THE EXPLOSION WILL BE THE SIZE OF A FIVE-STOREY BUILDING!

THE MAYOR EVACUATED EVERYONE?

THE SEWER POLICE TOOK CARE OF IT.

THOSE BASTARD ROGUES JUST AGREED TO LEAVE THEIR "HOME" WITHOUT A FIGHT?

HOW SHOULD I KNOW? I'M NOT THEIR NANNY! THEY'RE NOT MY PROBLEM.

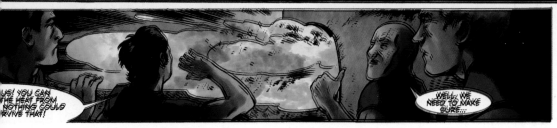

US! YOU CAN THE HEAT FROM NOTHING COULD RVIVE THAT!

WELL, WE NEED TO MAKE SURE...

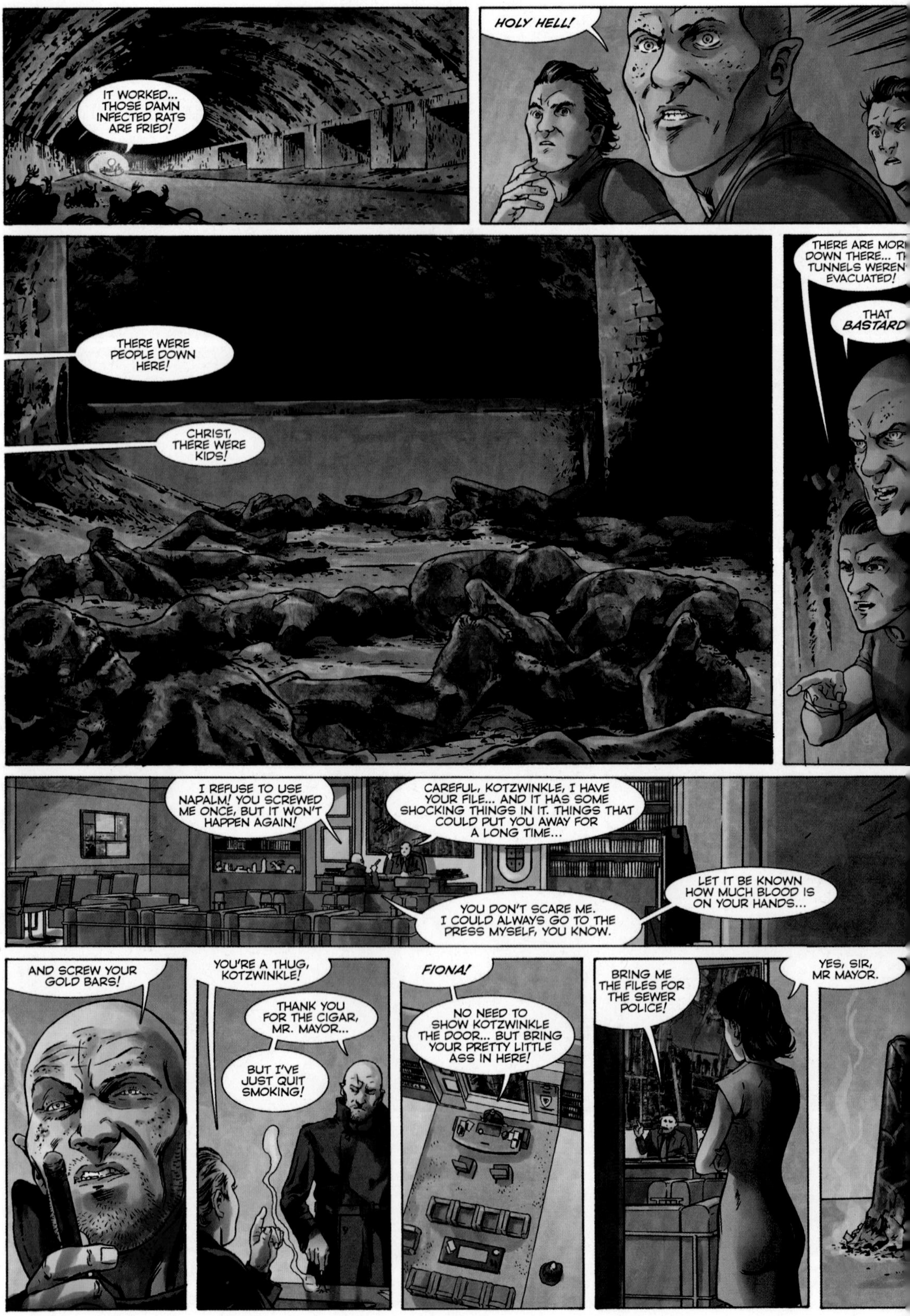
IT WORKED... THOSE DAMN INFECTED RATS ARE FRIED!
HOLY HELL!
THERE WERE PEOPLE DOWN HERE!
CHRIST, THERE WERE KIDS!
THERE ARE MOR DOWN THERE... T TUNNELS WEREN EVACUATED!
THAT BASTARD
I REFUSE TO USE NAPALM! YOU SCREWED ME ONCE, BUT IT WON'T HAPPEN AGAIN!
CAREFUL, KOTZWINKLE, I HAVE YOUR FILE... AND IT HAS SOME SHOCKING THINGS IN IT. THINGS THAT COULD PUT YOU AWAY FOR A LONG TIME...
YOU DON'T SCARE ME. I COULD ALWAYS GO TO THE PRESS MYSELF, YOU KNOW.
LET IT BE KNOWN HOW MUCH BLOOD IS ON YOUR HANDS...
AND SCREW YOUR GOLD BARS!
YOU'RE A THUG, KOTZWINKLE!
THANK YOU FOR THE CIGAR, MR. MAYOR...
BUT I'VE JUST QUIT SMOKING!
FIONA!
NO NEED TO SHOW KOTZWINKLE THE DOOR... BUT BRING YOUR PRETTY LITTLE ASS IN HERE!
BRING ME THE FILES FOR THE SEWER POLICE!
YES, SIR, MR MAYOR.

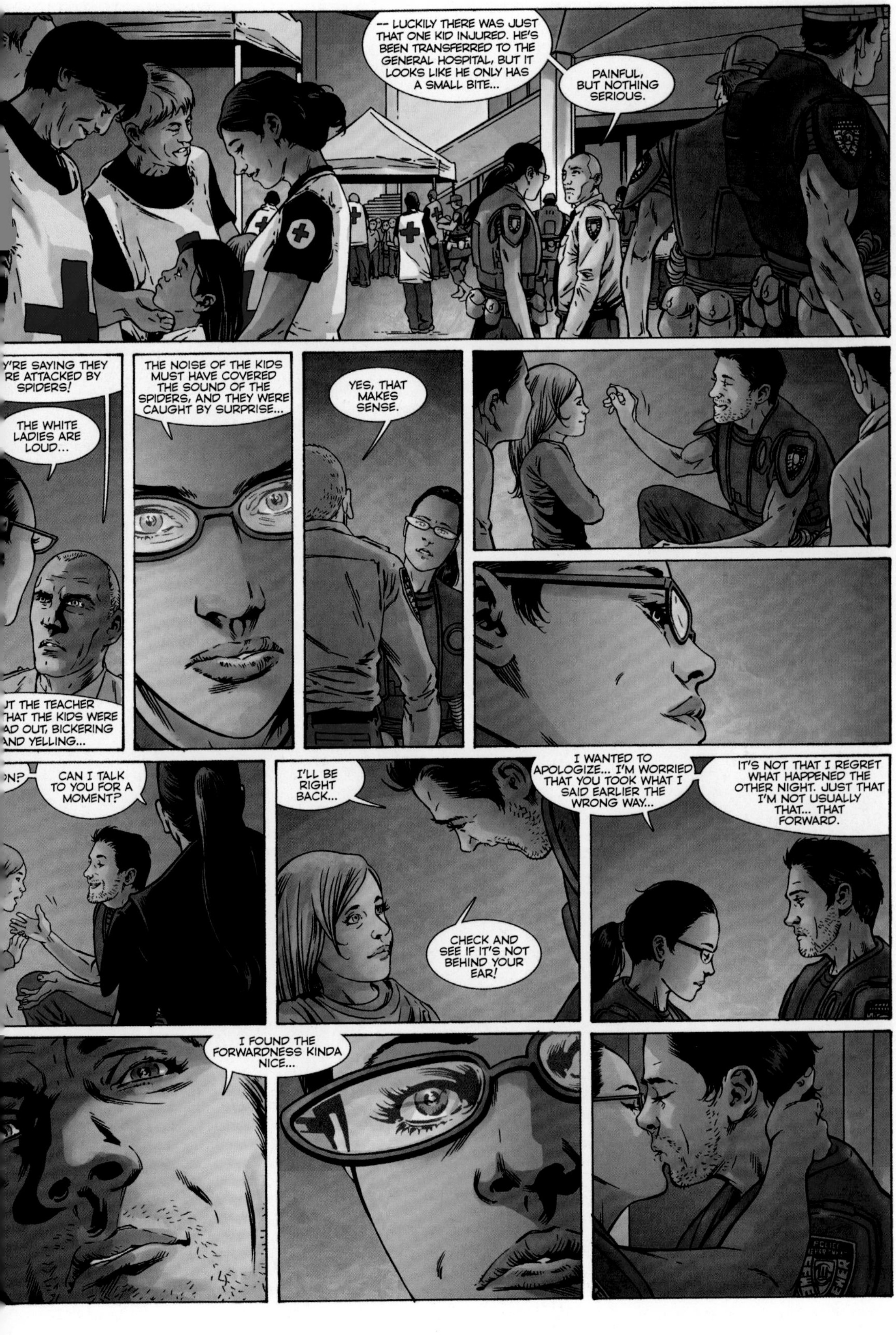

-- LUCKILY THERE WAS JUST THAT ONE KID INJURED. HE'S BEEN TRANSFERRED TO THE GENERAL HOSPITAL, BUT IT LOOKS LIKE HE ONLY HAS A SMALL BITE...
PAINFUL, BUT NOTHING SERIOUS.
Y'RE SAYING THEY RE ATTACKED BY SPIDERS!
THE WHITE LADIES ARE LOUD...
UT THE TEACHER THAT THE KIDS WERE AD OUT, BICKERING AND YELLING...
THE NOISE OF THE KIDS MUST HAVE COVERED THE SOUND OF THE SPIDERS, AND THEY WERE CAUGHT BY SURPRISE...
YES, THAT MAKES SENSE.
ON?
CAN I TALK TO YOU FOR A MOMENT?
I'LL BE RIGHT BACK...
CHECK AND SEE IF IT'S NOT BEHIND YOUR EAR!
I WANTED TO APOLOGIZE... I'M WORRIED THAT YOU TOOK WHAT I SAID EARLIER THE WRONG WAY...
IT'S NOT THAT I REGRET WHAT HAPPENED THE OTHER NIGHT. JUST THAT I'M NOT USUALLY THAT... THAT FORWARD.
I FOUND THE FORWARDNESS KINDA NICE...

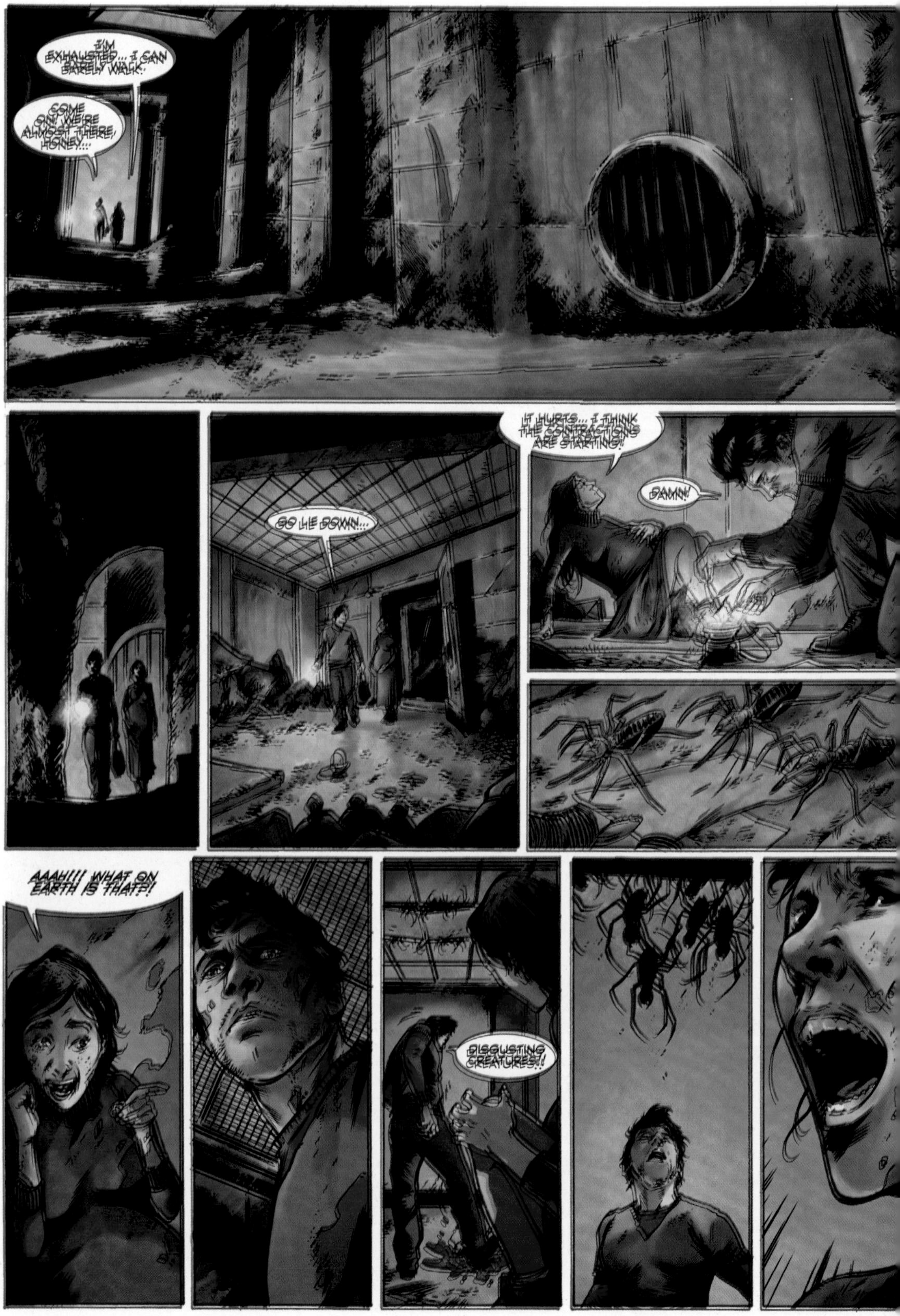
I'M EXHAUSTED... I CAN BARELY WALK.
COME ON! WE'RE ALMOST THERE, HONEY...
GO LIE DOWN...
IT HURTS... I THINK THE CONTRACTIONS ARE STARTING!
DAMN!
AAAH!!! WHAT ON EARTH IS THAT?!
DISGUSTING CREATURES!!

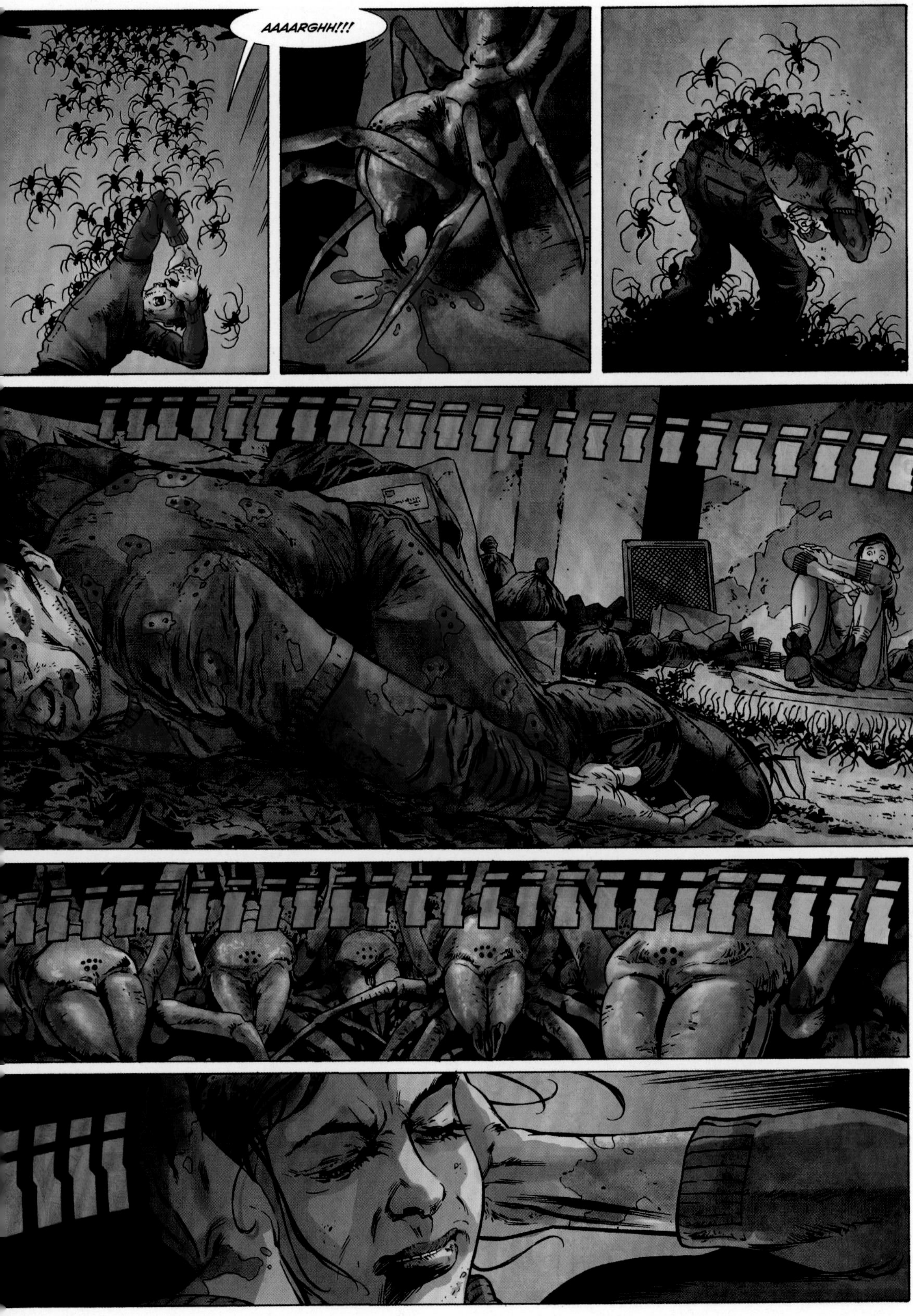
AAAARGHH!!!

I HAVE STUDIED YOUR FILE, LT. JERICHO...

IT'S UNFORTUNATE WHAT HAPPENED AT THE BANK... TO LOSE YOUR PARTNER UNDER SUCH CIRCUMSTANCES.

TELL ME ABOUT IT, MR. MAYOR.

AND THEN YOU WERE THROWN OUT BY THE ADMINISTRATION... HOW'S LIFE IN THE SEWERS?

HUMID, DIRTY, SMELLY... BUT I ALWAYS TRY TO DO THE BEST JOB I CAN.

YOU'RE THE BEST COP IN THE CITY, LIEUTENANT!

DON'T YOU EVER WANT TO COME BACK ABOVE GROUND AND SEE THE SUN?

WHAT D'YOU THINK?

GOOD. FIONA, BRING THE CASE PLEASE.

YES, SIR, MR MAYOR, RIGHT AWAY.

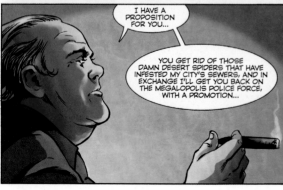

I HAVE A PROPOSITION FOR YOU...

YOU GET RID OF THOSE DAMN DESERT SPIDERS THAT HAVE INFESTED MY CITY'S SEWERS, AND IN EXCHANGE I'LL GET YOU BACK ON THE MEGALOPOLIS POLICE FORCE, WITH A PROMOTION...

AND GIVE YOU THIS AS A BONUS GIFT!

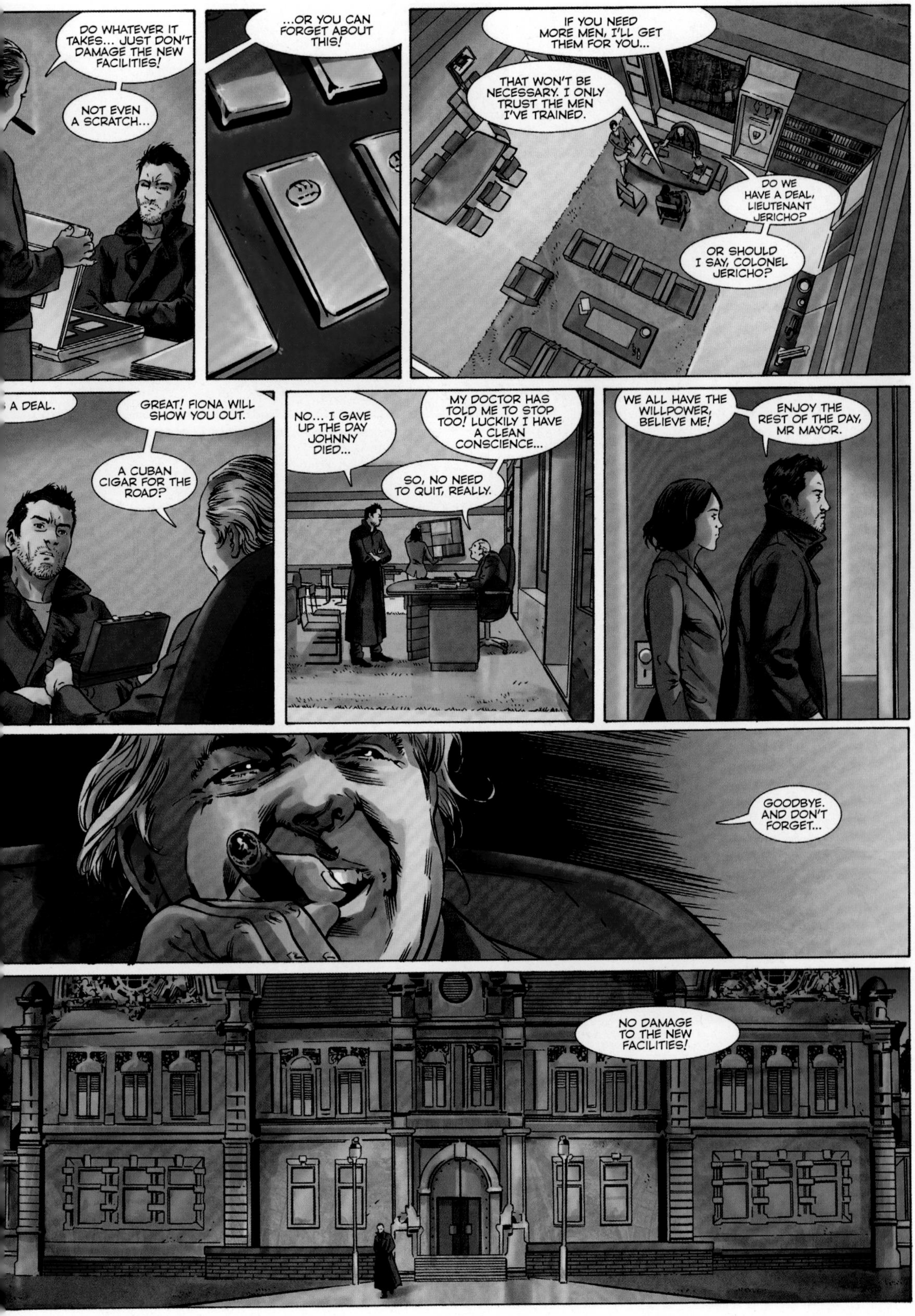
DO WHATEVER IT TAKES... JUST DON'T DAMAGE THE NEW FACILITIES!
NOT EVEN A SCRATCH...
...OR YOU CAN FORGET ABOUT THIS!
IF YOU NEED MORE MEN, I'LL GET THEM FOR YOU...
THAT WON'T BE NECESSARY. I ONLY TRUST THE MEN I'VE TRAINED.
DO WE HAVE A DEAL, LIEUTENANT JERICHO?
OR SHOULD I SAY, COLONEL JERICHO?
A DEAL.
GREAT! FIONA WILL SHOW YOU OUT.
A CUBAN CIGAR FOR THE ROAD?
NO... I GAVE UP THE DAY JOHNNY DIED...
MY DOCTOR HAS TOLD ME TO STOP TOO! LUCKILY I HAVE A CLEAN CONSCIENCE...
SO, NO NEED TO QUIT, REALLY.
WE ALL HAVE THE WILLPOWER, BELIEVE ME!
ENJOY THE REST OF THE DAY, MR MAYOR.
GOODBYE. AND DON'T FORGET...
NO DAMAGE TO THE NEW FACILITIES!

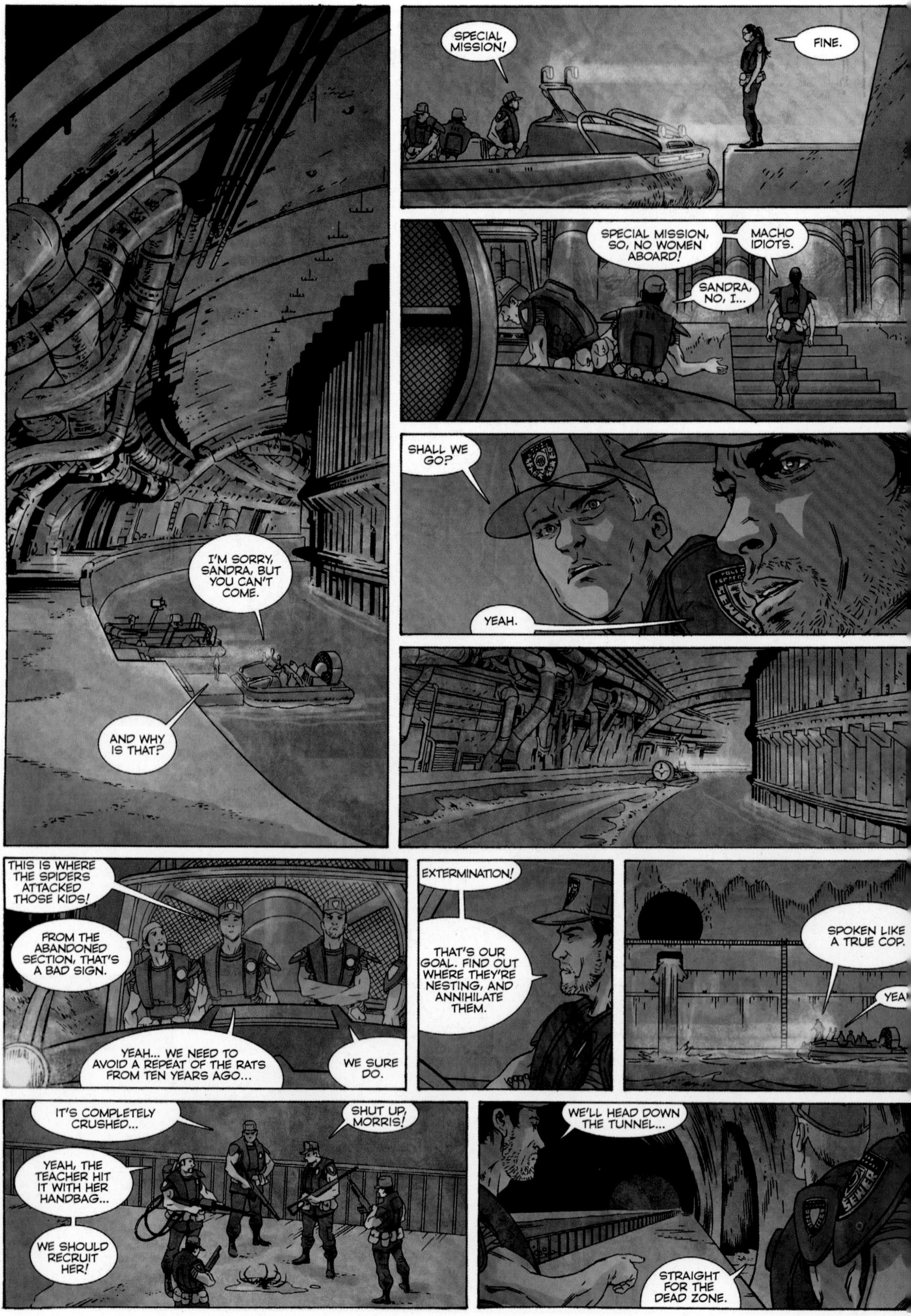
I'M SORRY, SANDRA, BUT YOU CAN'T COME.
AND WHY IS THAT?
SPECIAL MISSION!
FINE.
SPECIAL MISSION, SO, NO WOMEN ABOARD!
MACHO IDIOTS.
SANDRA, NO, I...
SHALL WE GO?
YEAH.
THIS IS WHERE THE SPIDERS ATTACKED THOSE KIDS!
FROM THE ABANDONED SECTION, THAT'S A BAD SIGN.
YEAH... WE NEED TO AVOID A REPEAT OF THE RATS FROM TEN YEARS AGO...
WE SURE DO.
EXTERMINATION!
THAT'S OUR GOAL. FIND OUT WHERE THEY'RE NESTING, AND ANNIHILATE THEM.
SPOKEN LIKE A TRUE COP.
IT'S COMPLETELY CRUSHED...
YEAH, THE TEACHER HIT IT WITH HER HANDBAG...
WE SHOULD RECRUIT HER!
SHUT UP, MORRIS!
WE'LL HEAD DOWN THE TUNNEL...
STRAIGHT FOR THE DEAD ZONE.

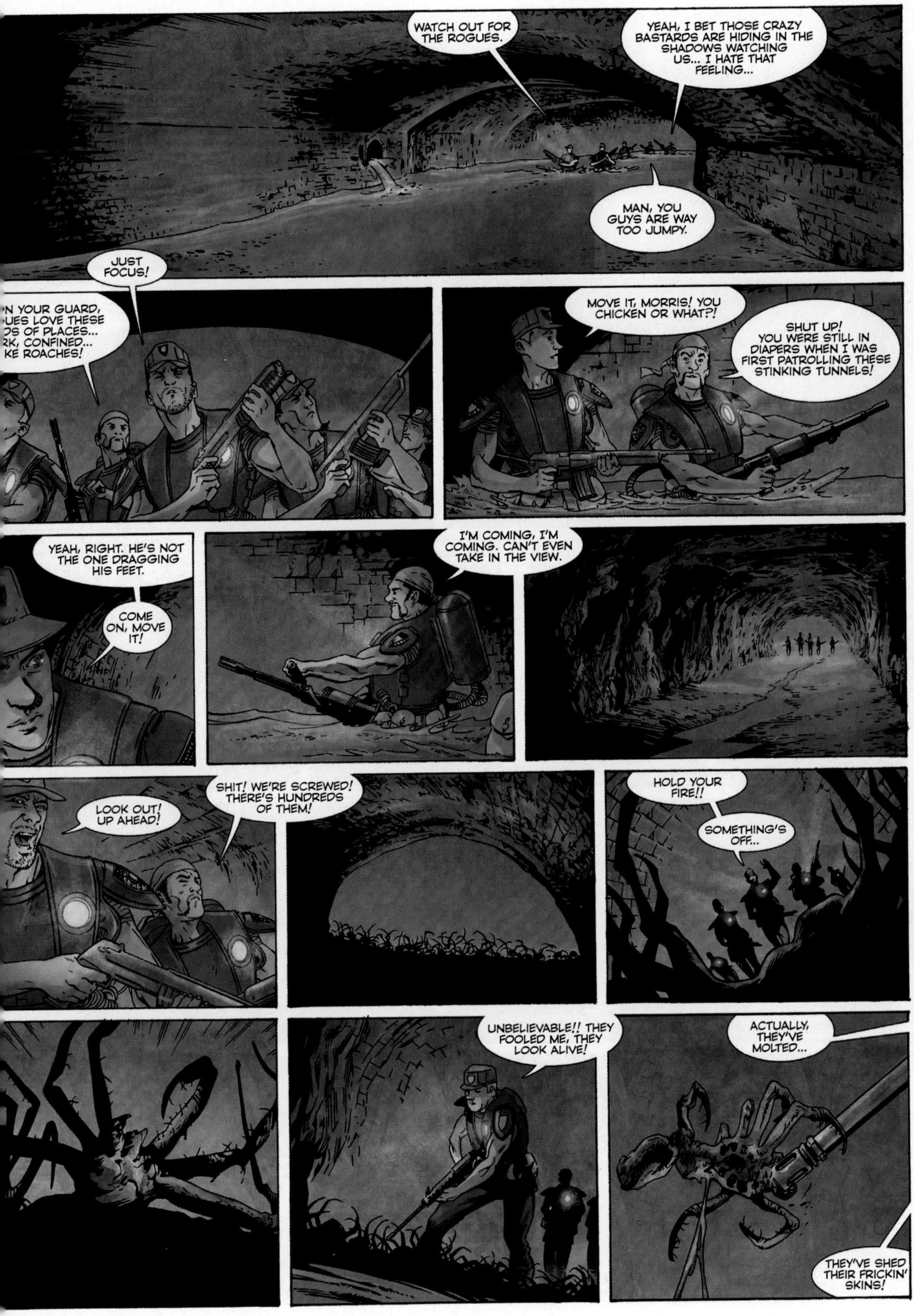
WATCH OUT FOR THE ROGUES.
YEAH, I BET THOSE CRAZY BASTARDS ARE HIDING IN THE SHADOWS WATCHING US... I HATE THAT FEELING...
MAN, YOU GUYS ARE WAY TOO JUMPY.
JUST FOCUS!
N YOUR GUARD, UES LOVE THESE DS OF PLACES... RK, CONFINED... KE ROACHES!
MOVE IT, MORRIS! YOU CHICKEN OR WHAT?!
SHUT UP! YOU WERE STILL IN DIAPERS WHEN I WAS FIRST PATROLLING THESE STINKING TUNNELS!
YEAH, RIGHT. HE'S NOT THE ONE DRAGGING HIS FEET.
COME ON, MOVE IT!
I'M COMING, I'M COMING. CAN'T EVEN TAKE IN THE VIEW.
LOOK OUT! UP AHEAD!
SHIT! WE'RE SCREWED! THERE'S HUNDREDS OF THEM!
HOLD YOUR FIRE!!
SOMETHING'S OFF...
UNBELIEVABLE!! THEY FOOLED ME, THEY LOOK ALIVE!
ACTUALLY, THEY'VE MOLTED...
THEY'VE SHED THEIR FRICKIN' SKINS!

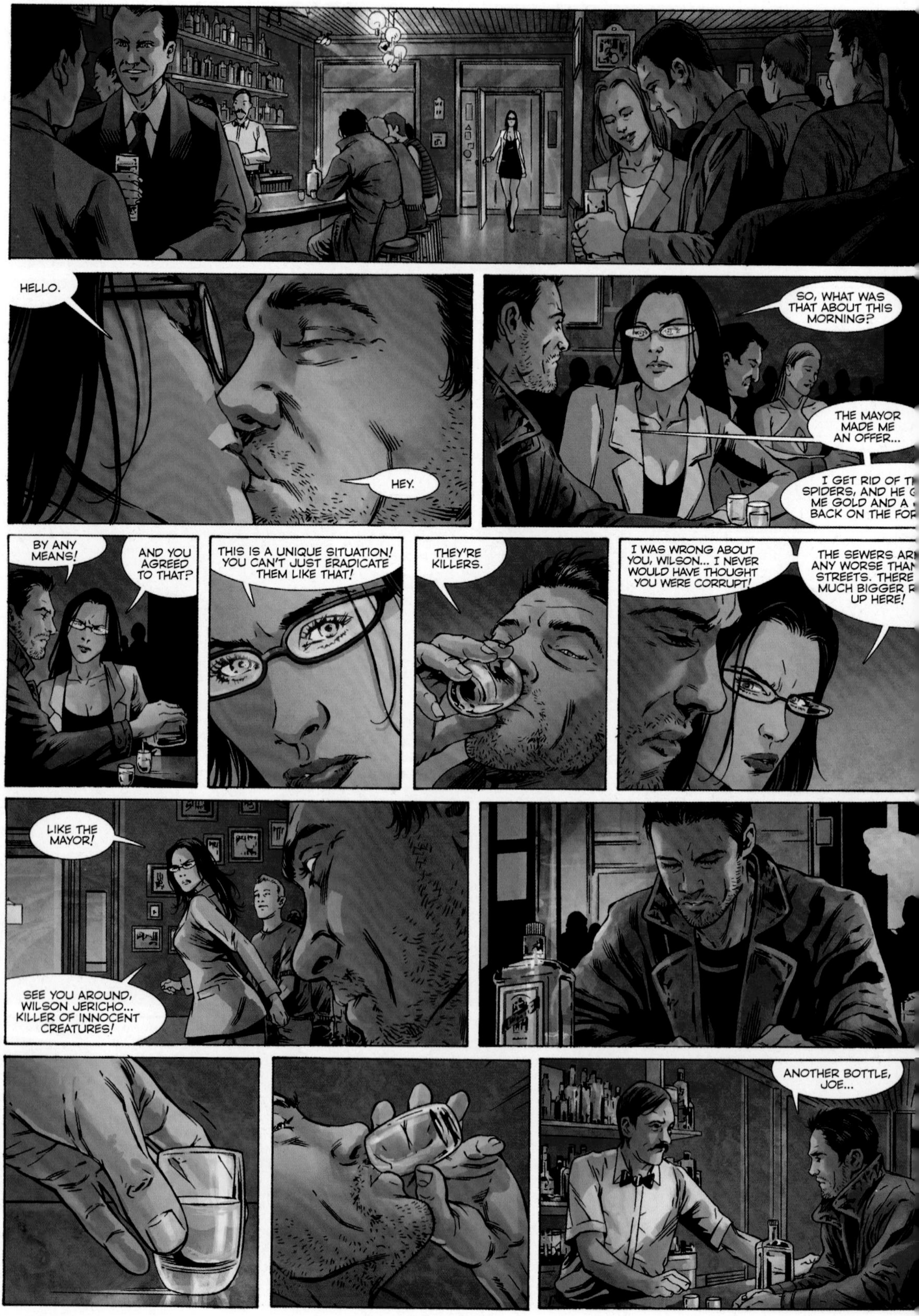
HELLO.
HEY.
SO, WHAT WAS THAT ABOUT THIS MORNING?
THE MAYOR MADE ME AN OFFER...
I GET RID OF T SPIDERS, AND HE G ME GOLD AND A BACK ON THE FOR
BY ANY MEANS!
AND YOU AGREED TO THAT?
THIS IS A UNIQUE SITUATION! YOU CAN'T JUST ERADICATE THEM LIKE THAT!
THEY'RE KILLERS.
I WAS WRONG ABOUT YOU, WILSON... I NEVER WOULD HAVE THOUGHT YOU WERE CORRUPT!
THE SEWERS AR ANY WORSE THAN STREETS. THERE MUCH BIGGER R UP HERE!
LIKE THE MAYOR!
SEE YOU AROUND, WILSON JERICHO... KILLER OF INNOCENT CREATURES!
ANOTHER BOTTLE, JOE...

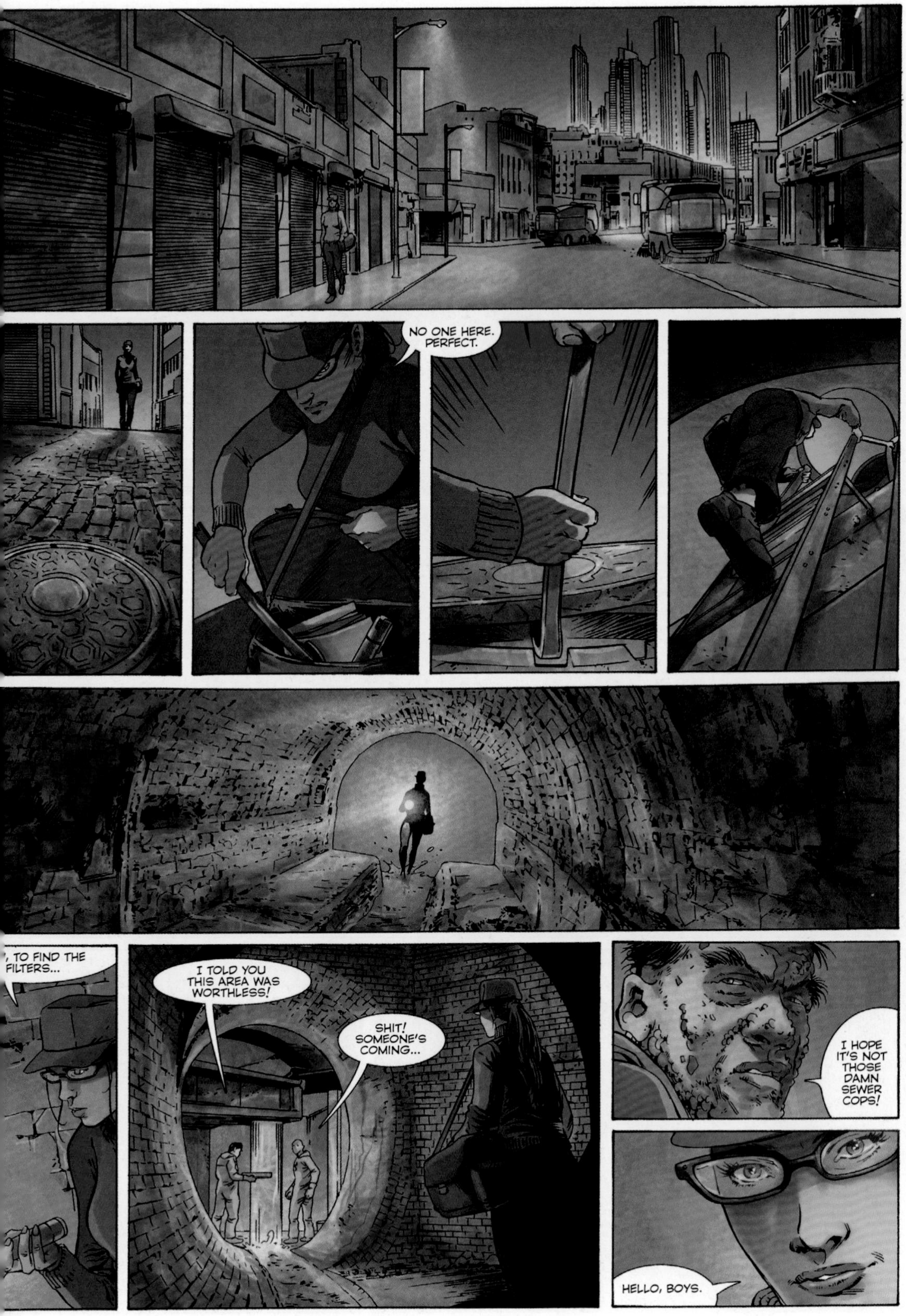
NO ONE HERE. PERFECT.
, TO FIND THE FILTERS...
I TOLD YOU THIS AREA WAS WORTHLESS!
SHIT! SOMEONE'S COMING...
I HOPE IT'S NOT THOSE DAMN SEWER COPS!
HELLO, BOYS.

I'M LOOKING FOR COCOONS.

HAVE YOU SEEN ANY HERE THE SEWERS?

LET'S SEE...

MAYBE, BUT I CAN'T QUITE SEEM TO REMEMBER...

DEFINITELY SEEN SOMETHING LIKE THAT...

SIGH...

OH, YEAH! IN ZONE 53!

RIGHT! ZONE 53!

CAREFUL LADY, IT'S RIGHT IN THE MIDDLE OF ROGUE TERRITORY IN THE DEAD ZONE...

WHATEVER YOU FIND THERE WON'T BE PRETTY.

ZONE 53, THAT'S...

I'LL POINT IT OUT ON YOUR MAP!

SHIT MAN, THESE CARCASSES MAKE ME WANT TO PUKE!

MORRIS, PLEASE!

WHY DO WE NEED ALL THESE DEAD COWS!?

TO ATTRACT THE SPIDERS...

HE READ IN SOME BOOK THAT THEY GO NUTS FOR CAMEL LIVER.

OKAY, BUT THIS IS A COW.

SO? A LIVER IS A LIVER!

STOP HERE! THIS IS ZONE 51!

LET'S HOPE MISS YEATMAN'S THEORY IS RIGHT...

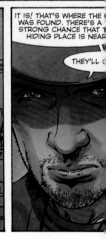
IT IS! THAT'S WHERE THE WAS FOUND. THERE'S A STRONG CHANCE THAT HIDING PLACE IS NEAR

THEY'LL

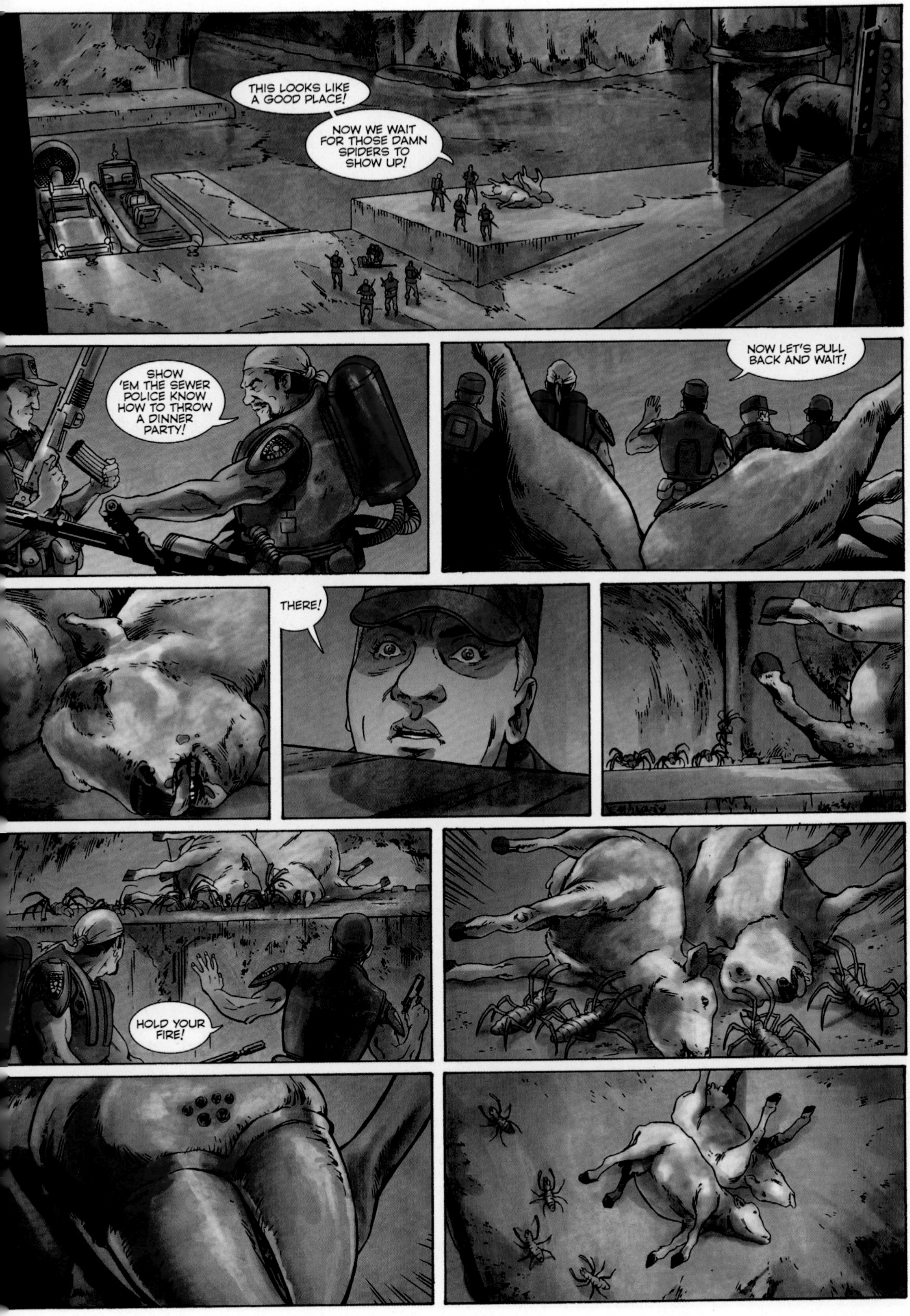
THIS LOOKS LIKE A GOOD PLACE!
NOW WE WAIT FOR THOSE DAMN SPIDERS TO SHOW UP!
SHOW 'EM THE SEWER POLICE KNOW HOW TO THROW A DINNER PARTY!
NOW LET'S PULL BACK AND WAIT!
THERE!
HOLD YOUR FIRE!

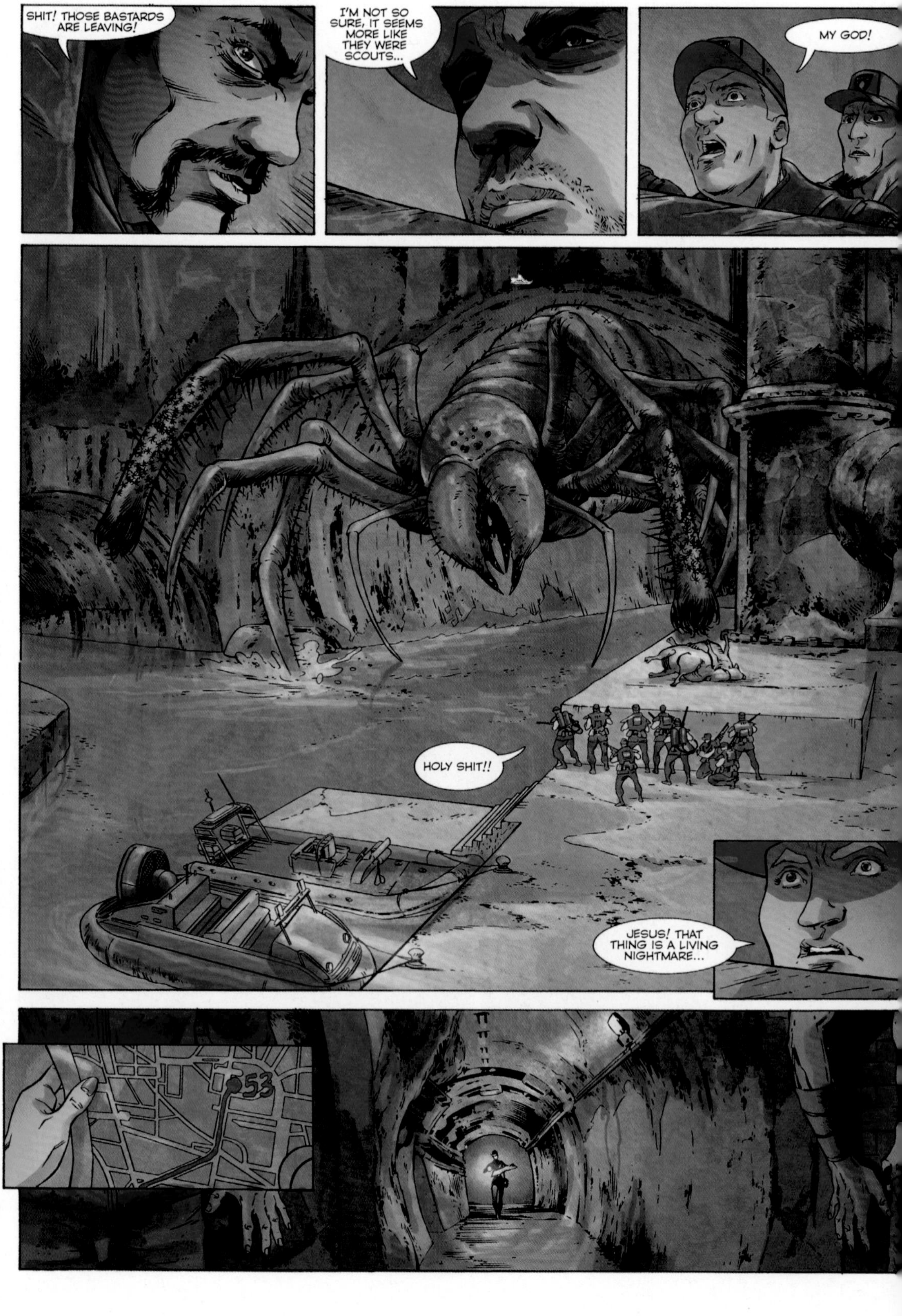
SHIT! THOSE BASTARDS ARE LEAVING!
I'M NOT SO SURE, IT SEEMS MORE LIKE THEY WERE SCOUTS...
MY GOD!
HOLY SHIT!!
JESUS! THAT THING IS A LIVING NIGHTMARE...
53

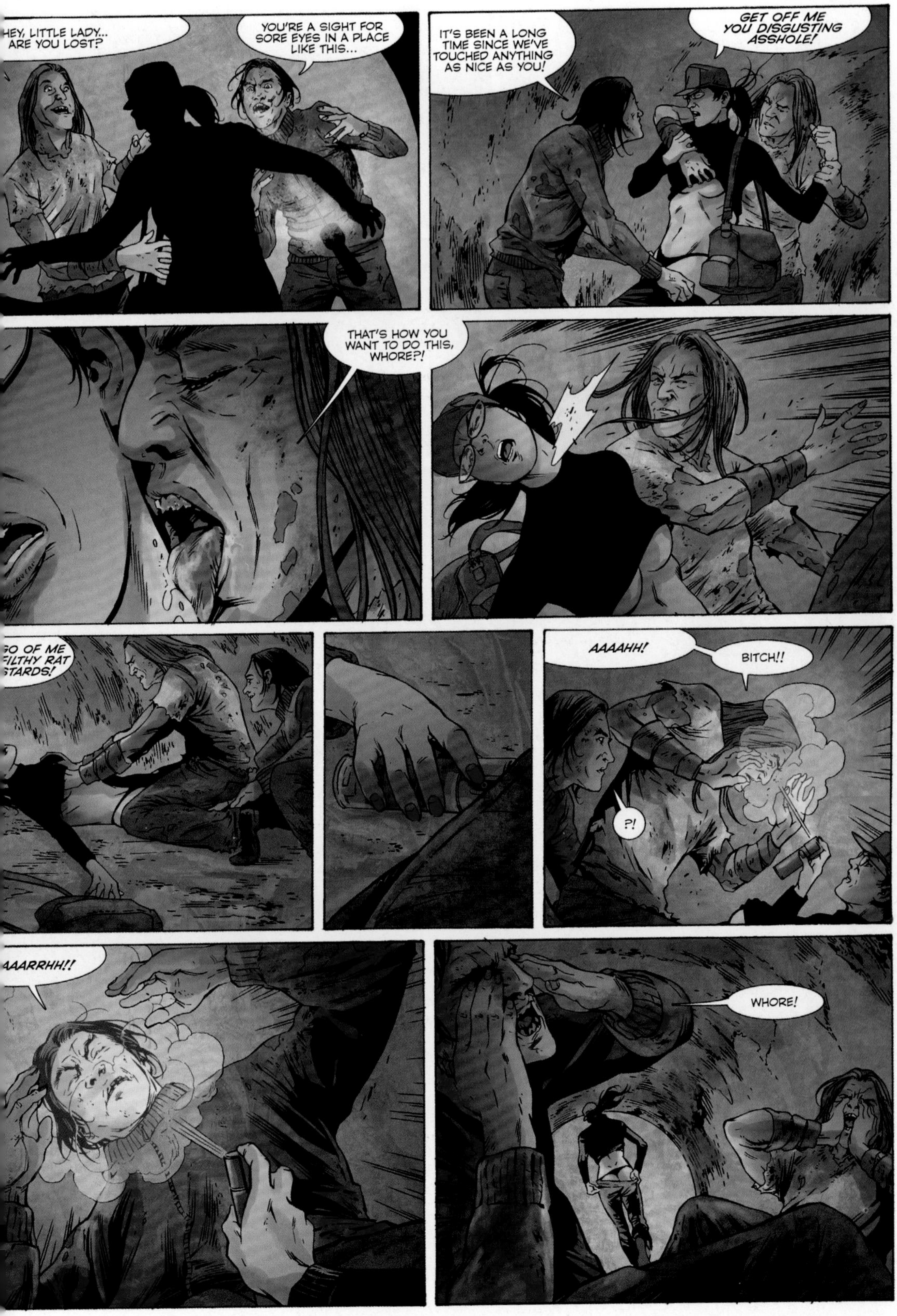
HEY, LITTLE LADY... ARE YOU LOST?
YOU'RE A SIGHT FOR SORE EYES IN A PLACE LIKE THIS...
IT'S BEEN A LONG TIME SINCE WE'VE TOUCHED ANYTHING AS NICE AS YOU!
GET OFF ME YOU DISGUSTING ASSHOLE!
THAT'S HOW YOU WANT TO DO THIS, WHORE?!
GO OF ME FILTHY RAT STARDS!
AAAAHH!
BITCH!!
?!
AAARRHH!!
WHORE!

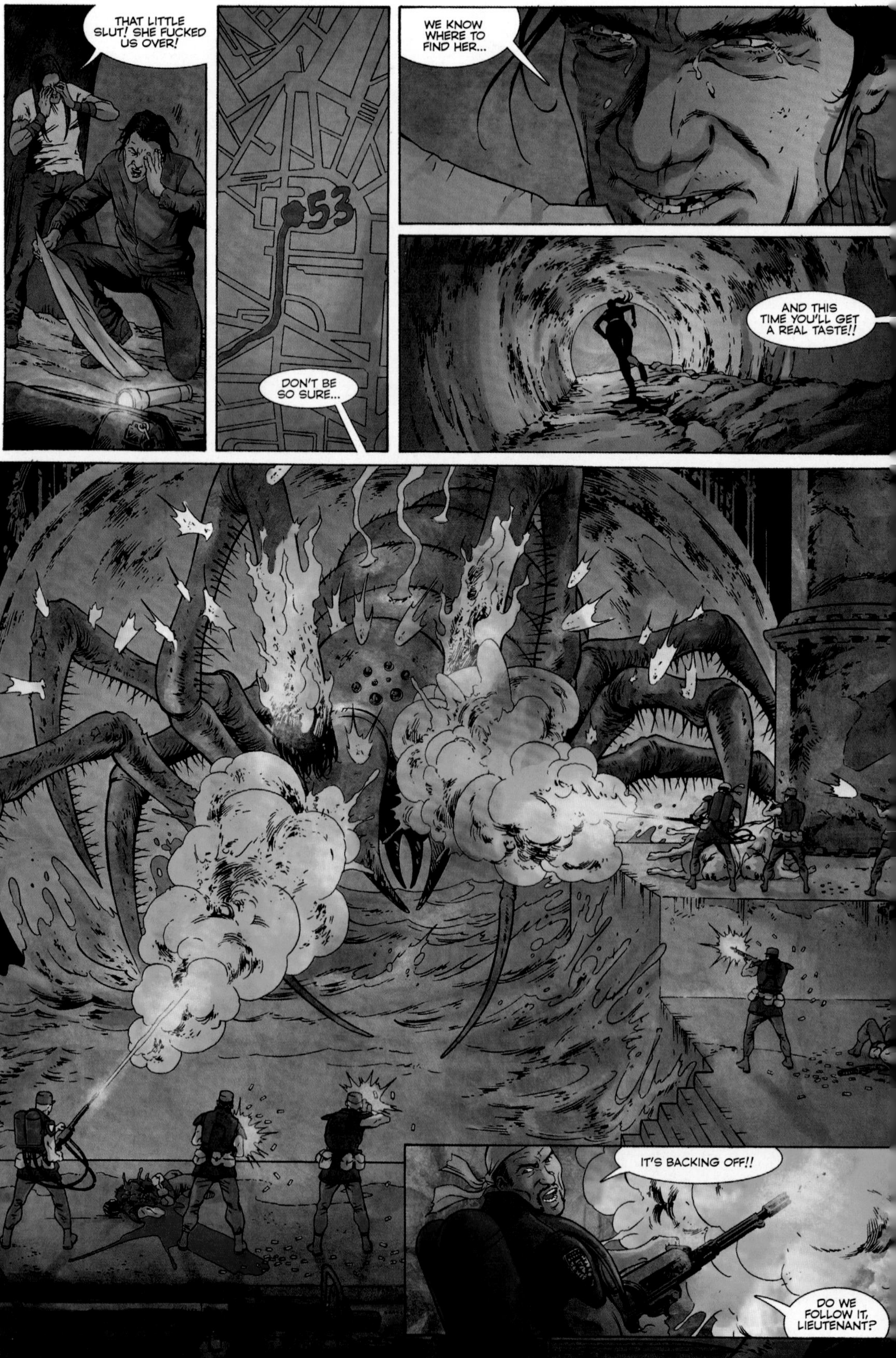
THAT LITTLE SLUT! SHE FUCKED US OVER!
DON'T BE SO SURE...
53
WE KNOW WHERE TO FIND HER...
AND THIS TIME YOU'LL GET A REAL TASTE!!
IT'S BACKING OFF!!
DO WE FOLLOW IT, LIEUTENANT?

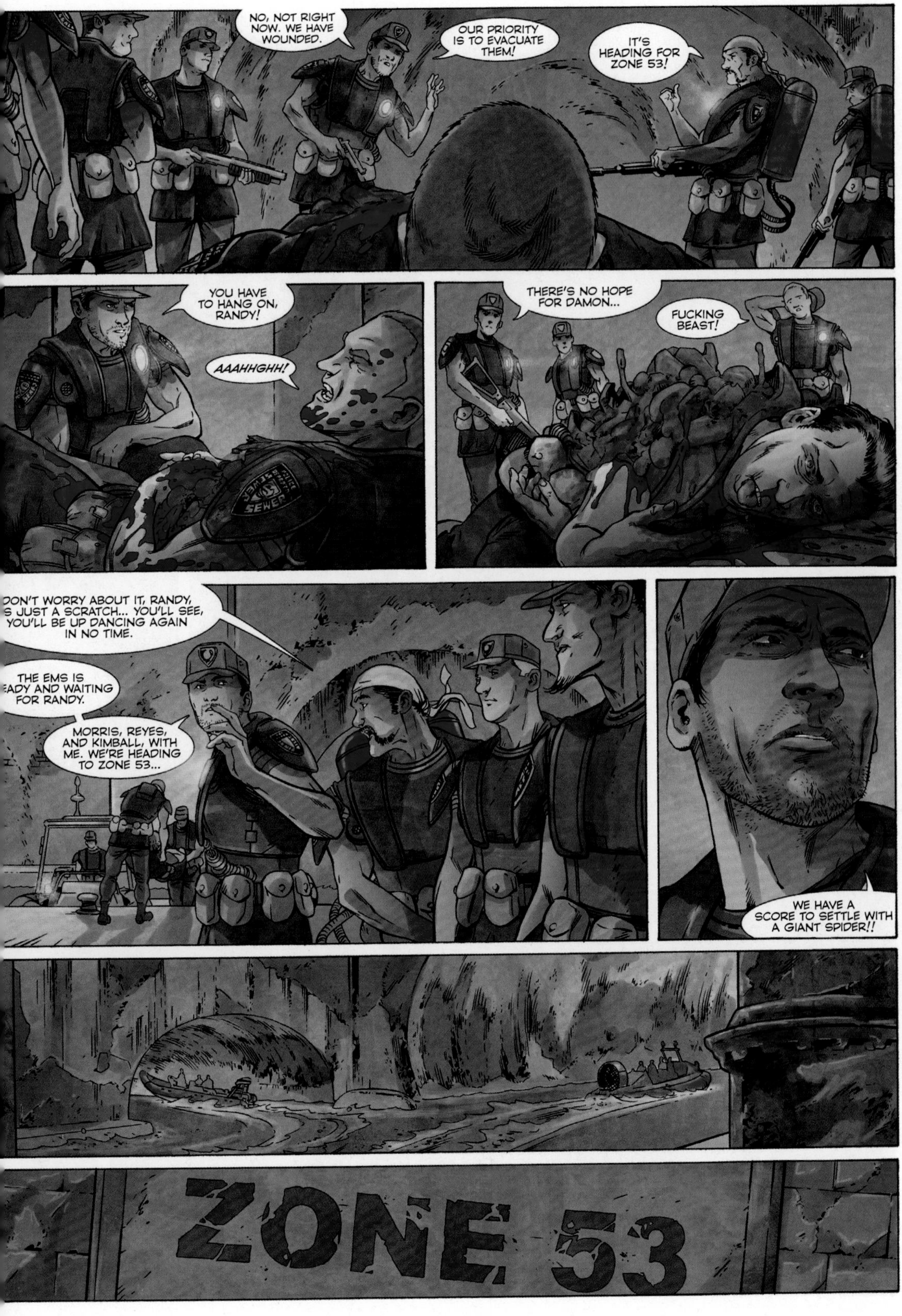
NO, NOT RIGHT NOW. WE HAVE WOUNDED.
OUR PRIORITY IS TO EVACUATE THEM!
IT'S HEADING FOR ZONE 53!
YOU HAVE TO HANG ON, RANDY!
AAAHHGHH!
THERE'S NO HOPE FOR DAMON...
FUCKING BEAST!
DON'T WORRY ABOUT IT, RANDY, 'S JUST A SCRATCH... YOU'LL SEE, YOU'LL BE UP DANCING AGAIN IN NO TIME.
THE EMS IS EADY AND WAITING FOR RANDY.
MORRIS, REYES, AND KIMBALL, WITH ME. WE'RE HEADING TO ZONE 53...
WE HAVE A SCORE TO SETTLE WITH A GIANT SPIDER!!
ZONE 53

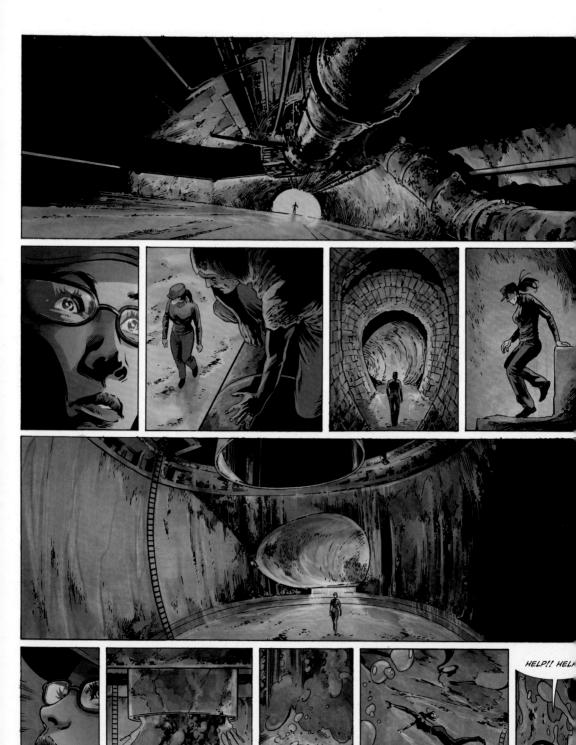

HELP!! HEL

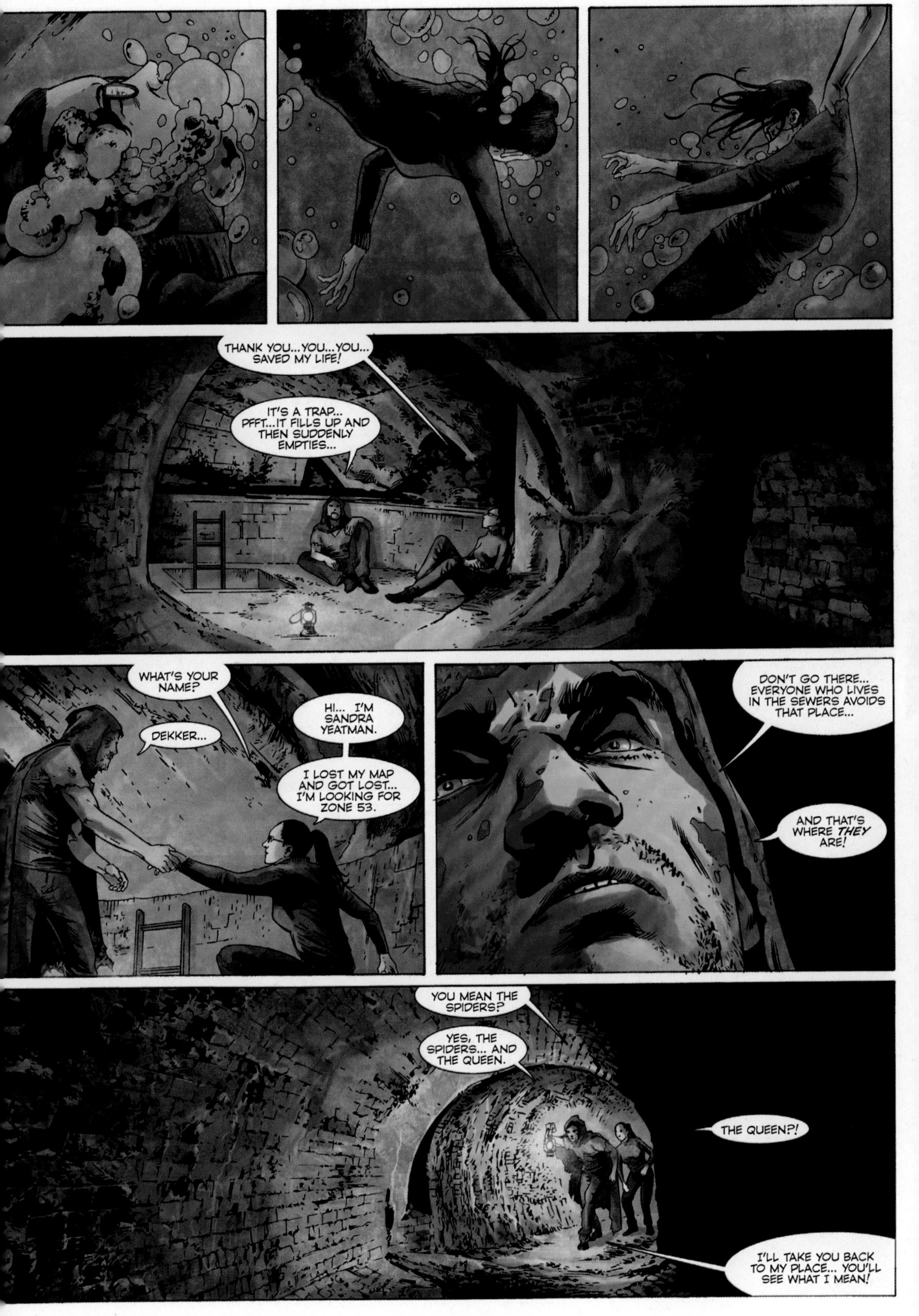
THANK YOU...YOU...YOU... SAVED MY LIFE!
IT'S A TRAP... PFFT...IT FILLS UP AND THEN SUDDENLY EMPTIES...
WHAT'S YOUR NAME?
DEKKER...
HI... I'M SANDRA YEATMAN.
I LOST MY MAP AND GOT LOST... I'M LOOKING FOR ZONE 53.
DON'T GO THERE... EVERYONE WHO LIVES IN THE SEWERS AVOIDS THAT PLACE...
AND THAT'S WHERE *THEY* ARE!
YOU MEAN THE SPIDERS?
YES, THE SPIDERS... AND THE QUEEN.
THE QUEEN?!
I'LL TAKE YOU BACK TO MY PLACE... YOU'LL SEE WHAT I MEAN!

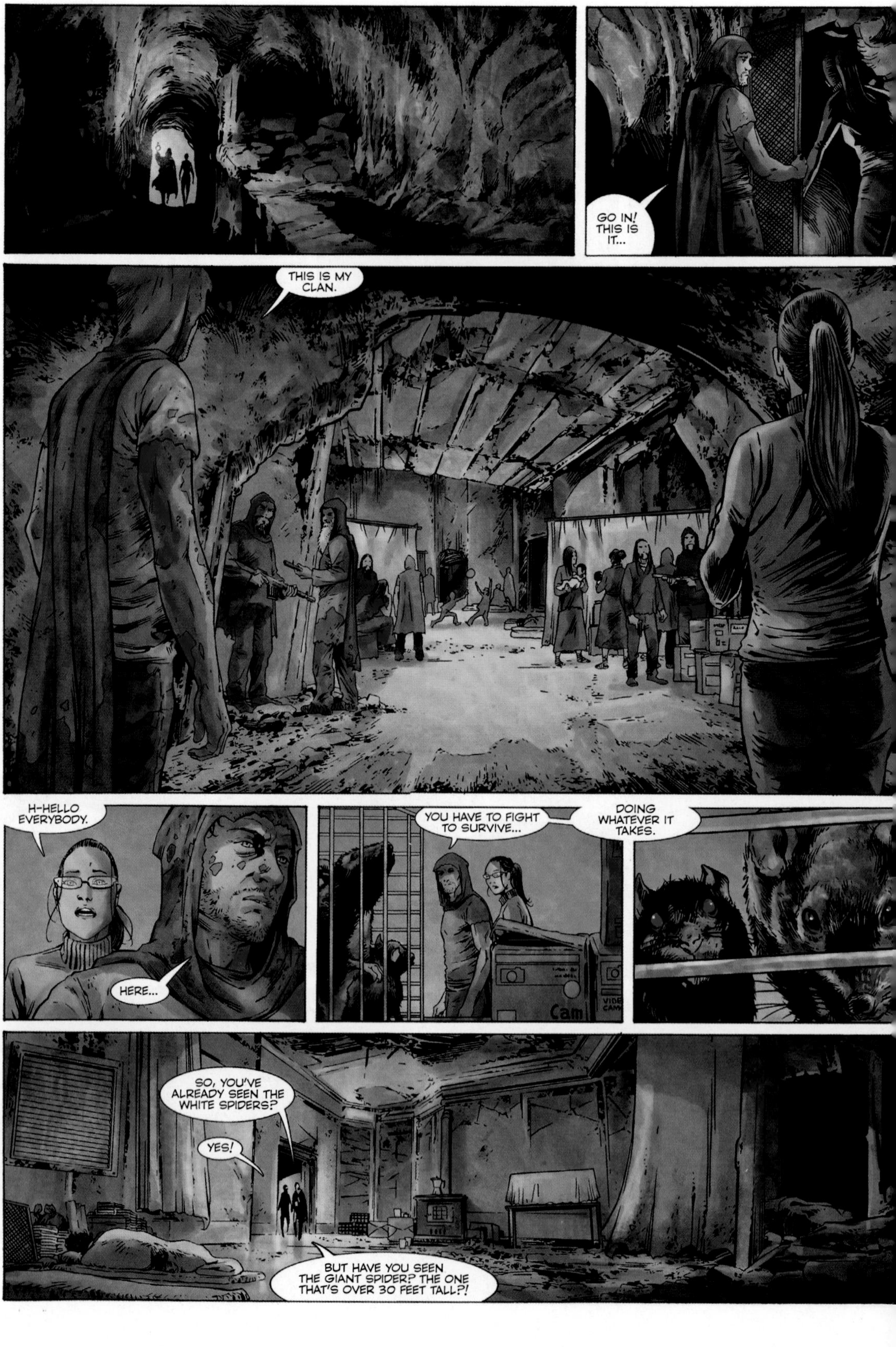
GO IN! THIS IS IT...
THIS IS MY CLAN.
H-HELLO EVERYBODY.
HERE...
YOU HAVE TO FIGHT TO SURVIVE...
DOING WHATEVER IT TAKES.
SO, YOU'VE ALREADY SEEN THE WHITE SPIDERS?
YES!
BUT HAVE YOU SEEN THE GIANT SPIDER? THE ONE THAT'S OVER 30 FEET TALL?!

...ARE CAMEL SPIDERS FROM ...E CALL THEM WHITE LADIES. ...E IN THE SEWERS OF THE ...GALOPOLIS, THEY MUTATED ...) ARE BIGGER THAN THEIR ...ATURAL SIZE, BUT NOT THAT BIG...

IT MUST BE THEIR ...DOWS THAT GAVE YOU THAT IMPRESSION.

SO YOU HAVEN'T SEEN IT THEN!

DONALD! WAKE UP YOU SLOTH!

DEKKER! WHAT DO YOU WANT NOW?!

I WAS DREAMING I WAS IN A STRIP CLUB AND THERE WAS A BEAUTIFUL DANCER...

I WANT TO SEE YOUR LEG!

I DON'T SHOW MY LEG TO YOUNG WOMEN!

I DON'T KNOW WHERE YOU FOUND HER, BUT SHE IS EXACTLY THE TYPE THAT DANCES THROUGH MY DREAMS...

COME ON, YOU OLD PERVERT... SHOW ME THAT LEG OR I'LL KICK YOUR ASS!

PATIENCE!

YOU KNOW, MY DEAR, NATURE HAS ALWAYS PROVEN THAT IT CAN CREATE MONSTERS... FIVE-LEGGED SHEEP, SIAMESE TWINS, GIANT SHARKS...

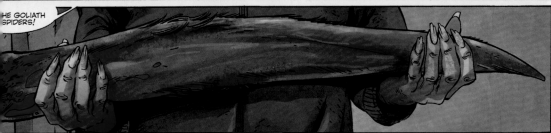

...HE GOLIATH ...PIDERS!

THAT'S INCREDIBLE! IT LOOKS COMPLETELY REAL! IT MUST HAVE MUTATED LIKE THE GOLIATH TARANTULA!

WHERE DID YOU FIND IT?

IN THE SEWERS OF ZONE 51.

THAT'S WHERE THE QUEEN'S FOOD STORES ARE.

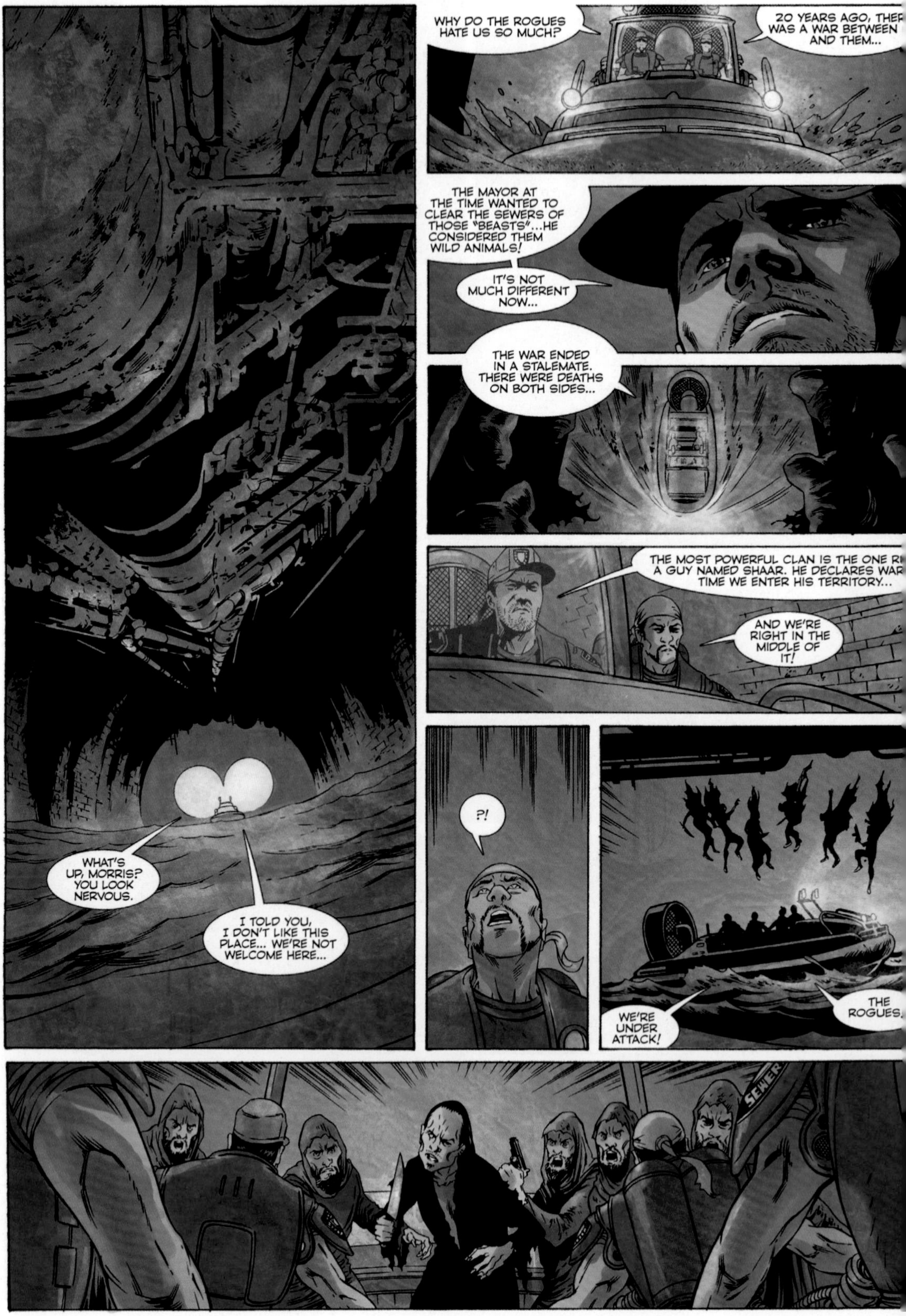

WHAT'S UP, MORRIS? YOU LOOK NERVOUS.
I TOLD YOU, I DON'T LIKE THIS PLACE... WE'RE NOT WELCOME HERE...
WHY DO THE ROGUES HATE US SO MUCH?
20 YEARS AGO, THER WAS A WAR BETWEEN AND THEM...
THE MAYOR AT THE TIME WANTED TO CLEAR THE SEWERS OF THOSE "BEASTS"...HE CONSIDERED THEM WILD ANIMALS!
IT'S NOT MUCH DIFFERENT NOW...
THE WAR ENDED IN A STALEMATE. THERE WERE DEATHS ON BOTH SIDES...
THE MOST POWERFUL CLAN IS THE ONE R A GUY NAMED SHAAR. HE DECLARES WAR TIME WE ENTER HIS TERRITORY...
AND WE'RE RIGHT IN THE MIDDLE OF IT!
?!
WE'RE UNDER ATTACK!
THE ROGUES.
SEWER

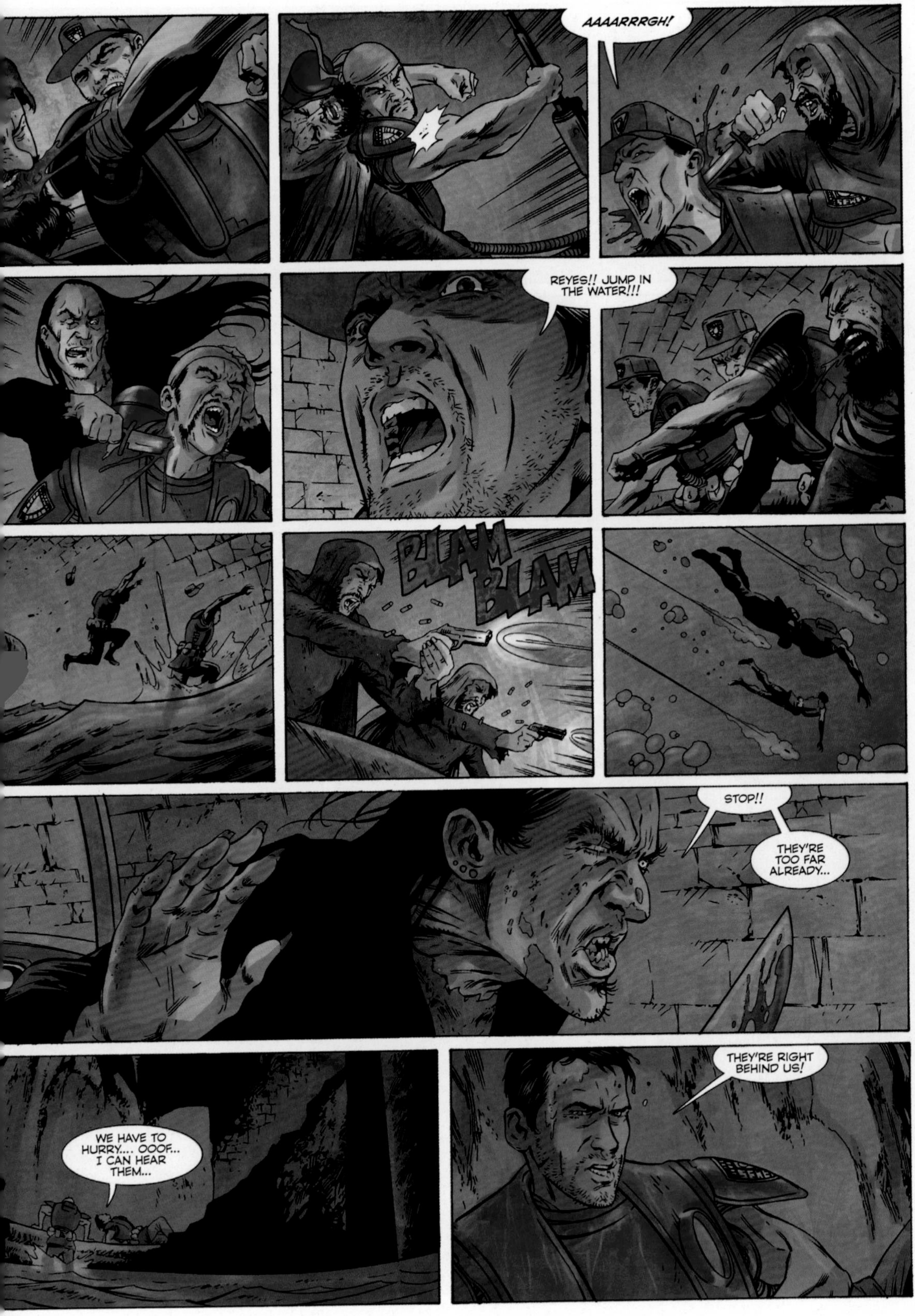
AAAARRRGH!
REYES!! JUMP IN THE WATER!!!
BLAM BLAM
STOP!!
THEY'RE TOO FAR ALREADY...
WE HAVE TO HURRY.... OOOF... I CAN HEAR THEM...
THEY'RE RIGHT BEHIND US!

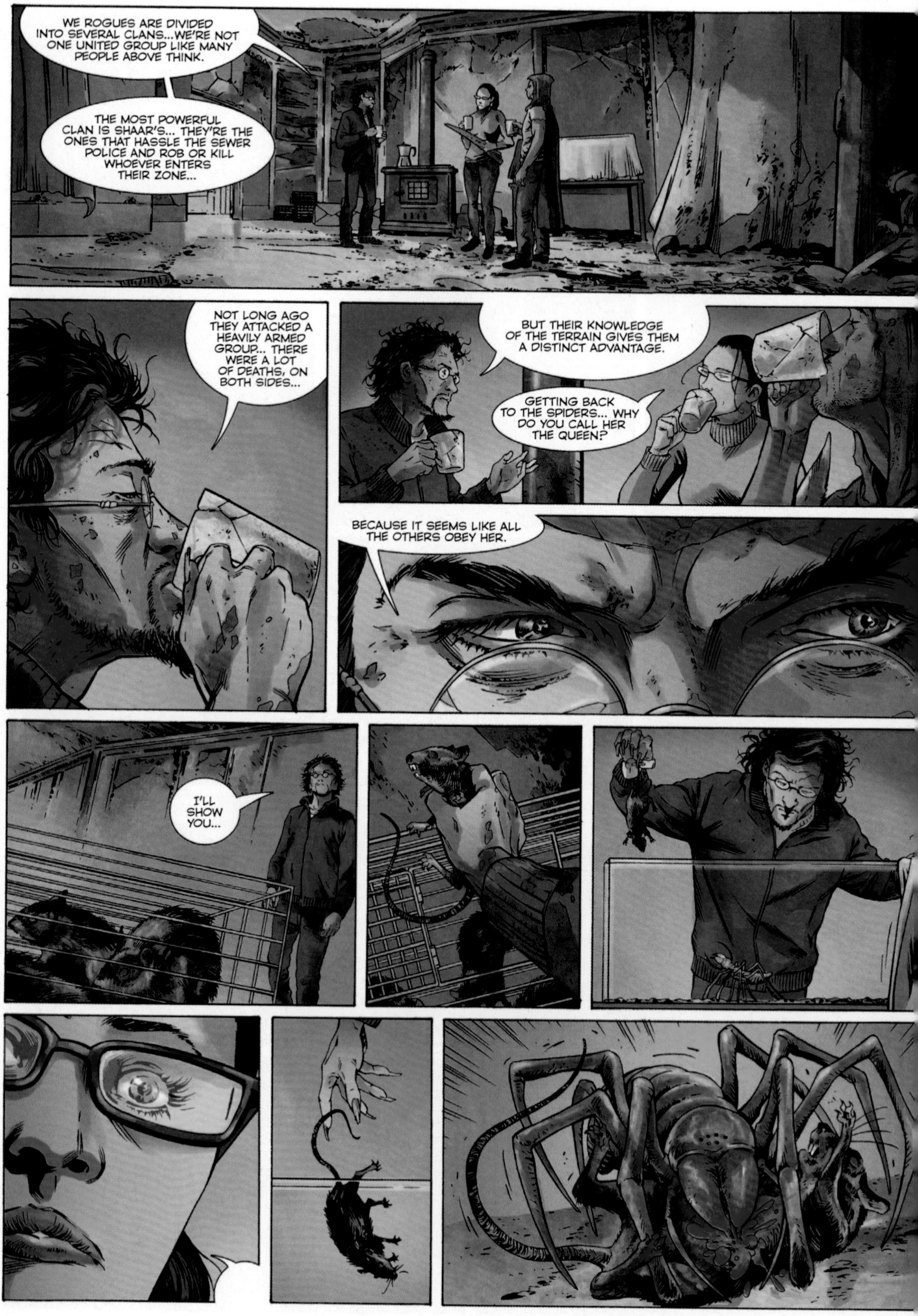
WE ROGUES ARE DIVIDED INTO SEVERAL CLANS...WE'RE NOT ONE UNITED GROUP LIKE MANY PEOPLE ABOVE THINK.
THE MOST POWERFUL CLAN IS SHAAR'S... THEY'RE THE ONES THAT HASSLE THE SEWER POLICE AND ROB OR KILL WHOEVER ENTERS THEIR ZONE...
NOT LONG AGO THEY ATTACKED A HEAVILY ARMED GROUP... THERE WERE A LOT OF DEATHS, ON BOTH SIDES...
BUT THEIR KNOWLEDGE OF THE TERRAIN GIVES THEM A DISTINCT ADVANTAGE.
GETTING BACK TO THE SPIDERS... WHY DO YOU CALL HER THE QUEEN?
BECAUSE IT SEEMS LIKE ALL THE OTHERS OBEY HER.
I'LL SHOW YOU...

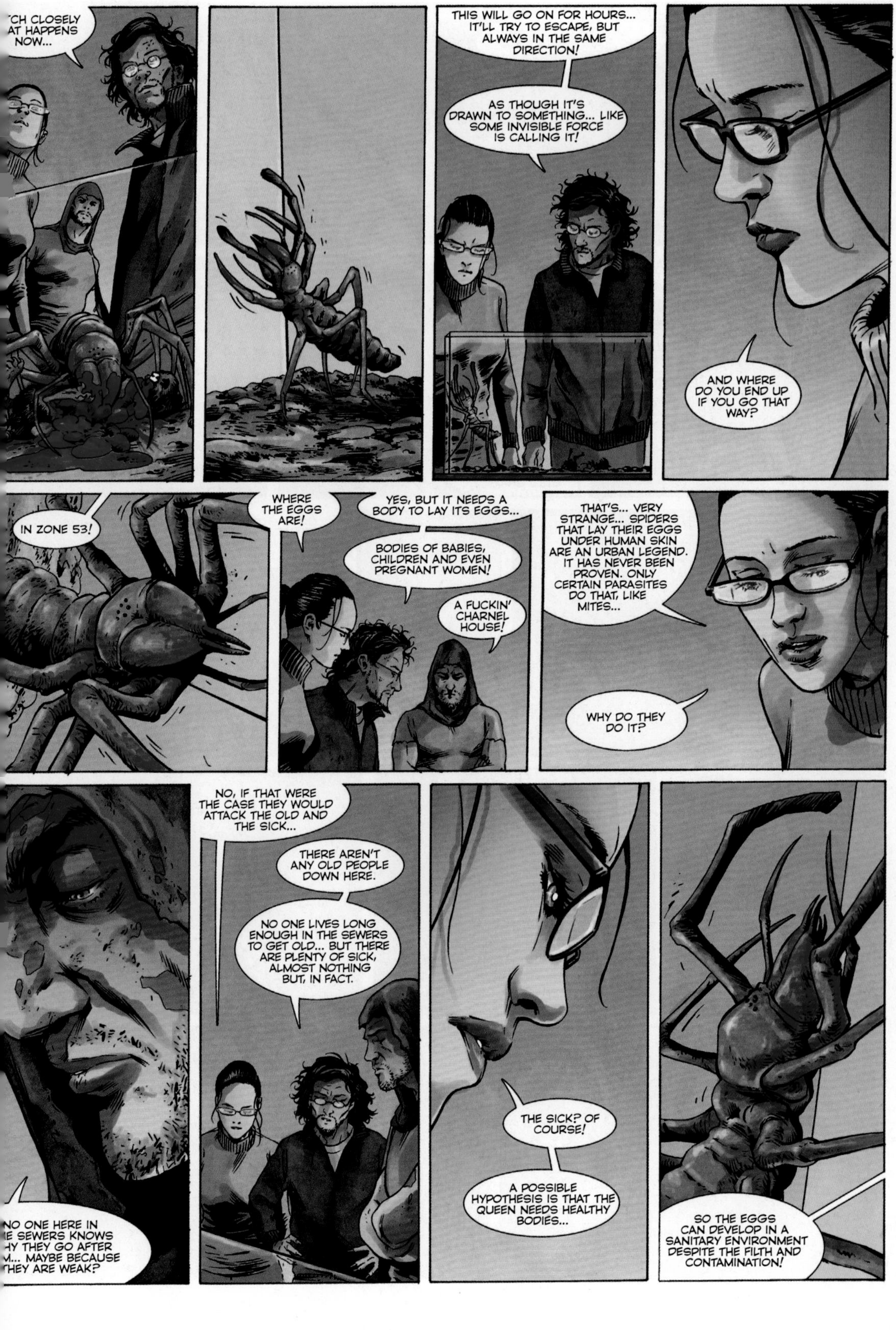
TCH CLOSELY AT HAPPENS NOW...
THIS WILL GO ON FOR HOURS... IT'LL TRY TO ESCAPE, BUT ALWAYS IN THE SAME DIRECTION!
AS THOUGH IT'S DRAWN TO SOMETHING... LIKE SOME INVISIBLE FORCE IS CALLING IT!
AND WHERE DO YOU END UP IF YOU GO THAT WAY?
IN ZONE 53!
WHERE THE EGGS ARE!
YES, BUT IT NEEDS A BODY TO LAY ITS EGGS...
BODIES OF BABIES, CHILDREN AND EVEN PREGNANT WOMEN!
A FUCKIN' CHARNEL HOUSE!
THAT'S... VERY STRANGE... SPIDERS THAT LAY THEIR EGGS UNDER HUMAN SKIN ARE AN URBAN LEGEND. IT HAS NEVER BEEN PROVEN. ONLY CERTAIN PARASITES DO THAT, LIKE MITES...
WHY DO THEY DO IT?
NO ONE HERE IN E SEWERS KNOWS HY THEY GO AFTER M... MAYBE BECAUSE THEY ARE WEAK?
NO, IF THAT WERE THE CASE THEY WOULD ATTACK THE OLD AND THE SICK...
THERE AREN'T ANY OLD PEOPLE DOWN HERE.
NO ONE LIVES LONG ENOUGH IN THE SEWERS TO GET OLD... BUT THERE ARE PLENTY OF SICK, ALMOST NOTHING BUT, IN FACT.
THE SICK? OF COURSE!
A POSSIBLE HYPOTHESIS IS THAT THE QUEEN NEEDS HEALTHY BODIES...
SO THE EGGS CAN DEVELOP IN A SANITARY ENVIRONMENT DESPITE THE FILTH AND CONTAMINATION!

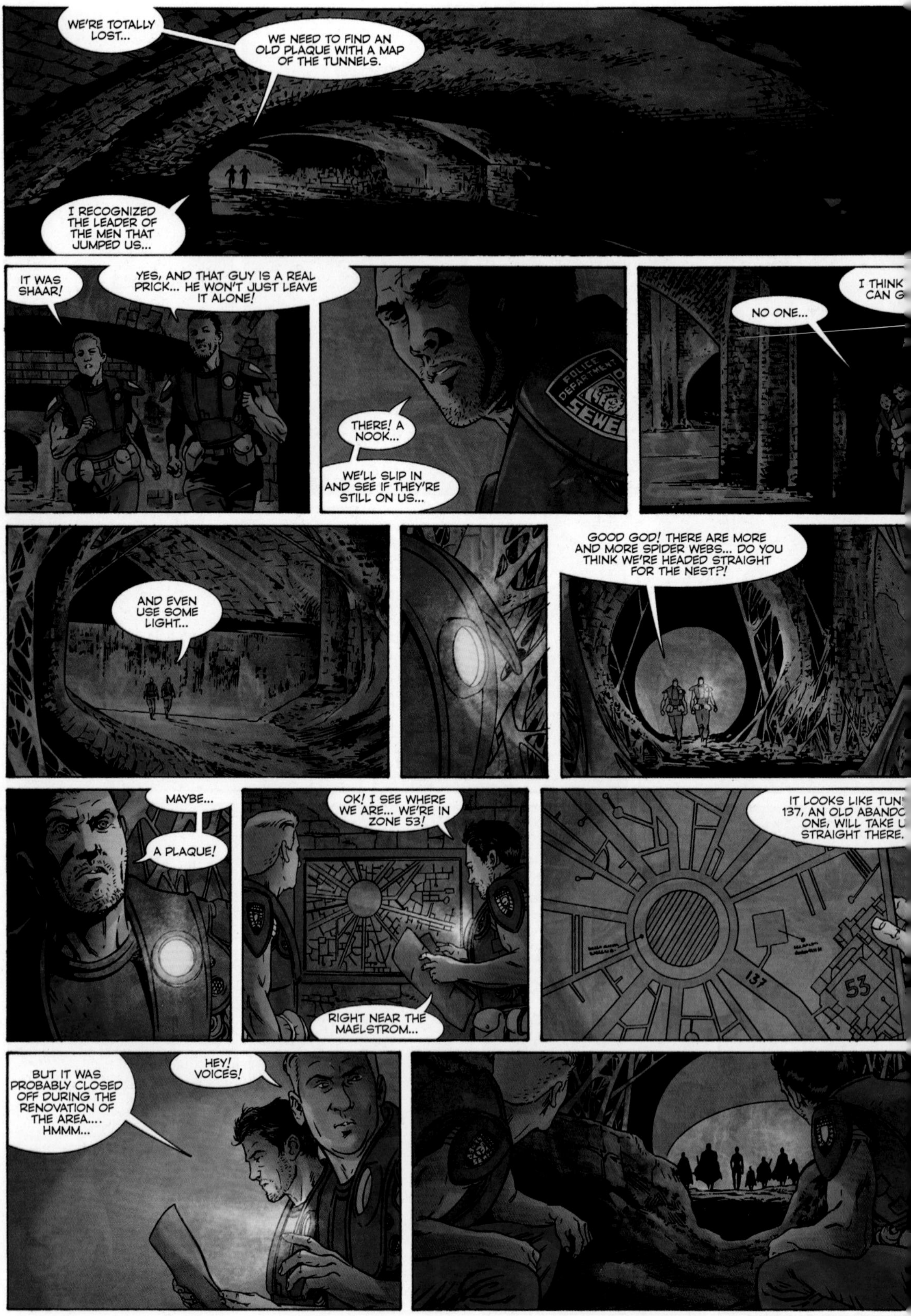
WE'RE TOTALLY LOST...
WE NEED TO FIND AN OLD PLAQUE WITH A MAP OF THE TUNNELS.
I RECOGNIZED THE LEADER OF THE MEN THAT JUMPED US...
IT WAS SHAAR!
YES, AND THAT GUY IS A REAL PRICK... HE WON'T JUST LEAVE IT ALONE!
POLICE DEPARTMENT SEWE
THERE! A NOOK...
WE'LL SLIP IN AND SEE IF THEY'RE STILL ON US...
NO ONE...
I THINK CAN G
AND EVEN USE SOME LIGHT...
GOOD GOD! THERE ARE MORE AND MORE SPIDER WEBS... DO YOU THINK WE'RE HEADED STRAIGHT FOR THE NEST?!
MAYBE...
A PLAQUE!
OK! I SEE WHERE WE ARE... WE'RE IN ZONE 53!
RIGHT NEAR THE MAELSTROM...
IT LOOKS LIKE TUN 137, AN OLD ABANDO ONE, WILL TAKE U STRAIGHT THERE.
137
53
BUT IT WAS PROBABLY CLOSED OFF DURING THE RENOVATION OF THE AREA.... HMMM...
HEY! VOICES!

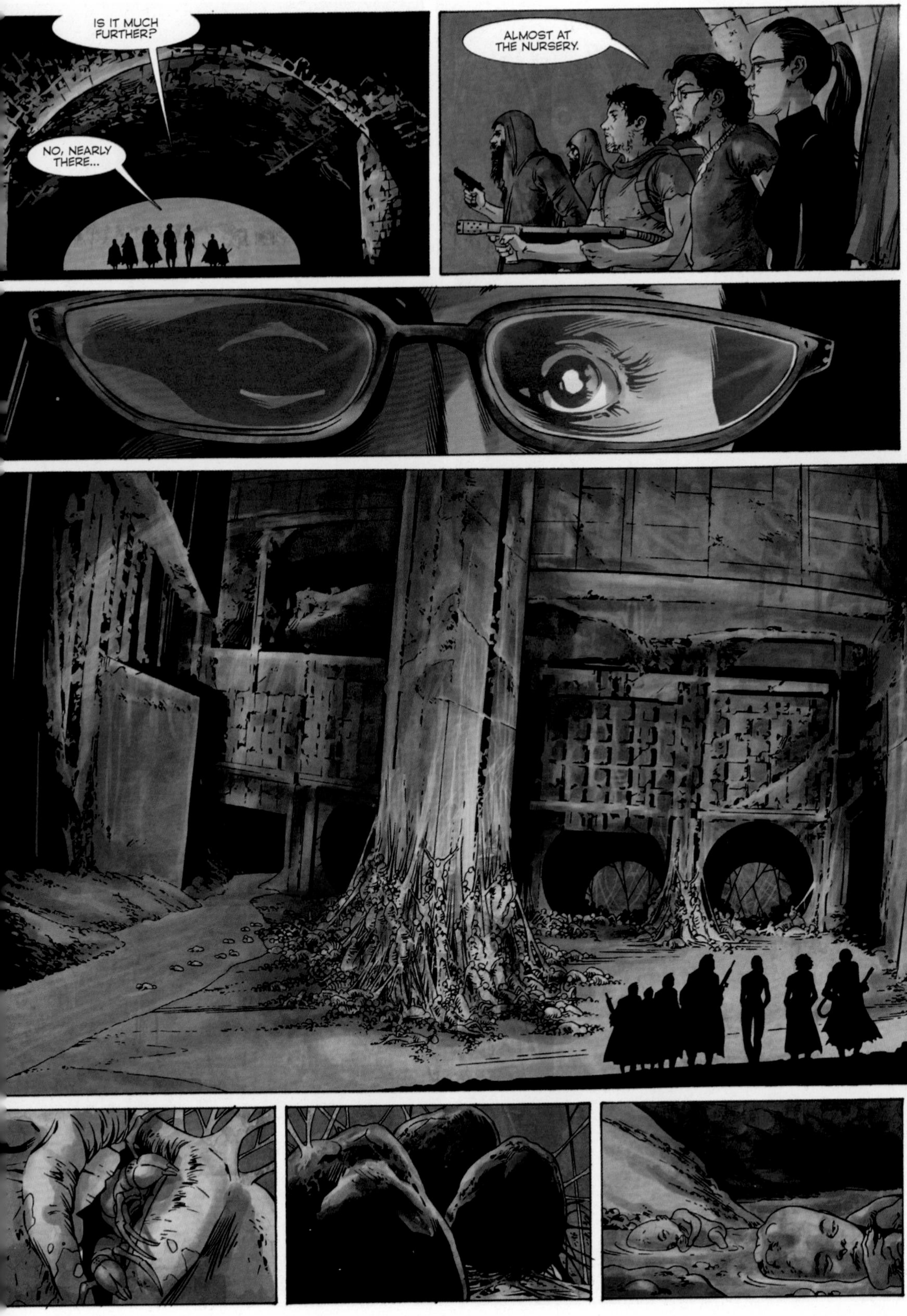
IS IT MUCH FURTHER?
NO, NEARLY THERE...
ALMOST AT THE NURSERY.

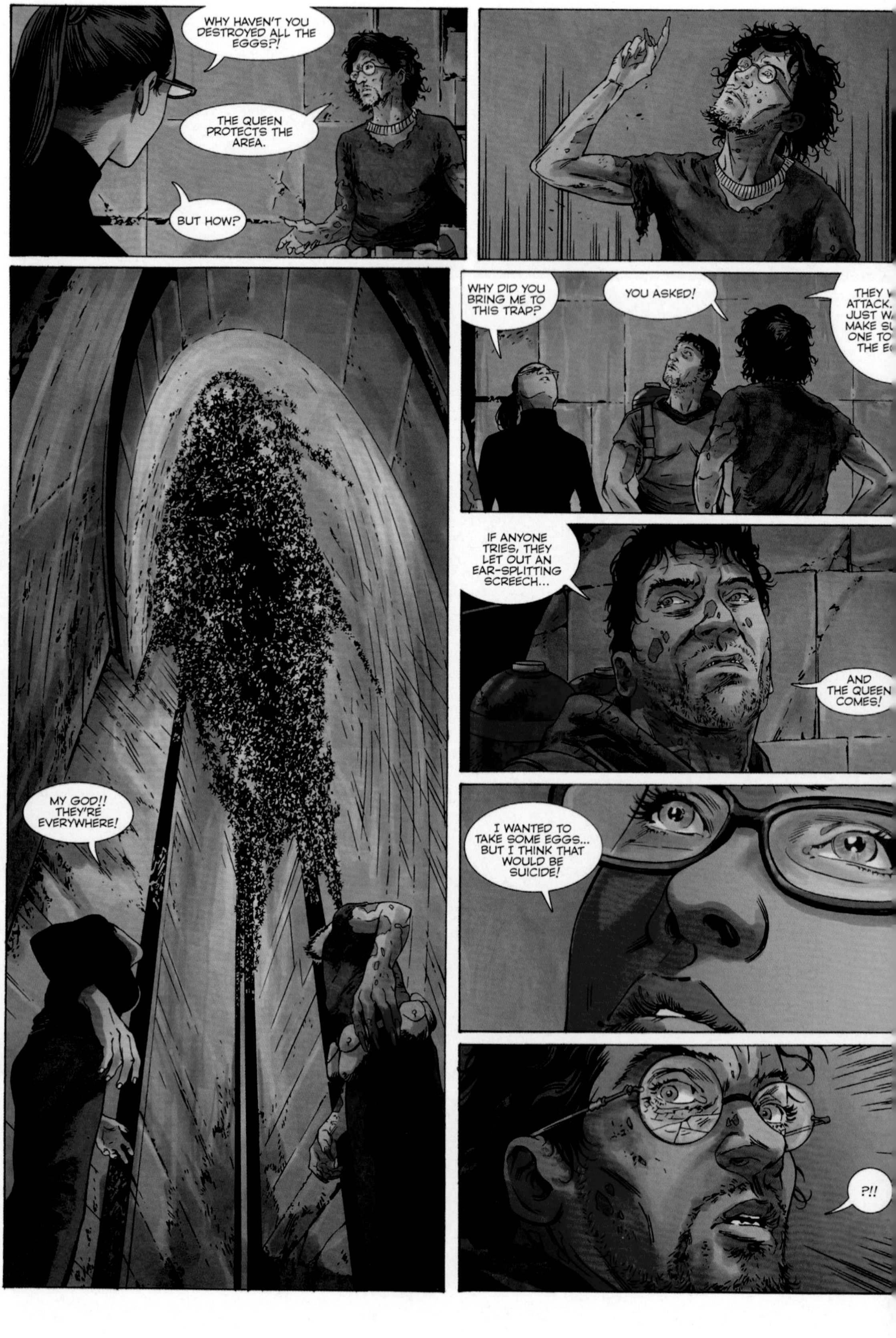
WHY HAVEN'T YOU DESTROYED ALL THE EGGS?!
THE QUEEN PROTECTS THE AREA.
BUT HOW?
WHY DID YOU BRING ME TO THIS TRAP?
YOU ASKED!
MY GOD!! THEY'RE EVERYWHERE!
IF ANYONE TRIES, THEY LET OUT AN EAR-SPLITTING SCREECH...
AND THE QUEEN COMES!
I WANTED TO TAKE SOME EGGS... BUT I THINK THAT WOULD BE SUICIDE!
?!!

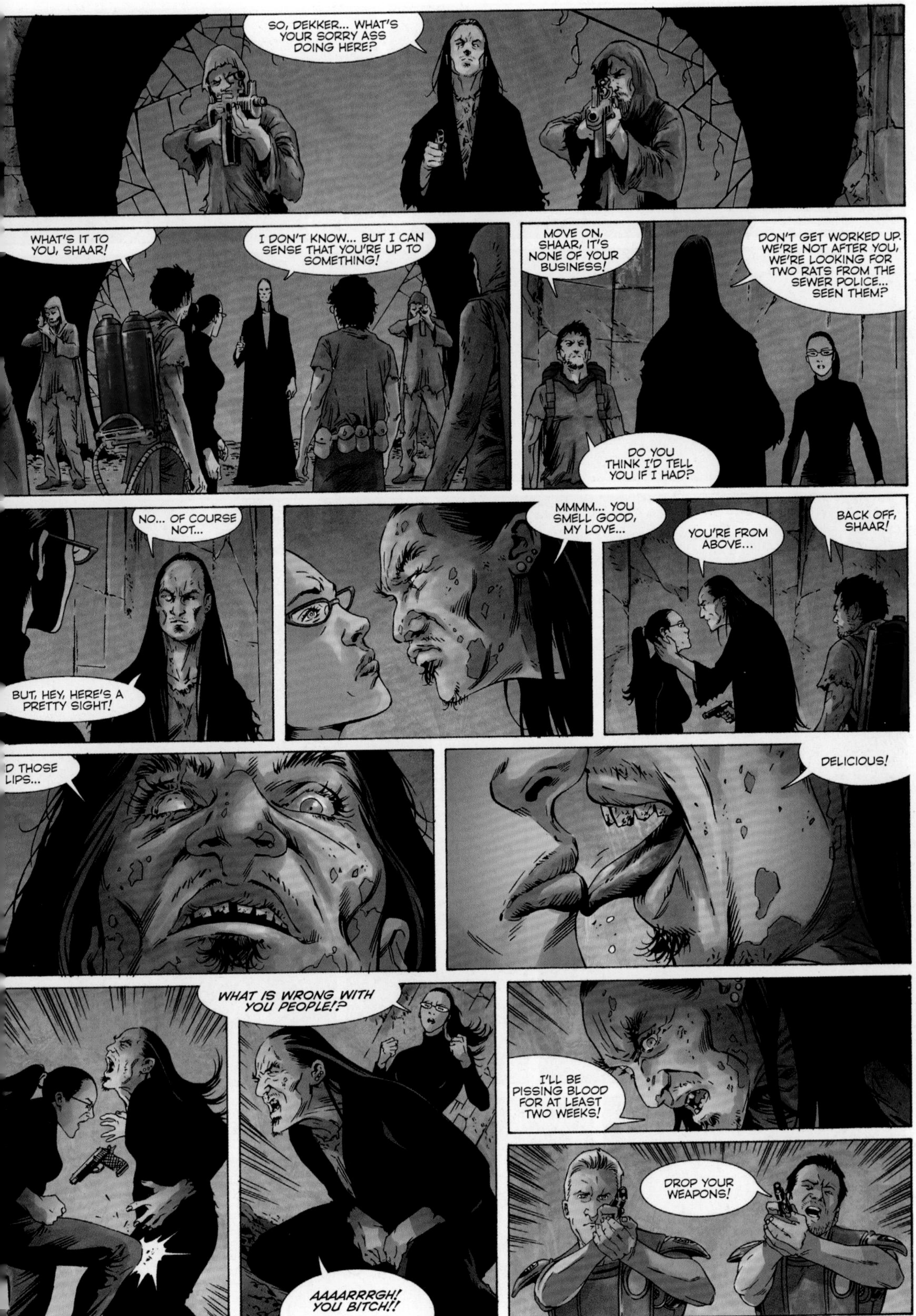
SO, DEKKER... WHAT'S YOUR SORRY ASS DOING HERE?
WHAT'S IT TO YOU, SHAAR!
I DON'T KNOW... BUT I CAN SENSE THAT YOU'RE UP TO SOMETHING!
MOVE ON, SHAAR, IT'S NONE OF YOUR BUSINESS!
DON'T GET WORKED UP. WE'RE NOT AFTER YOU, WE'RE LOOKING FOR TWO RATS FROM THE SEWER POLICE... SEEN THEM?
DO YOU THINK I'D TELL YOU IF I HAD?
NO... OF COURSE NOT...
BUT, HEY, HERE'S A PRETTY SIGHT!
MMMM... YOU SMELL GOOD, MY LOVE...
YOU'RE FROM ABOVE...
BACK OFF, SHAAR!
D THOSE LIPS...
DELICIOUS!
WHAT IS WRONG WITH YOU PEOPLE!?
AAAARRRGH! YOU BITCH!!
I'LL BE PISSING BLOOD FOR AT LEAST TWO WEEKS!
DROP YOUR WEAPONS!

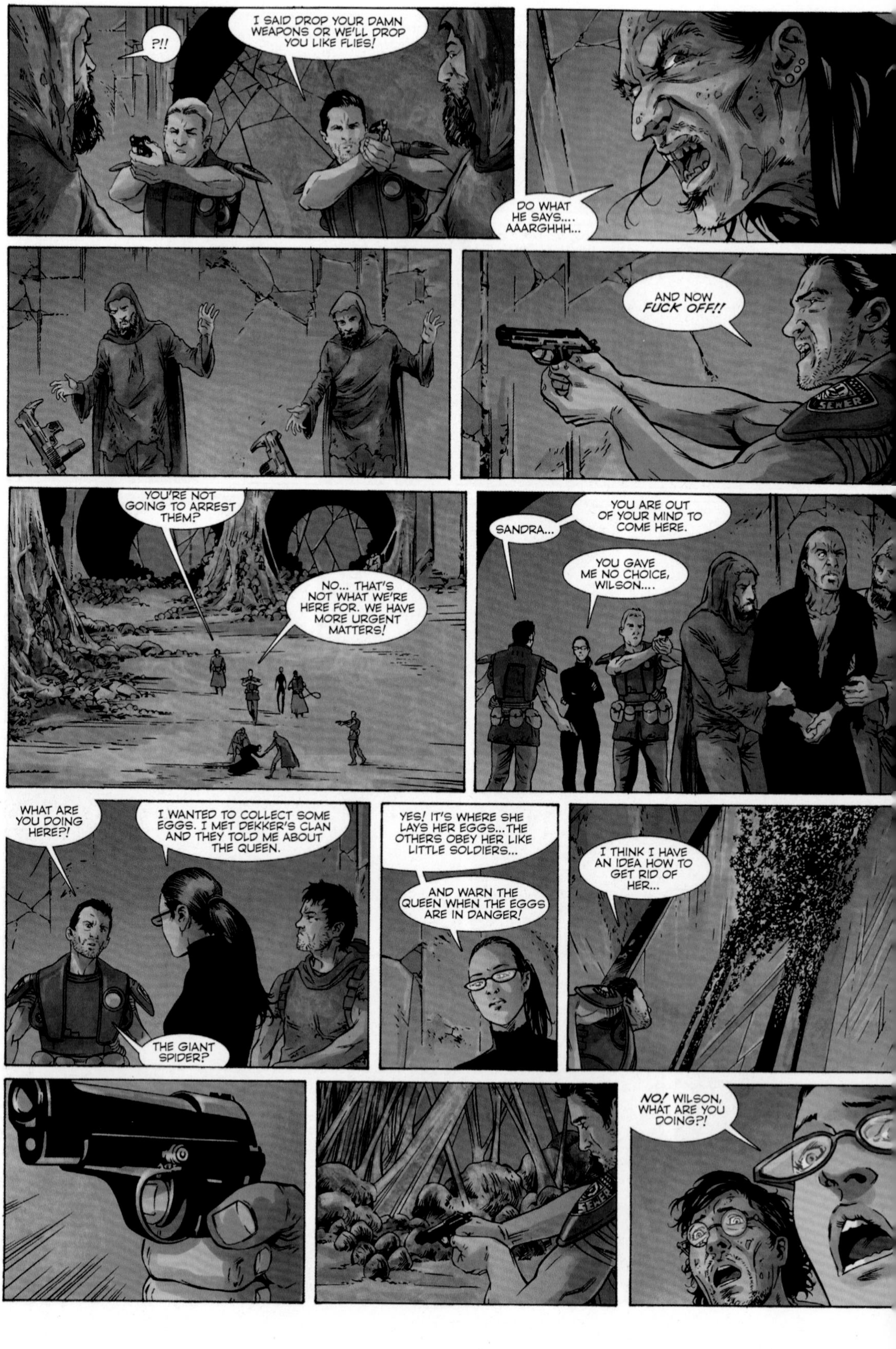
?!!
I SAID DROP YOUR DAMN WEAPONS OR WE'LL DROP YOU LIKE FLIES!
DO WHAT HE SAYS.... AAARGHHH...
AND NOW FUCK OFF!!
SEWER
YOU'RE NOT GOING TO ARREST THEM?
NO... THAT'S NOT WHAT WE'RE HERE FOR. WE HAVE MORE URGENT MATTERS!
SANDRA...
YOU ARE OUT OF YOUR MIND TO COME HERE.
YOU GAVE ME NO CHOICE, WILSON....
WHAT ARE YOU DOING HERE?!
I WANTED TO COLLECT SOME EGGS. I MET DEKKER'S CLAN AND THEY TOLD ME ABOUT THE QUEEN.
THE GIANT SPIDER?
YES! IT'S WHERE SHE LAYS HER EGGS...THE OTHERS OBEY HER LIKE LITTLE SOLDIERS...
AND WARN THE QUEEN WHEN THE EGGS ARE IN DANGER!
I THINK I HAVE AN IDEA HOW TO GET RID OF HER...
NO! WILSON, WHAT ARE YOU DOING?!

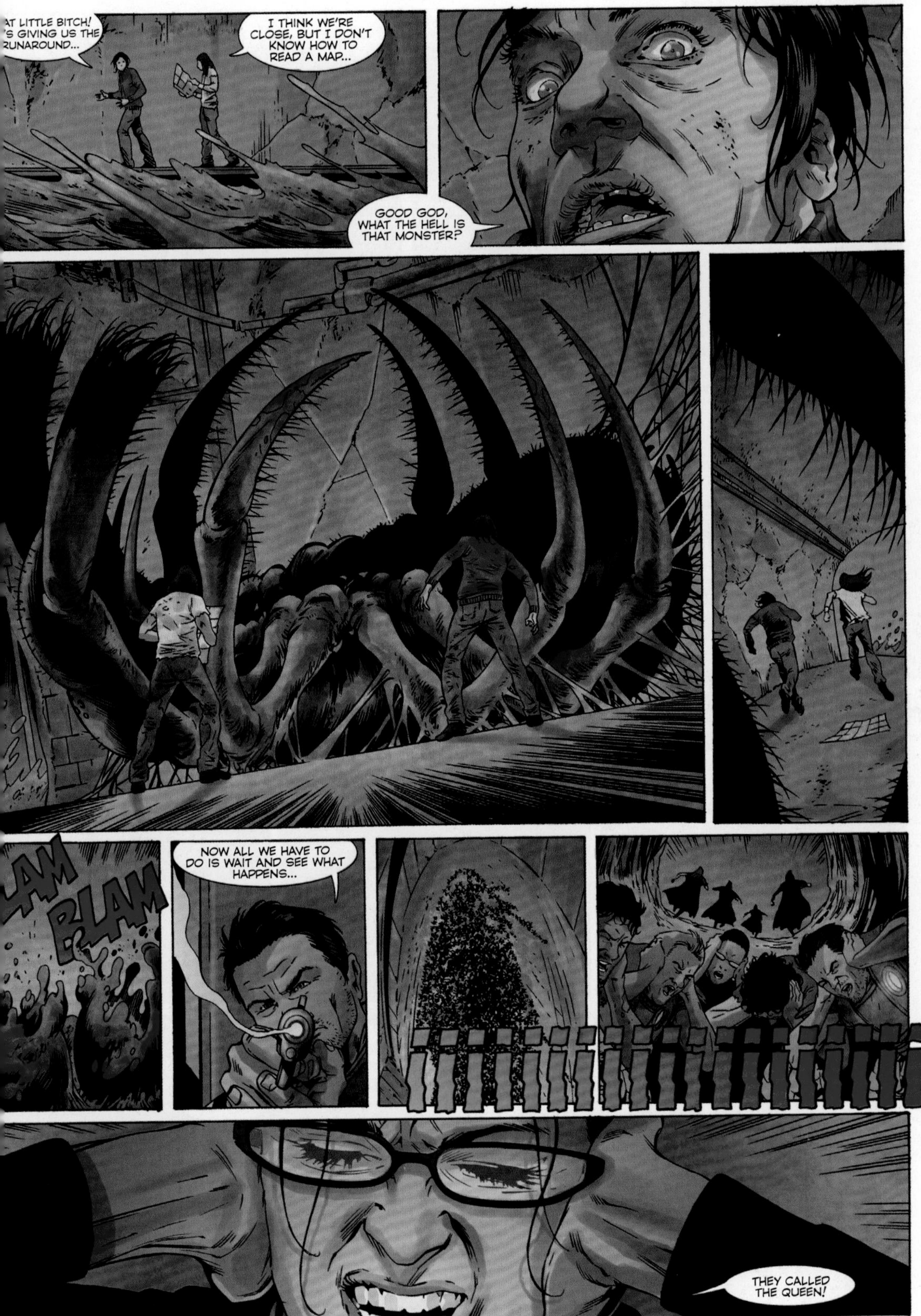
AT LITTLE BITCH! 'S GIVING US THE RUNAROUND...
I THINK WE'RE CLOSE, BUT I DON'T KNOW HOW TO READ A MAP...
GOOD GOD, WHAT THE HELL IS THAT MONSTER?
LAM
BLAM
NOW ALL WE HAVE TO DO IS WAIT AND SEE WHAT HAPPENS...
iiiiiiiiiiiiiiiiiiiiii
THEY CALLED THE QUEEN!

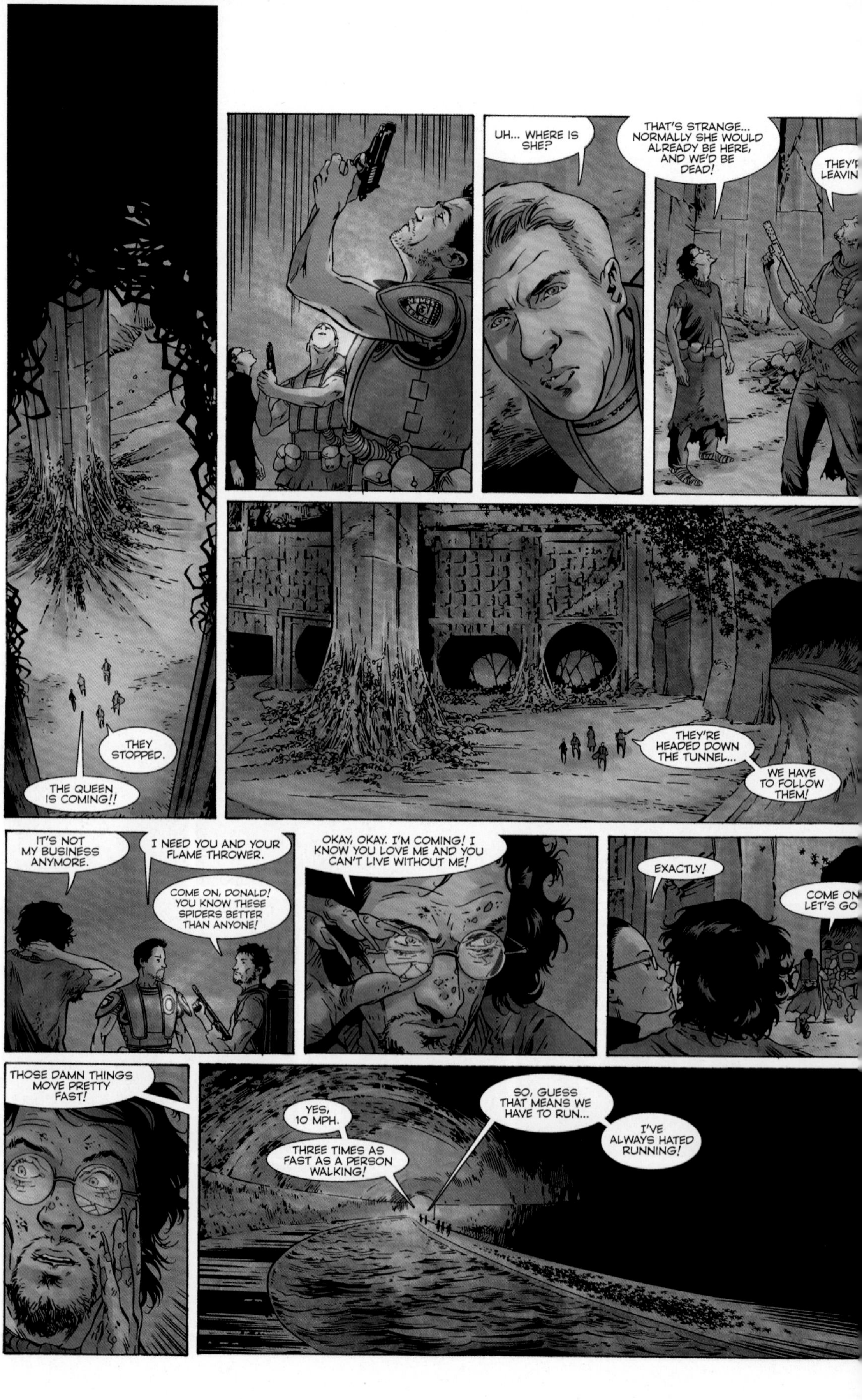
THEY STOPPED.
THE QUEEN IS COMING!!
UH... WHERE IS SHE?
THAT'S STRANGE... NORMALLY SHE WOULD ALREADY BE HERE, AND WE'D BE DEAD!
THEY'R LEAVIN
THEY'RE HEADED DOWN THE TUNNEL...
WE HAVE TO FOLLOW THEM!
IT'S NOT MY BUSINESS ANYMORE.
I NEED YOU AND YOUR FLAME THROWER.
COME ON, DONALD! YOU KNOW THESE SPIDERS BETTER THAN ANYONE!
OKAY, OKAY. I'M COMING! I KNOW YOU LOVE ME AND YOU CAN'T LIVE WITHOUT ME!
EXACTLY!
COME ON LET'S GO
THOSE DAMN THINGS MOVE PRETTY FAST!
YES, 10 MPH.
THREE TIMES AS FAST AS A PERSON WALKING!
SO, GUESS THAT MEANS WE HAVE TO RUN...
I'VE ALWAYS HATED RUNNING!

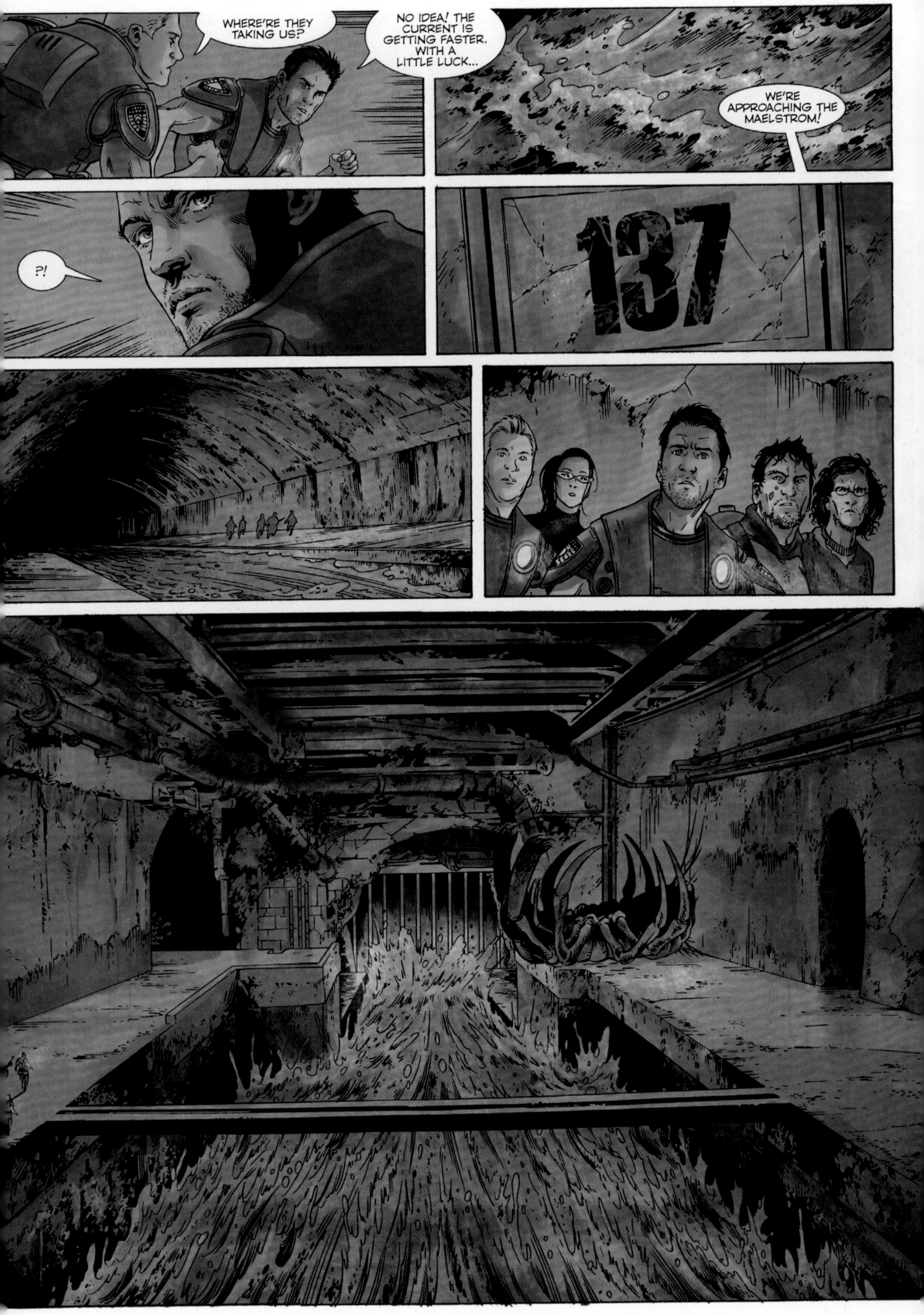
WHERE'RE THEY TAKING US?
NO IDEA! THE CURRENT IS GETTING FASTER. WITH A LITTLE LUCK...
WE'RE APPROACHING THE MAELSTROM!
?!
137

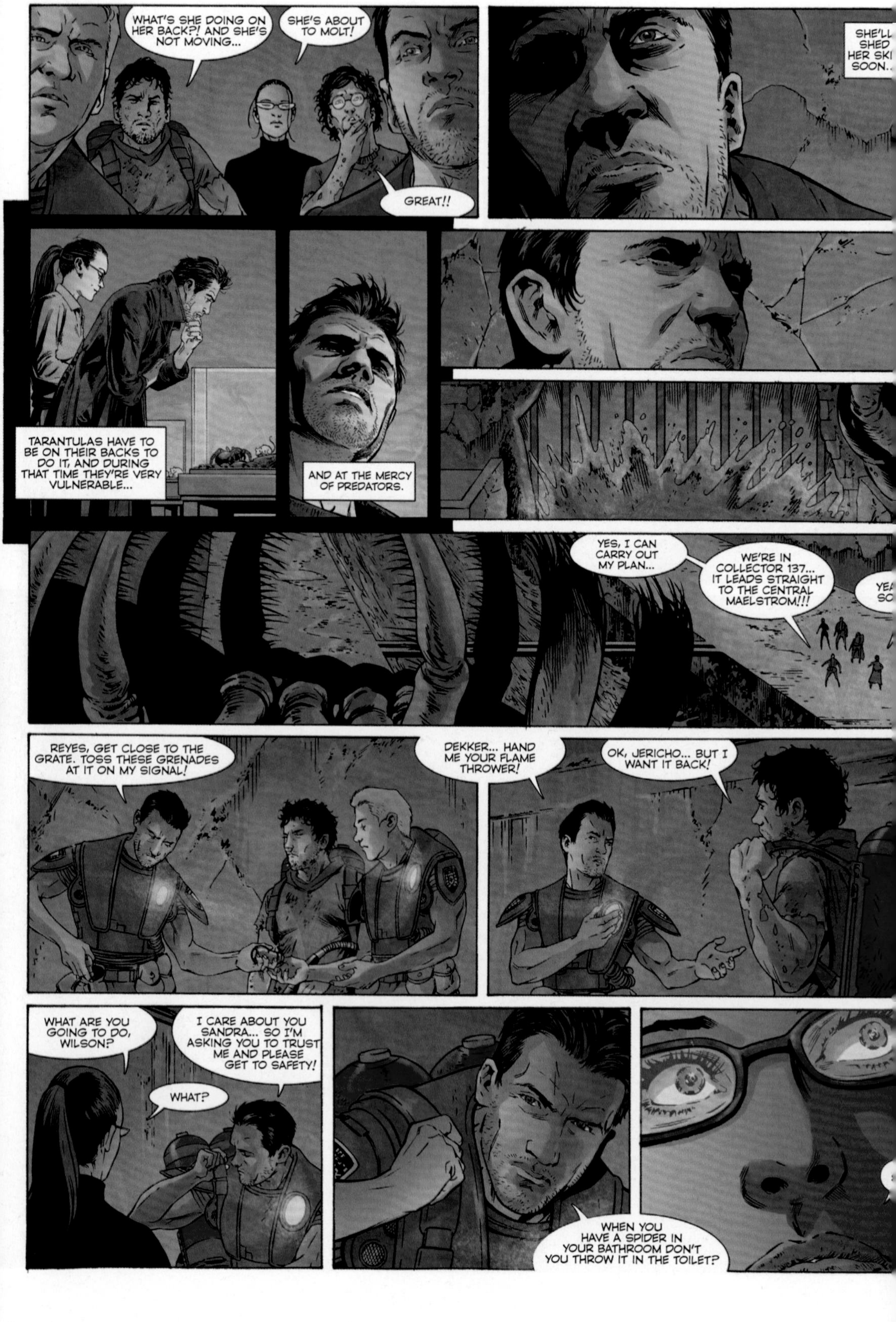
WHAT'S SHE DOING ON HER BACK?! AND SHE'S NOT MOVING...
SHE'S ABOUT TO MOLT!
GREAT!!
SHE'LL SHED HER SKI SOON...
TARANTULAS HAVE TO BE ON THEIR BACKS TO DO IT, AND DURING THAT TIME THEY'RE VERY VULNERABLE...
AND AT THE MERCY OF PREDATORS.
YES, I CAN CARRY OUT MY PLAN...
WE'RE IN COLLECTOR 137... IT LEADS STRAIGHT TO THE CENTRAL MAELSTROM!!!
REYES, GET CLOSE TO THE GRATE. TOSS THESE GRENADES AT IT ON MY SIGNAL!
DEKKER... HAND ME YOUR FLAME THROWER!
OK, JERICHO... BUT I WANT IT BACK!
WHAT ARE YOU GOING TO DO, WILSON?
I CARE ABOUT YOU SANDRA... SO I'M ASKING YOU TO TRUST ME AND PLEASE GET TO SAFETY!
WHAT?
WHEN YOU HAVE A SPIDER IN YOUR BATHROOM DON'T YOU THROW IT IN THE TOILET?

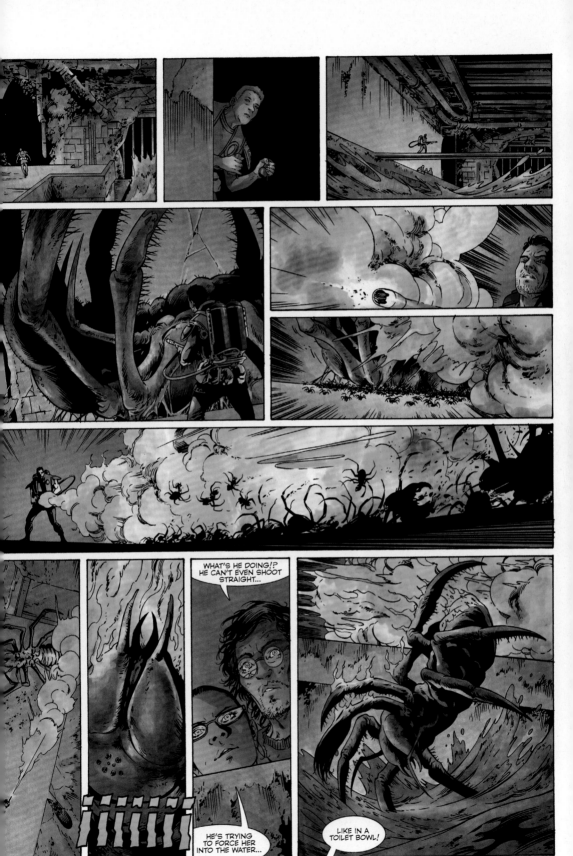

WHAT'S HE DOING!?
HE CAN'T EVEN SHOOT
STRAIGHT...

HE'S TRYING
TO FORCE HER
INTO THE WATER...

LIKE IN A
TOILET BOWL!

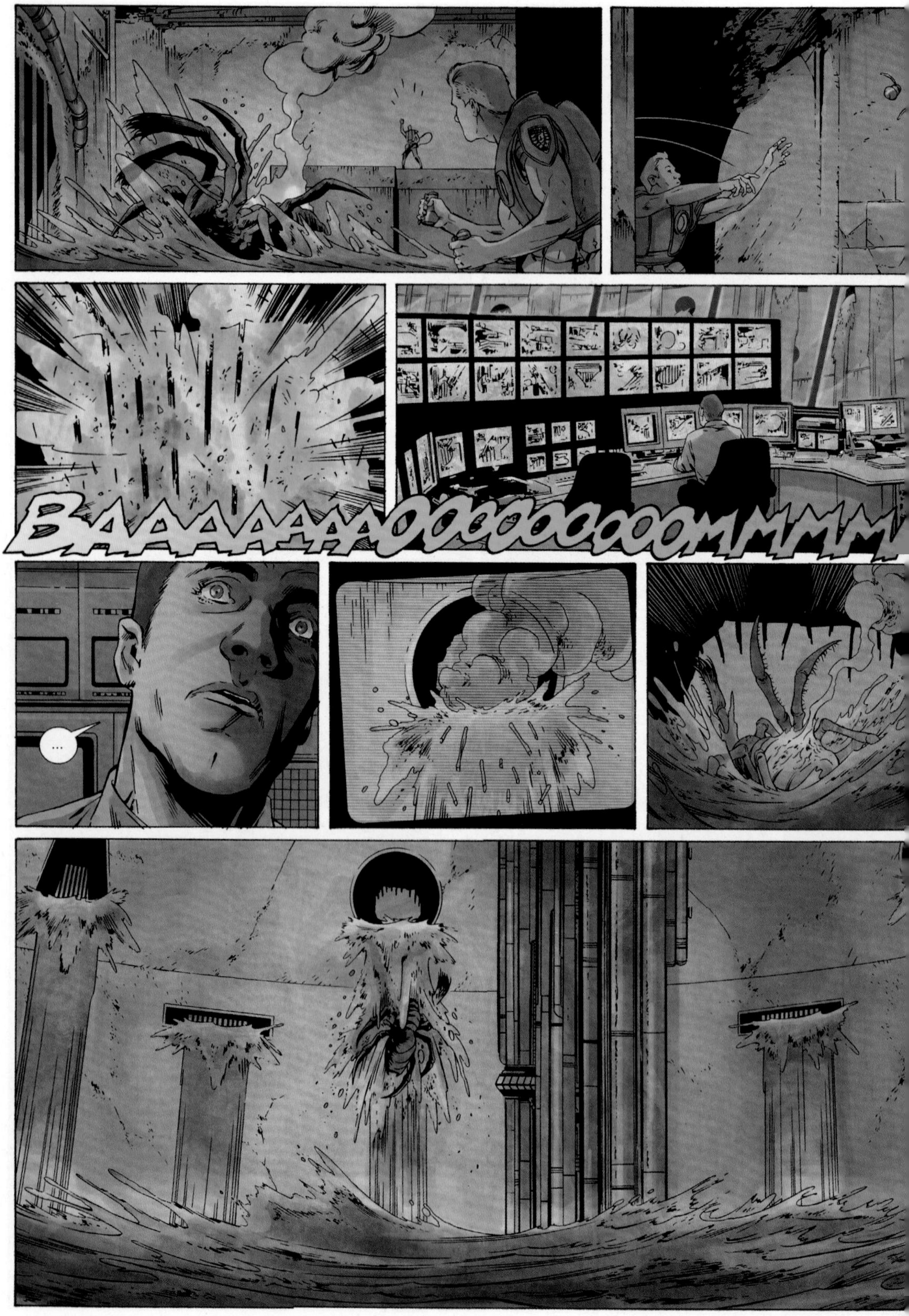
BAAAAAAOOOOOOOOMMMMM
...

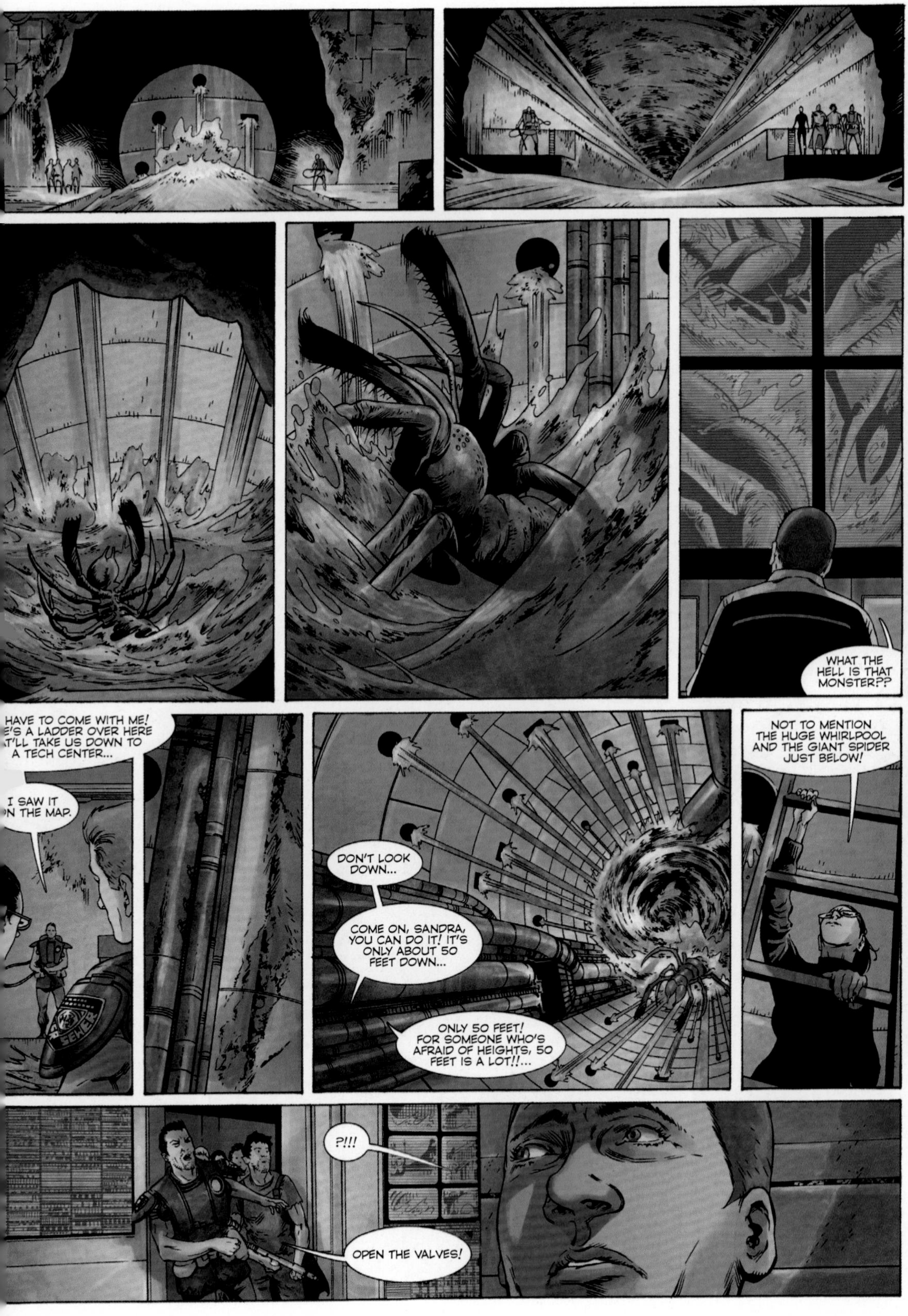
WHAT THE HELL IS THAT MONSTER??
HAVE TO COME WITH ME! E'S A LADDER OVER HERE T'LL TAKE US DOWN TO A TECH CENTER...
I SAW IT N THE MAP.
DON'T LOOK DOWN...
COME ON, SANDRA, YOU CAN DO IT! IT'S ONLY ABOUT 50 FEET DOWN...
ONLY 50 FEET! FOR SOMEONE WHO'S AFRAID OF HEIGHTS, 50 FEET IS A LOT!!...
NOT TO MENTION THE HUGE WHIRLPOOL AND THE GIANT SPIDER JUST BELOW!
?!!!
OPEN THE VALVES!

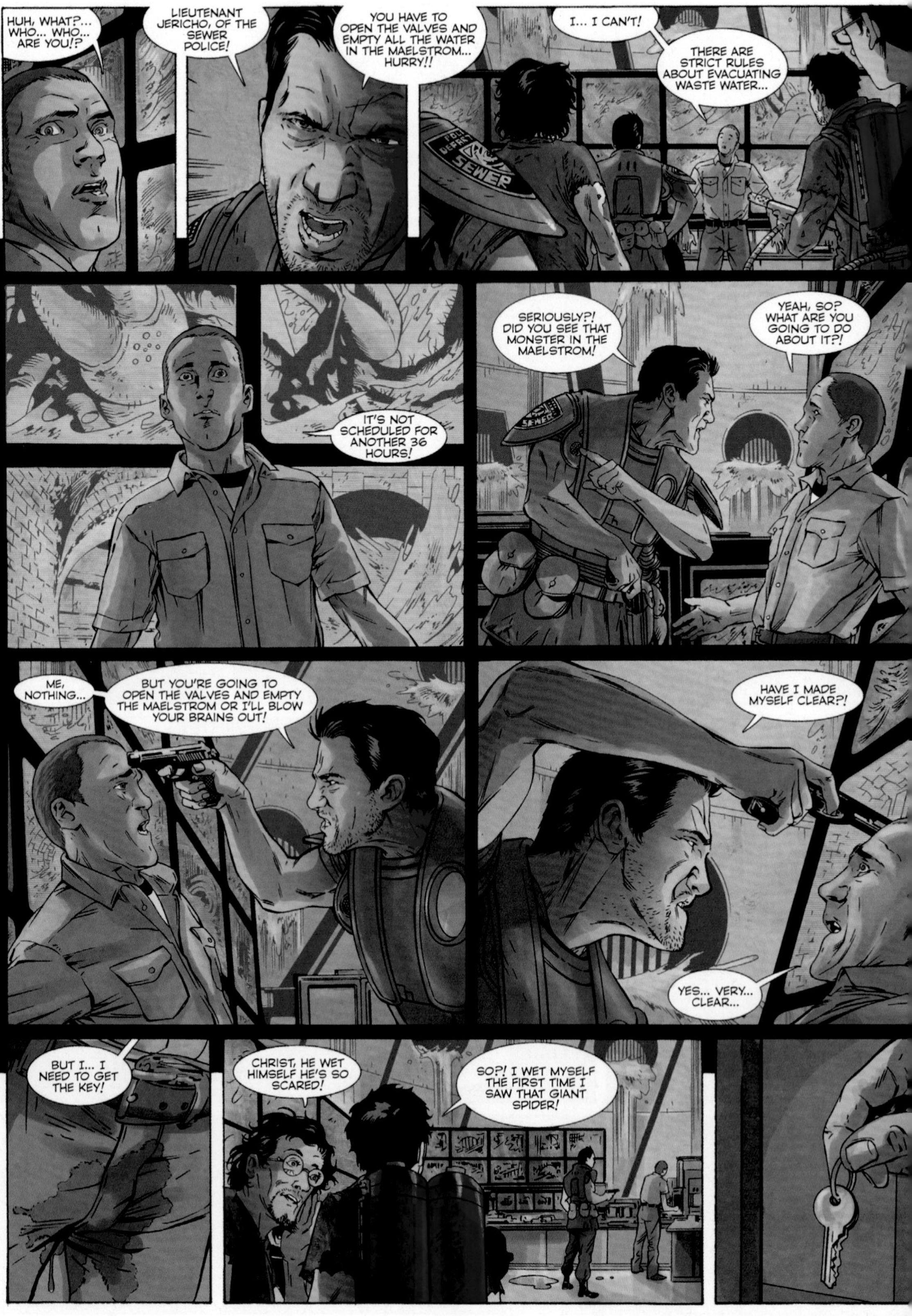
HUH, WHAT?... WHO... WHO... ARE YOU!?
LIEUTENANT JERICHO, OF THE SEWER POLICE!
YOU HAVE TO OPEN THE VALVES AND EMPTY ALL THE WATER IN THE MAELSTROM... HURRY!!
I... I CAN'T!
THERE ARE STRICT RULES ABOUT EVACUATING WASTE WATER...
SEWER
IT'S NOT SCHEDULED FOR ANOTHER 36 HOURS!
SERIOUSLY?! DID YOU SEE THAT MONSTER IN THE MAELSTROM!
YEAH, SO? WHAT ARE YOU GOING TO DO ABOUT IT?!
ME, NOTHING...
BUT YOU'RE GOING TO OPEN THE VALVES AND EMPTY THE MAELSTROM OR I'LL BLOW YOUR BRAINS OUT!
HAVE I MADE MYSELF CLEAR?!
YES... VERY... CLEAR...
BUT I... I NEED TO GET THE KEY!
CHRIST, HE WET HIMSELF HE'S SO SCARED!
SO?! I WET MYSELF THE FIRST TIME I SAW THAT GIANT SPIDER!

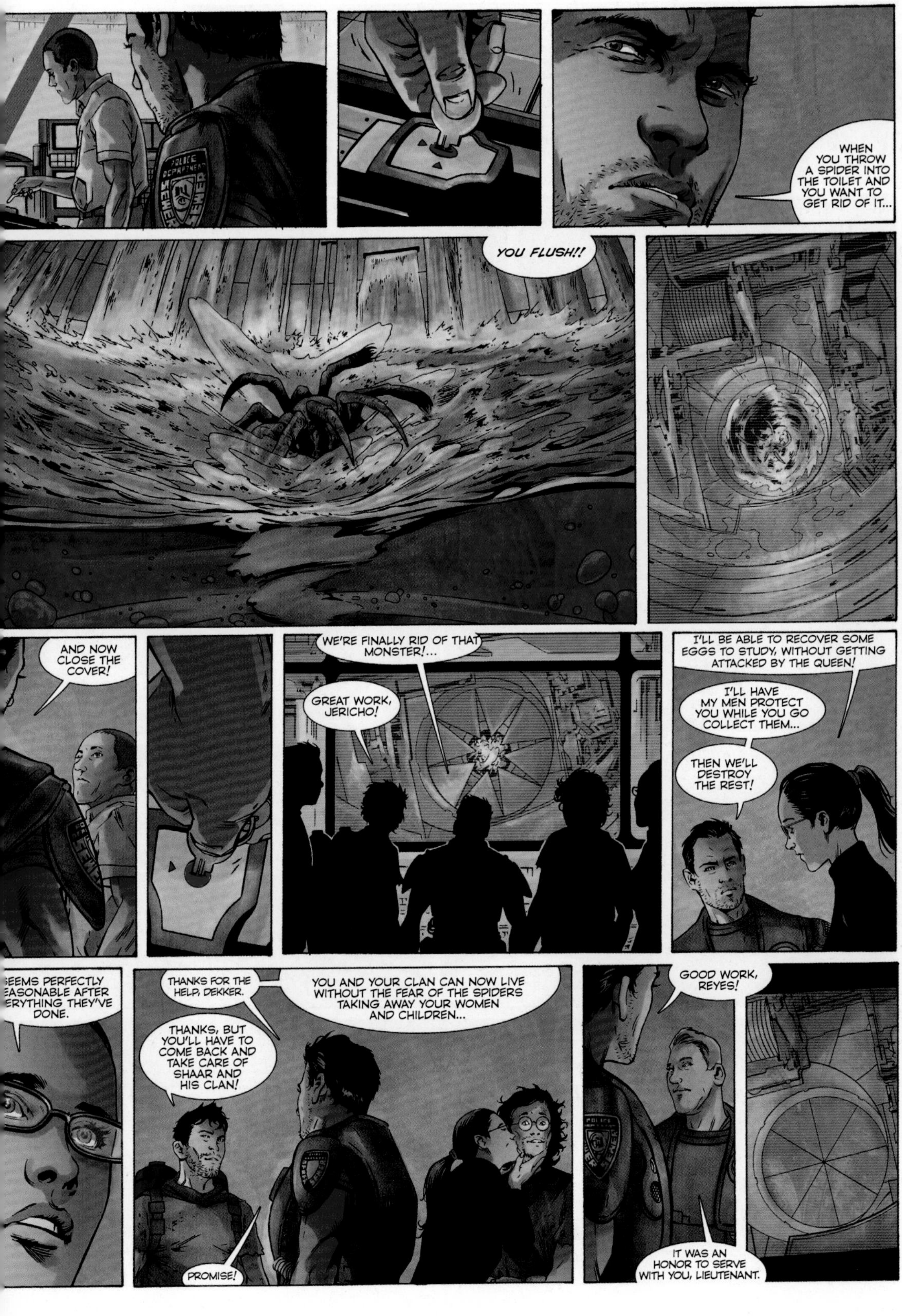
WHEN YOU THROW A SPIDER INTO THE TOILET AND YOU WANT TO GET RID OF IT...
YOU FLUSH!!
AND NOW CLOSE THE COVER!
WE'RE FINALLY RID OF THAT MONSTER!...
GREAT WORK, JERICHO!
I'LL BE ABLE TO RECOVER SOME EGGS TO STUDY, WITHOUT GETTING ATTACKED BY THE QUEEN!
I'LL HAVE MY MEN PROTECT YOU WHILE YOU GO COLLECT THEM...
THEN WE'LL DESTROY THE REST!
SEEMS PERFECTLY EASONABLE AFTER ERYTHING THEY'VE DONE.
THANKS FOR THE HELP, DEKKER.
YOU AND YOUR CLAN CAN NOW LIVE WITHOUT THE FEAR OF THE SPIDERS TAKING AWAY YOUR WOMEN AND CHILDREN...
THANKS, BUT YOU'LL HAVE TO COME BACK AND TAKE CARE OF SHAAR AND HIS CLAN!
PROMISE!
GOOD WORK, REYES!
IT WAS AN HONOR TO SERVE WITH YOU, LIEUTENANT.

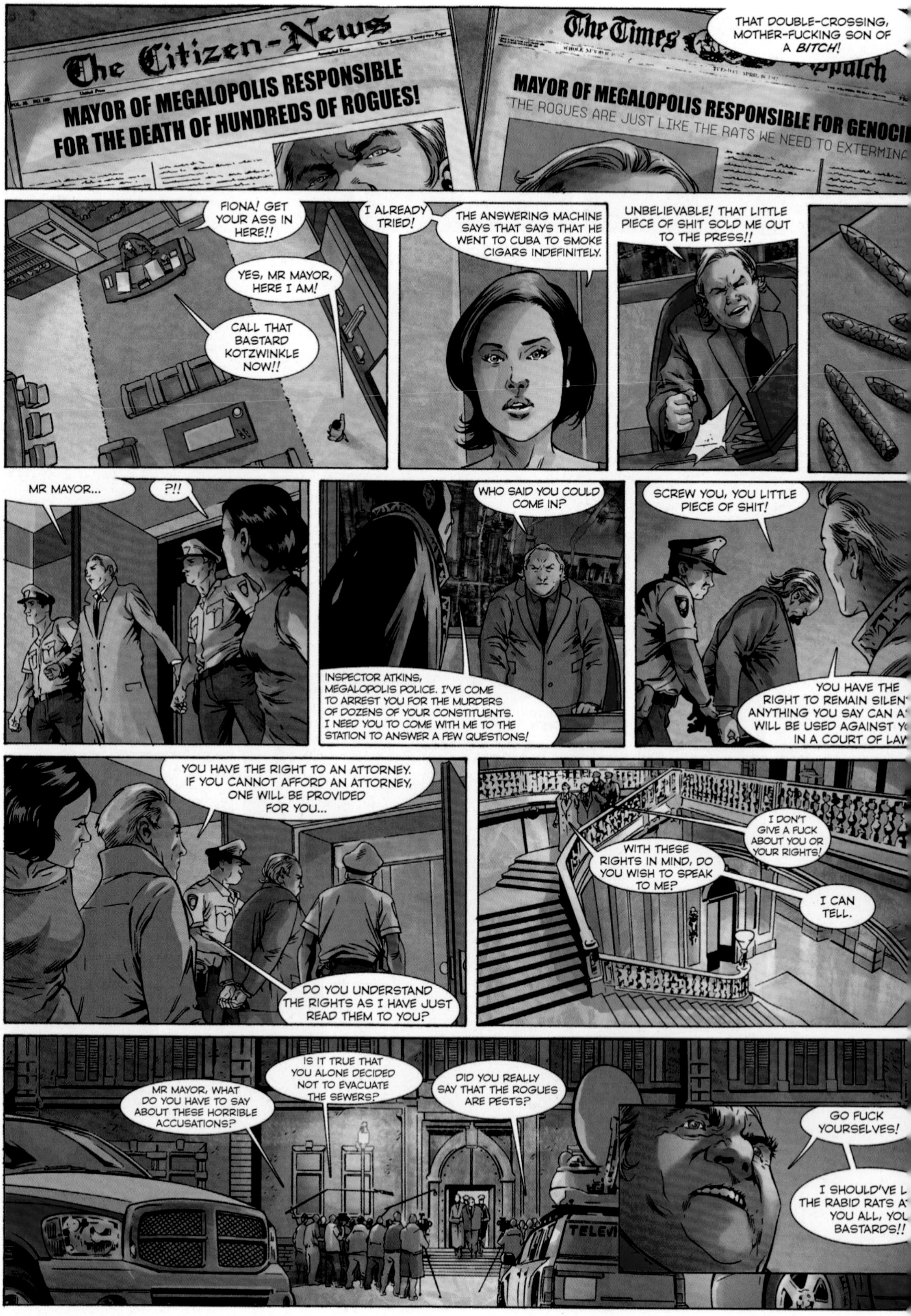
The Citizen-News
MAYOR OF MEGALOPOLIS RESPONSIBLE FOR THE DEATH OF HUNDREDS OF ROGUES!
The Times
MAYOR OF MEGALOPOLIS RESPONSIBLE FOR GENOCI
"THE ROGUES ARE JUST LIKE THE RATS WE NEED TO EXTERMINA
THAT DOUBLE-CROSSING, MOTHER-FUCKING SON OF A *BITCH*!
FIONA! GET YOUR ASS IN HERE!!
YES, MR MAYOR, HERE I AM!
CALL THAT BASTARD KOTZWINKLE NOW!!
I ALREADY TRIED!
THE ANSWERING MACHINE SAYS THAT SAYS THAT HE WENT TO CUBA TO SMOKE CIGARS INDEFINITELY.
UNBELIEVABLE! THAT LITTLE PIECE OF SHIT SOLD ME OUT TO THE PRESS!!
MR MAYOR...
?!!
WHO SAID YOU COULD COME IN?
INSPECTOR ATKINS, MEGALOPOLIS POLICE. I'VE COME TO ARREST YOU FOR THE MURDERS OF DOZENS OF YOUR CONSTITUENTS. I NEED YOU TO COME WITH ME TO THE STATION TO ANSWER A FEW QUESTIONS!
SCREW YOU, YOU LITTLE PIECE OF SHIT!
YOU HAVE THE RIGHT TO REMAIN SILEN ANYTHING YOU SAY CAN A WILL BE USED AGAINST Y IN A COURT OF LAW
YOU HAVE THE RIGHT TO AN ATTORNEY. IF YOU CANNOT AFFORD AN ATTORNEY, ONE WILL BE PROVIDED FOR YOU...
DO YOU UNDERSTAND THE RIGHTS AS I HAVE JUST READ THEM TO YOU?
WITH THESE RIGHTS IN MIND, DO YOU WISH TO SPEAK TO ME?
I DON'T GIVE A FUCK ABOUT YOU OR YOUR RIGHTS!
I CAN TELL.
MR MAYOR, WHAT DO YOU HAVE TO SAY ABOUT THESE HORRIBLE ACCUSATIONS?
IS IT TRUE THAT YOU ALONE DECIDED NOT TO EVACUATE THE SEWERS?
DID YOU REALLY SAY THAT THE ROGUES ARE PESTS?
TELEVI
GO FUCK YOURSELVES!
I SHOULD'VE L THE RABID RATS A YOU ALL, YOU BASTARDS!!

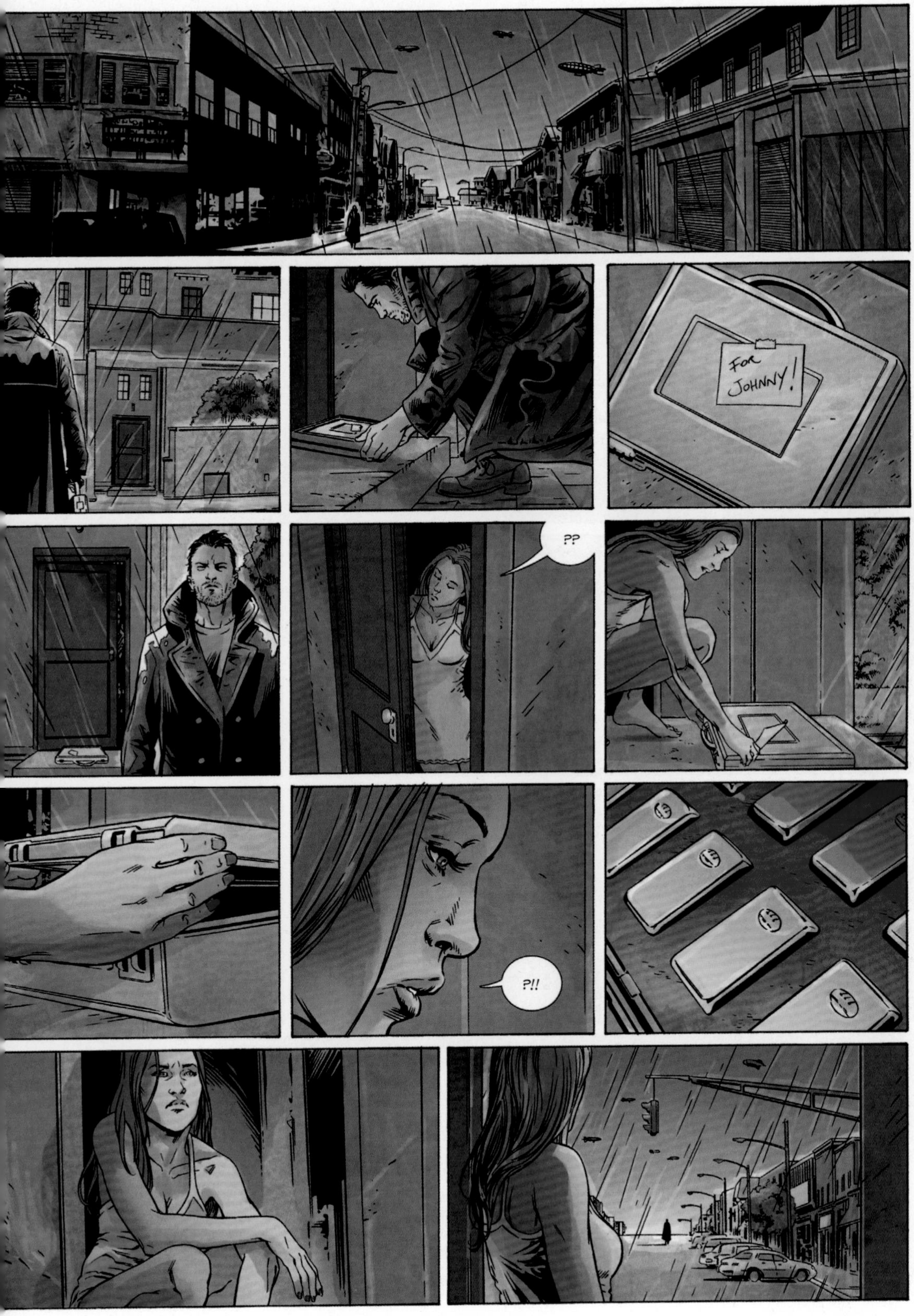
FOR JOHNNY!
??
?!!

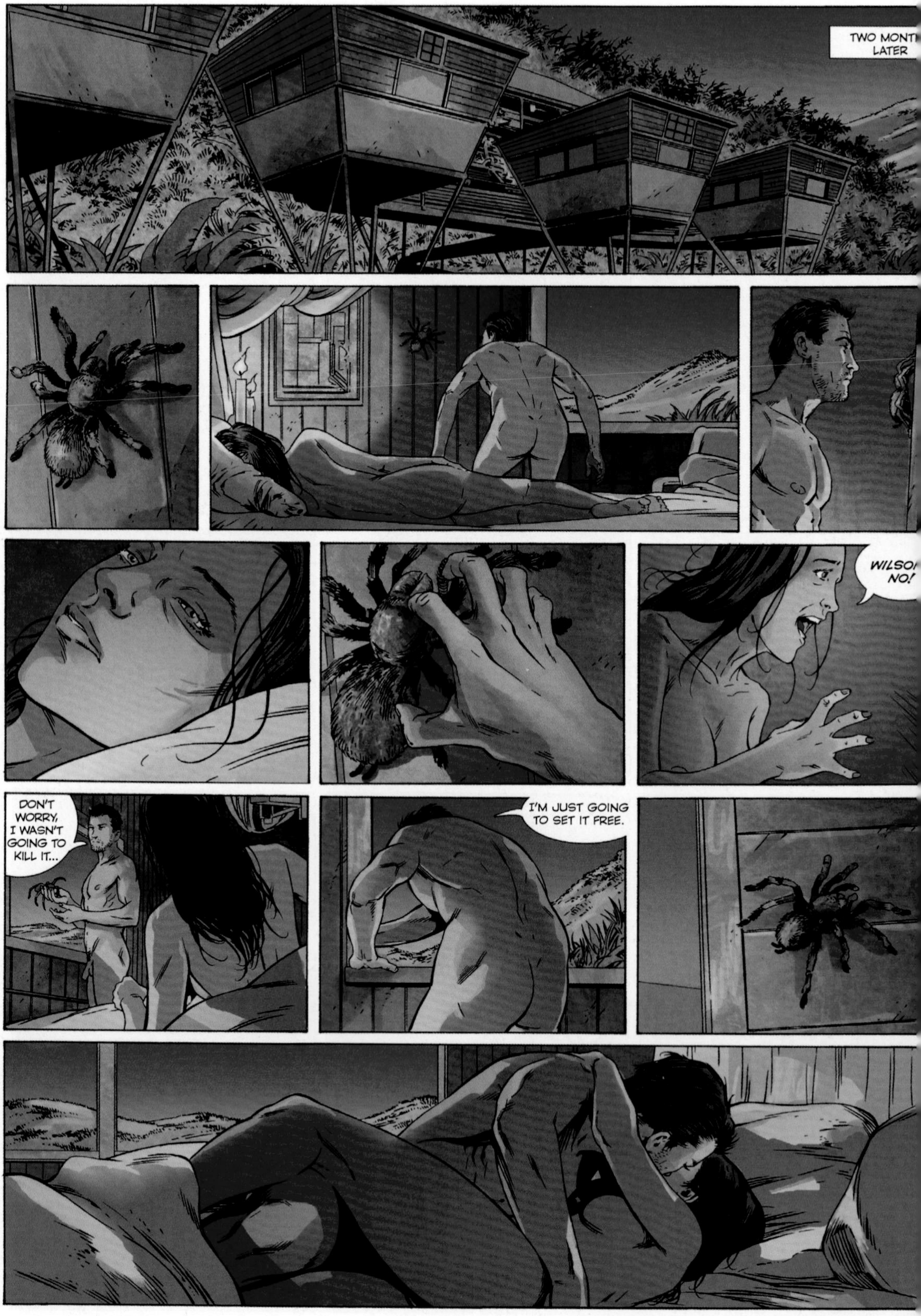
TWO MONT
LATER
WILSO
NO!
DON'T WORRY, I WASN'T GOING TO KILL IT...
I'M JUST GOING TO SET IT FREE.

HI GUYS!

HEY, COLONEL!

GOOD WEEKEND?

YEAH, PRETTY GOOD. WENT FOR A NICE LITTLE STROLL IN THE MEGALOPOLIS PARK...

BIDIP BIDIP

EXCUSE ME...

HELLO?

IT'S ME, HONEY...

HOW IS MY LOVELY WIFE THIS MORNING?

TAKE CARE, SEE YOU TONIGHT...I LOVE YOU.

ME TOO. BIG KISS!

A LITTLE STROLL... WE KNOW WHO WITH!

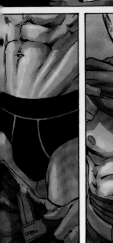

COME ON, YOU GUYS, ENOUGH CHAT...

LET'S GO!

LIEUTENANT REYES... ARE THE BOATS READY TO PATROL ZONE 51?

YES, COLONEL JERICHO, THEY'RE READY!

UH, COLONEL... I GOT A MESSAGE FROM ACKERMAN.

EVEN IF DESK LIFE ISN'T FOR YOU... HE SAYS DON'T TAKE TOO LONG TO FINISH THE PAPERWORK...THAT'S STILL PART OF THE JOB WHEN PROMOTED TO A COLONEL!

HA HA! GOOD OLD ACKERMAN... HE WAS A GREAT ONE.

BUT NO GOOD ON THE GROUND LIKE YOU!

HE WISHES LUCK AND SAID TH DOESN'T REGRET RET FOR ONE SECOND

NOW HE CAN DEDICATE HIMSELF TO HIS PASSION...

CATCHING THE BIG ONES!

BEC - RAFFAELE - FAVRELLE 2011

THE END...?

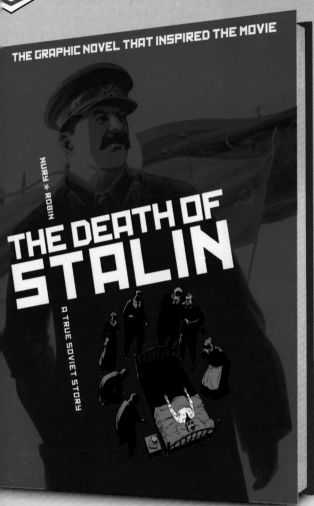

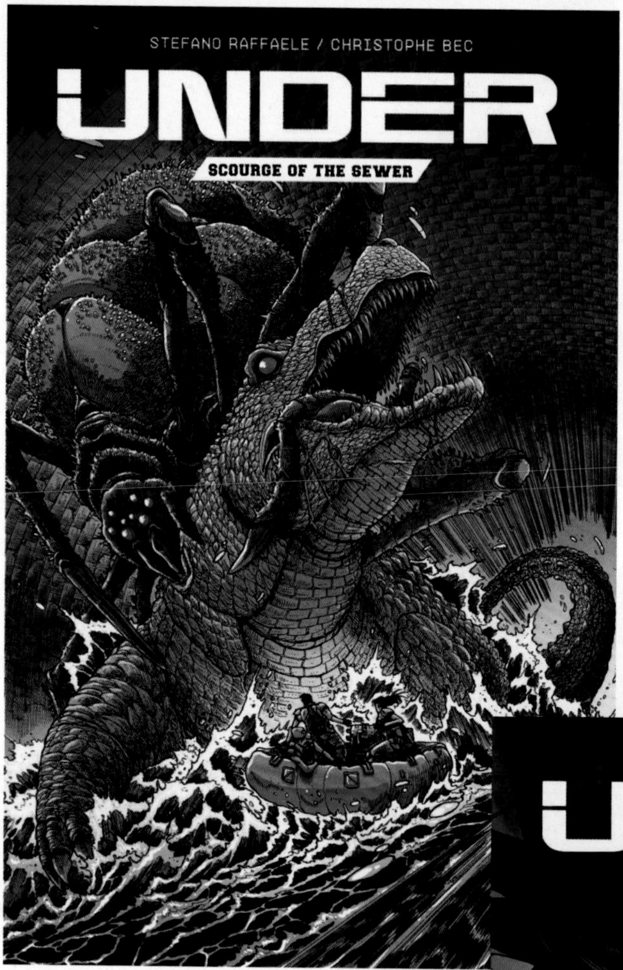
STEFANO RAFFAELE / CHRISTOPHE BEC
UNDER
SCOURGE OF THE SEWER

#1 COVER A
JAMES STOKOE

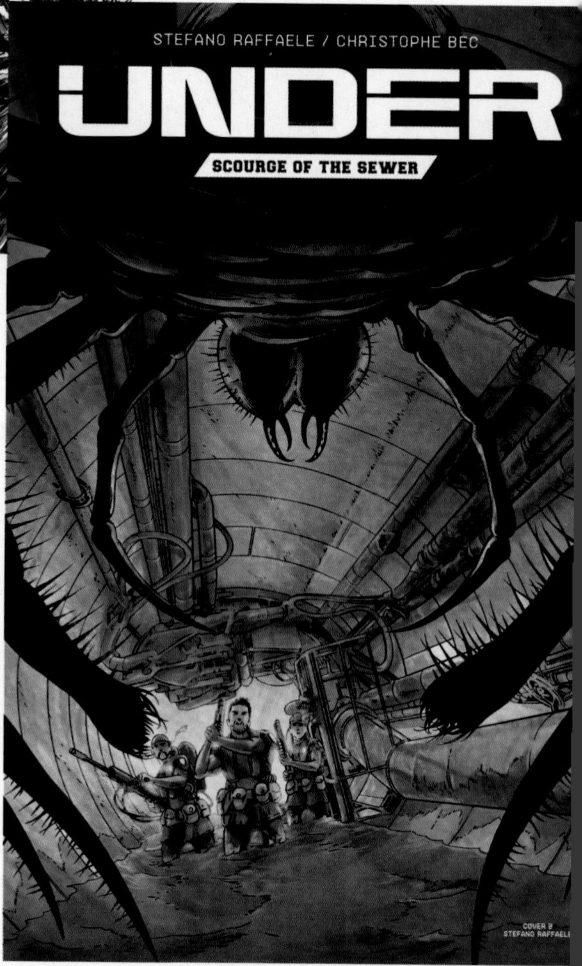
STEFANO RAFFAELE / CHRISTOPHE BEC
UNDER
SCOURGE OF THE SEWER

#1 COVER B
STEFANO RAFFAELE

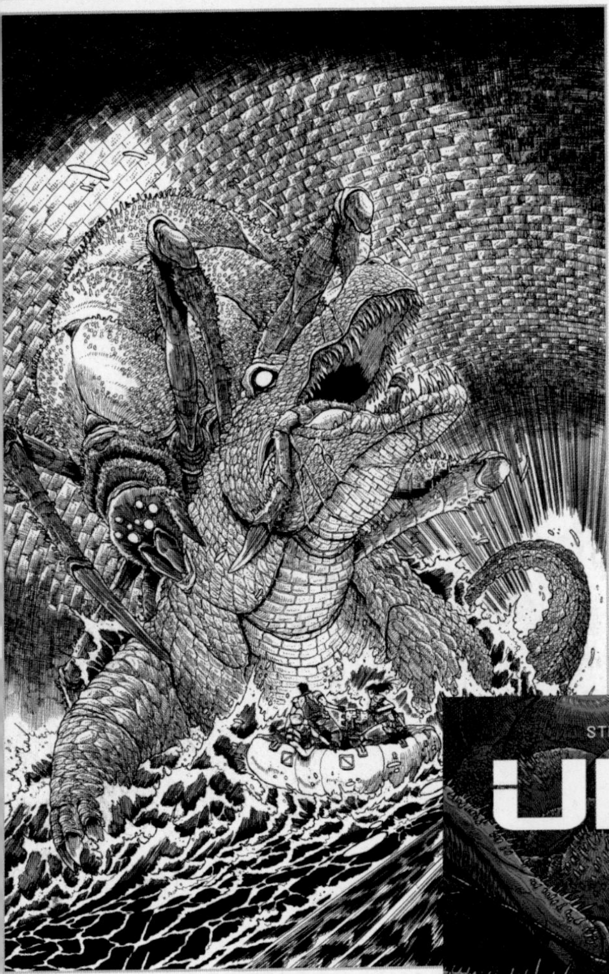

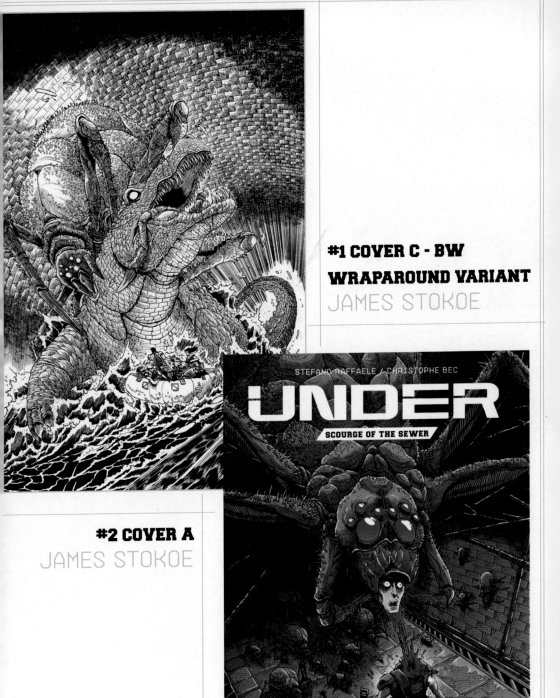

#1 COVER C - BW WRAPAROUND VARIANT

JAMES STOKOE

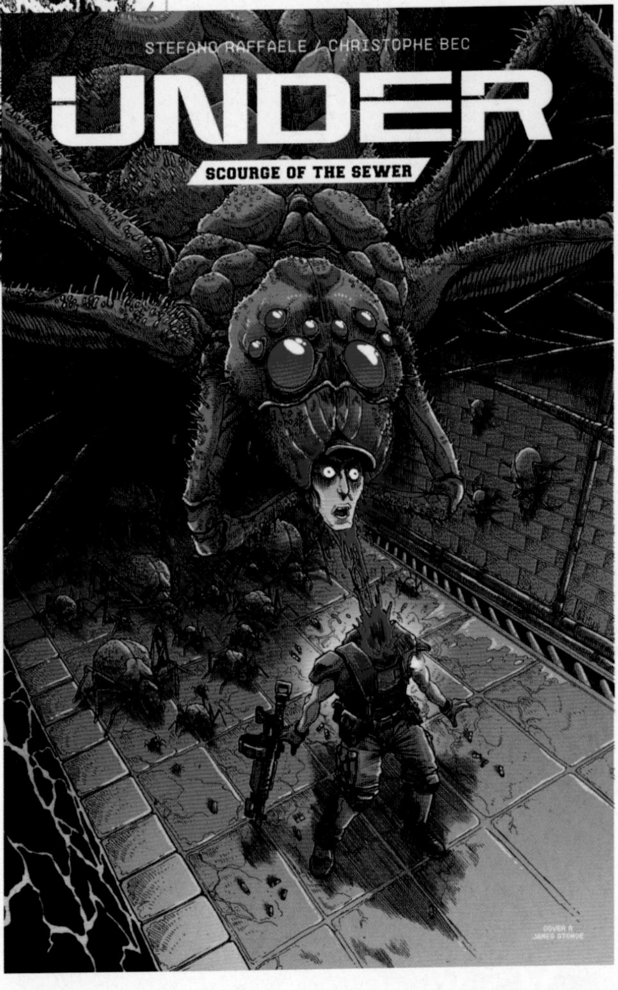
STEFANO RAFFAELE / CHRISTOPHE BEC
UNDER
SCOURGE OF THE SEWER

#2 COVER A

JAMES STOKOE

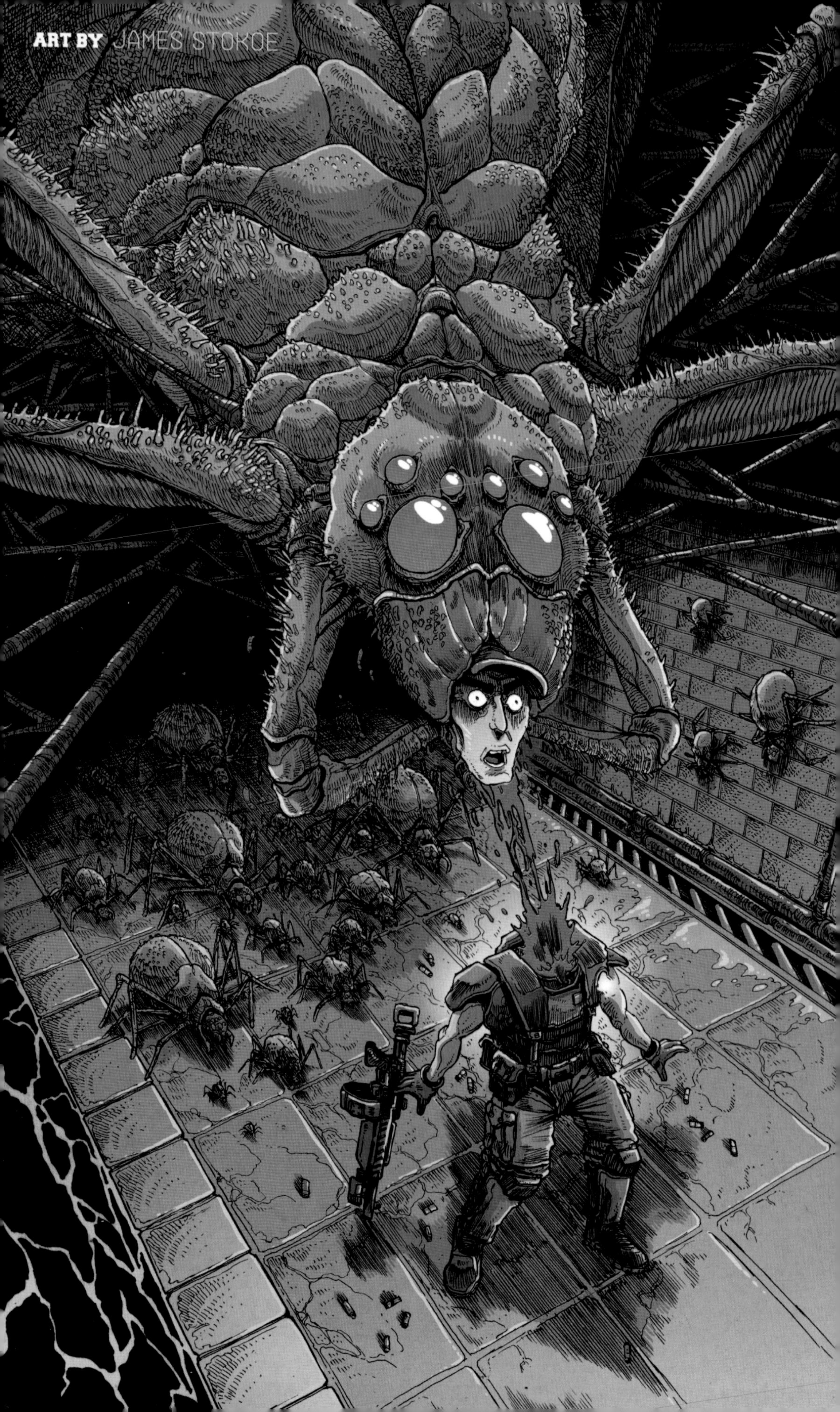

ART BY JAMES STOKOE